W9-AAT-094

"Fred Bergsten has a special knack for focusing on the right issues at the right time. This new book challenges the policymakers to respond to the need for fresh thinking to deal with financial volatility."
—**Paul A. Volcker, former Chairman of The Board of Governors, The Federal Reserve System**

"Fred Bergsten makes a powerful case for the G-7 to reinvigorate its interest in, and leadership of, the global economy."
—**Stanley Fischer, First Deputy Managing Director, International Monetary Fund**

"This is an important book. [Its] analysis of the decline of the G-7 . . . is disturbingly accurate. Restoring G-7 cooperation is essential to strengthening world growth without inflation or currency instability."
—**David C. Mulford, Chairman, CS First Boston, and former Under Secretary of the Treasury for International Affairs**

"The G-7 is fast becoming a ceremonial artifact. So it is timely that [this book] explains why, and offers ideas of what could be done to revive international economic cooperation among the major players."
—**Robert B. Zoellick, Executive Vice President and General Counsel, Federal National Mortgage Association, and former Under Secretary of State and Economic Summit "Sherpa"**

". . . makes a strong case for a 'revised G-7' as the best available option to provide effective economic leadership to the world when it will be most urgently needed [and] outlines an agenda for improvements that is both ambitious and realistic."
—**Wolfgang Rieke, former Head of the International Division, Deutsche Bundesbank**

"After sharply criticizing the present G-7, which has downsized to a 'nonaggression pact' among the world's leading economic powers, this book presents dynamic proposals to revitalize it as the effective steering committee for global economic management with a more disciplined surveillance mechanism, more involvement by central banks, from the IMF and non-7, and more determination to establish a new framework of flexible but stable exchange rates."
—**Shijuro Ogata, former Executive Director, Bank of Japan**

"This incisive and thoughtful analysis of international policy coordination of the major economic powers points at the grave dangers to the world economy of the decline and lack of that coordination. This book presents a convincing argument and a practical strategy to restore coordination to the benefit of world economic growth and stability and to counter the powerful forces of economic materialism and protectionism."

—**Rimmer de Vries, former Managing Director and Chief Economist of J. P. Morgan**

". . . an informative, constructive, and provocative book aimed at improving economic performance in this increasingly interdependent world."

—**Robert Solomon, the Brookings Institution**

C. FRED BERGSTEN
C. RANDALL HENNING

GLOBAL ECONOMIC LEADERSHIP
and the Group of Seven

INSTITUTE FOR INTERNATIONAL ECONOMICS
Washington, DC
June 1996

C. Fred Bergsten is Director of the Institute for International Economics, Chairman of the Competitiveness Policy Council, and Chairman of the APEC Eminent Persons Group throughout its existence (1993–95). He was Assistant Secretary for International Affairs of the US Treasury (1977–81); Assistant for International Economic Affairs to the National Security Council (1969–71); and a Senior Fellow at the Brookings Institution (1972–76), the Carnegie Endowment for International Peace (1981), and the Council on Foreign Relations (1967–68). He is the author or editor of 26 books on a wide range of international economic issues including *Reconcilable Differences? United States-Japan Economic Conflict* with Marcus Noland (1993), *Pacific Dynamism and the International Economic System* with Marcus Noland (1993), *America in the World Economy: A Strategy for the 1990s* (1988), *Trade Policy in the 1980s* with William Cline (1984), *American Multinationals and American Interests* (1978), *The Dilemmas of the Dollar* (1976), and *World Politics and International Economics* (1975).

C. Randall Henning, Visiting Fellow, is Associate Professor at the School of International Service, American University. He is the author of *Currencies and Politics in the United States, Germany, and Japan* (1994) and *Macroeconomic Diplomacy in the 1980s: Domestic Politics and International Conflict Among the United States, Japan, and Europe* (1987), coeditor of *Reviving the European Union* (1994), and coauthor of *Dollar Politics: Exchange Rate Policymaking in the United States* (1989) and *Can Nations Agree? Issues in International Economic Cooperation* (1989). He has also taught international and comparative political economy at Georgetown and Johns Hopkins Universities.

INSTITUTE FOR INTERNATIONAL ECONOMICS
11 Dupont Circle, NW
Washington, DC 20036-1207
(202) 328-9000 FAX: (202) 328-5432
http://www.iie.com
orders@iie.com

C. Fred Bergsten, *Director*
Christine F. Lowry, *Director of Publications*

Cover design by Michelle M. Fleitz
Typesetting by Automated Graphic Systems
Printing by Automated Graphic Systems

Copyright © 1996 by the Institute for International Economics. All rights reserved. No part of this book may be reproduced or utilized in any form or by any means, electronic or mechanical, including photocopying, recording, or by information storage or retrieval system, without permission from the Institute.

For reprints/permission to photocopy please contact the APS customer service department at CCC Academic Permissions Service, 27 Congress Street, Salem, MA 01970

Printed in the United States of America
98 97 96 5 4 3 2 1

Library of Congress Cataloging-in-Publication Data

Bergsten, C. Fred, 1941–
    Global Economic Leadership and the Group of Seven / C. Fred Bergsten, C. Randall Henning.
    p. cm.
    Includes bibliographical references and index.
    1. International foreign relations.
    2. Economic policy—International cooperation.   3. Monetary policy—International cooperation. 4. Group of Seven (Organization)   I. Henning, C. Randall.   II. Title.
HF1359.B445   1995   95-17295
337—dc20   CIP

ISBN 0-88132-218-0

Marketed and Distributed outside the USA and Canada by Longman Group UK Limited, London

The views expressed in this publication are those of the authors. This publication is part of the overall program of the Institute, as endorsed by its Board of Directors, but does not necessarily reflect the views of individual members of the Board or the Advisory Committee.

TO PAUL A. VOLCKER

For his lifelong dedication to a stable and prosperous world economy and to more effective international economic cooperation.

His wisdom and support have been a source of inspiration and encouragement to the Institute in all our work on these topics.

Contents

Preface   xi

Acknowledgments   xv

1   Summary and Conclusions   1

2   The Role and Record of the G-7   13
    The G-7 as an Institution   13
    The Responsibilities of the G-7   15
    Past Successes   20

3   The Decline of the G-7   27
    World Growth and Stability   27
    Exchange Rates   30
    International Imbalances   34
    External Relations   35
    The International Economic System   39
    The Legitimacy of the G-7   43
    The Bottom Line   49

4   The Sources of G-7 Decline: Traditional Tensions   55
    Growth vs. Stability   55
    Surplus vs. Deficit Countries   59

Globalism vs. Regionalism   68

The Politics of the G-7   73

A Summing Up   80

5 The Sources of G-7 Decline: The New Consensus   **83**

The Immobilization of Fiscal Policy   86

The Primacy of the Central Banks   87

The Growth and Spread of Private Capital Flows   89

The Downgrading of the IMF   91

The Abdication of Responsibility   92

6 Reviving the G-7   **97**

Resolving the Traditional Differences   97

Immobilization of Fiscal Policy and Coordination of Monetary Policy   100

The Role of the Central Banks   109

Coping with Private Capital Movements   112

The Bureaucratic Politics of Monetary Reform   117

A Summing Up   120

7 An Action Program   **123**

A New Exchange Rate Regime   124

Avoiding "Future Mexicos"   134

Enhancing the Legitimacy of the G-7   138

Conclusion   140

Appendix A: International Economic Coordination   **143**

References   **149**

Index   **158**

Boxes

Box 1.1 International Economic Organizations   2

Box 2.1 The Three Groups   16

Box 2.2 The General Arrangements to Borrow   22

Tables

Table 3.1a G-7 share of world merchandise exports, 1950–94   45

Table 3.1b G-7 share of world merchandise imports, 1950–94   45

Table 3.2 Share of G-5 currencies in world foreign exchange reserves, 1973–94   46

Table 3.3 Shares of major currencies in world private transactions 46
Table 3.4 G-7 share of total international monetary reserves, 1973–95 47
Table 3.5 G-7 share of total IMF quotas, 1950–95 47
Table 7.1 G-7 performance on proposed cooperation criteria, 1995–97 132

Figures

Figure 2.1 G-7 share of gross world output, 1960–94 17
Figure 3.1 Yen per dollar, 4 January 1988 through 22 April 1996 31
Figure 3.2 Monthly real trade-weighted dollar exchange rate against 101 trading partners, January 1988–December 1995 49
Figure 3.3 Monthly real trade-weighted dollar exchange rate versus other G-7 countries, January 1988–November 1995 50
Figure 4.1 United States: current account and merchandise trade balance, 1970–95 60
Figure 4.2 Germany: current account and merchandise trade balance, 1970–95 60
Figure 4.3 Japan: current account and merchandise trade balance, 1970–95 61
Figure 4.4 United Kingdom: current account and merchandise trade balance, 1970–95 61
Figure 4.5 France: current account and merchandise trade balance, 1970–95 62
Figure 4.6 Italy: current account and merchandise trade balance, 1970–95 62
Figure 4.7 EU, Japan, and US: trade in goods and services, 1960–94 64
Figure 4.8 Current account surpluses by country share, 1994 66
Figure 7.1 Deutsche marks per dollar, 4 January 1988 through 22 April 1996 125

Preface

The issue of international economic cooperation has been near the top of the agenda of the Institute for International Economics throughout its history. Leadership of the global system has been a recurrent theme. Some of our studies have addressed cooperation and leadership within the context of a particular functional component of the world economy, such as the trading system or international monetary affairs (including Yoichi Funabashi's earlier account of the G-7, *Managing the Dollar: From the Plaza to the Louvre*, in 1988). Some have addressed the role of key individual countries, such as the United States (my *America in the World Economy* in 1988) and Japan (*Japan in the World Economy*, by Bela Balassa and Marcus Noland, also in 1988). We held a conference on these issues in 1994 to mark the 50th anniversary of the creation of the Bretton Woods institutions, from which emerged a series of papers on the most important components of the system (*Managing the World Economy: Fifty Years After Bretton Woods*, edited by Peter B. Kenen).

This book addresses the central leadership group in the entire process of international economic cooperation: the Group of Seven, or G-7, especially at the operational level of finance ministers and central bank governors. The book traces the evolution of the group's success in promoting global prosperity and stability, concludes that it has declined sharply in recent years, analyzes the reasons for that decline, and recommends steps to revive the process. It addresses the wide range of substantive issues that the G-7 attempts to cover, blends the economic and political dimensions of the question, and relates the "finance G-7" both to the broader global financial institutions (especially the International Monetary Fund) and to the G-7 summits of political leaders. Many of the book's recommendations are in fact addressed to the summiteers, beginning with their session at Lyon, France, in late June 1996.

This book benefited even more than most Institute publications from the authors' discussions with policymakers. A number of past and present participants in the G-7 process, as listed in the acknowledgments, generously shared with us their own observations and recollections. Needless to say, they do not necessarily endorse our conclusions or recommendations, and the authors take full responsibility for all material in the volume.

The Institute for International Economics is a private nonprofit institution for the study and discussion of international economic policy. Its purpose is to analyze important issues in that area and to develop and communicate practical new approaches for dealing with them. The Institute is completely nonpartisan.

The Institute is funded largely by philanthropic foundations. Major institutional grants are now being received from the German Marshall Fund of the United States, which created the Institute with a generous commitment of funds in 1981, and from the Ford Foundation, the Andrew Mellon Foundation, and the C. V. Starr Foundation. A number of other foundations and private corporations also contribute to the highly diversified financial resources of the Institute. About 16 percent of the Institute's resources in our latest fiscal year were provided by contributors outside the United States, including about 7 percent from Japan.

The Board of Directors bears overall responsibility for the Institute and gives general guidance and approval to its research program—including identification of topics that are likely to become important to international economic policymakers over the medium run (generally, one to three years), and which thus should be addressed by the Institute. The Director, working closely with the staff and outside Advisory Committee, is responsible for the development of particular projects and makes the final decision to publish an individual study.

The Institute hopes that its studies and other activities will contribute to building a stronger foundation for international economic policy around the world. We invite readers of these publications to let us know how they think we can best accomplish this objective.

C. FRED BERGSTEN
Director
May 1996

INSTITUTE FOR INTERNATIONAL ECONOMICS
11 Dupont Circle, NW, Washington, DC 20036-1207
(202) 328-9000 Fax: (202) 328-5432

C. Fred Bergsten, *Director*

BOARD OF DIRECTORS

*Peter G. Peterson, *Chairman*
*Anthony M. Solomon, *Chairman,*
   Executive Committee

Leszek Balcerowicz
Raymond Barre
W. Michael Blumenthal
Miguel de la Madrid
George David
*Jessica Einhorn
George M. C. Fisher
Maurice R. Greenberg
*Carla A. Hills
W. M. Keck II
Nigel Lawson
Lee Kuan Yew
*Frank E. Loy
Donald F. McHenry
Ruben F. Mettler
Minoru Murofushi
Kaneo Nakamura
Suliman S. Olayan
Paul H. O'Neill
I. G. Patel
Karl Otto Pöhl
Edzard Reuter
David Rockefeller
Stephan Schmidheiny
Paul A. Volcker
*Dennis Weatherstone
Marina v.N. Whitman
Lynn R. Williams
Andrew Young

Ex officio
*C. Fred Bergsten

Honorary Directors
Alan Greenspan
Reginald H. Jones
Akio Morita
George P. Shultz

ADVISORY COMMITTEE

Robert Baldwin
Barry P. Bosworth
Susan M. Collins
Rimmer de Vries
Wendy Dobson
Juergen B. Donges
Rudiger Dornbusch
Gerhard Fels
Robert J. Flanagan
Isaiah Frank
Jacob A. Frenkel
David D. Hale
Mahbub ul Haq
Dale E. Hathaway
Nurul Islam
Peter B. Kenen
Lawrence R. Klein
Lawrence B. Krause
Anne O. Krueger
Paul R. Krugman
Roger M. Kubarych
Robert Z. Lawrence
Jessica T. Mathews
Rachel McCulloch
Isamu Miyazaki
Michael Mussa
Richard R. Nelson
Sylvia Ostry
Rudolph A. Oswald
Tommaso Padoa-Schioppa
Jacques J. Polak
Dani Rodrik
Jeffrey D. Sachs
Lawrence H. Summers
Alan Wm. Wolff
Robert B. Zoellick

*Member of the Executive Committee

Acknowledgments

The authors would like to thank the following for providing valuable comments on early drafts of the manuscript: Nicholas Bayne, William R. Cline, Richard N. Cooper, Bowman Cutter, Charles Dallara, Rimmer de Vries, Wendy Dobson, Jessica Einhorn, Robert Fauver, Gerhard Fels, Stanley Fischer, Jeffrey A. Frankel, Yoichi Funabashi, Timothy Geithner, Manuel Guitian, Morris Goldstein, Bill Helkie, G. John Ikenberry, Miles Kahler, Peter B. Kenen, Mervyn King, Roger Kubarych, Reynold Levy, David Lipton, James Lister, Catherine Mann, Stephen Marris, David C. Mulford, Marcus Noland, Shijuro Ogata, Henry Owen, Jacques J. Polak, Wolfgang Rieke, Richard Smyser, Anthony Solomon, Robert Solomon, Lawrence H. Summers, Hans Tietmeyer, Jean-Claude Trichet, Edwin M. Truman, Paul A. Volcker, Nigel Wicks, John Williamson, and Robert Zoellick.

We also gratefully acknowledge the research assistance of Alan Kackmeister, Albert Kim, and Tracy Temanson. Finally, we thank Alda Seubert for her tireless assistance in processing the many drafts and helping to manage the project; Valerie Norville for her superb editing; and Brigitte Coulton, Helen Kim, and Christine Lowry for ensuring timely publication.

Needless to say, the authors alone bear full responsibility for the analysis and conclusions contained in this book.

1

Summary and Conclusions

The Group of Seven (G-7) comprises Canada, France, Germany, Italy, Japan, the United Kingdom, and the United States. These seven industrial democracies account for about two-thirds of global output.[1] They (or similar predecessor groups) have been meeting regularly, at several different levels, for more than 30 years to try to lead the world economy toward prosperity and stability.

International economic cooperation is clearly desirable. A central feature of the entire postwar order was the institutionalization of such cooperation in the International Monetary Fund (IMF), World Bank, and International Trade Organization, which became the General Agreement on Tariffs and Trade (GATT), and now the World Trade Organization, or WTO (see box 1.1). The goal, which antedated the Cold War and was a wholly separate element of the postwar structure (Ikenberry 1996), was to avoid any replication of the international economic chaos of the 1930s that both deepened the Great Depression and helped bring on World War II.

It has always been essential for a smaller group with a systemic perspective to assume leadership of international economic policy and operations. The United States played the leadership role alone in the early postwar years as a kind of G-1, but it needed help to deal with its own external deficits and dollar crises by the early 1960s. As Europe recovered from

---

1. This is based on calculations using market exchange rates. The G-7 countries account for only about one-half of world output on the basis of purchasing power parities, but their share has not declined significantly over the postwar period on either measure (figure 2.1).

1

Box 1.1 International Economic Organizations

The chief international economic organizations are in principle functionally special-
ized. In practice, their missions are closely related and overlap to some extent. Their
country memberships also overlap, although different executive agencies represent
national governments in the different organizations. The organizations that are particularly relevant to the G-7 are described below.

International Monetary Fund (IMF)

The IMF was created along with the World Bank by agreement among 44 countries
at Bretton Woods, New Hampshire, in July 1944. The founding members were determined to avoid the disruption of trade and other international transactions that had
been caused to a large extent by the breakdown of the foreign currency exchanges
and the collapse of monetary and credit systems in the interwar period. They dedi-
cated the IMF to the achievement and maintenance of currency convertibility for
current (as opposed to capital) transactions under a system of fixed but adjustable
exchange rates. To help pursue this goal, they provided substantial resources to the
IMF to enable it to help finance member countries' balance of payments deficits.

The IMF's mission has evolved to include surveillance of members' economic and
exchange rate policies. The conditions it attaches to its lending programs have a
major impact on economic policy in borrowing countries, and the Fund's approval of
a country's policies (as frequently expressed by the existence of a lending or standby
program) is extremely important to the markets' determination of that country's creditworthiness. The IMF has focused on economic liberalization, stabilization, and reform in the developing countries (especially debtor countries in the 1980s) and, in
addition, in Eastern Europe and the former Soviet Union in the 1990s. The IMF has
181 members and is located in Washington.

World Bank

The Washington-based World Bank was originally created to finance postwar reconstruction but grew to become the world's premier organization for economic development. The Bank group has several components: the International Bank for Reconstruction and Development (IBRD) for development financing at market interest rates,

---

the war and then Japan joined the ranks of industrial countries, the G-7
evolved to meet the world's need for an informal steering committee. The
global institutions themselves created smaller steering groups, notably
the Interim Committee for the IMF and the Development Committee for
the World Bank, but they were still too large and too heterogeneous to
play an effective leadership role.

The G-7 has never been successful in creating systemic arrangements
that would prevent global economic problems. It has instead generally
resorted to ad hoc reactions to whatever issues came to the fore. Nevertheless, it has recorded major accomplishments.

The G-7 finance ministers and central bank governors, on which this
book focuses and to which we usually refer in using the term "G-7," have
been a useful firefighting brigade, responding to international currency

Box 1.1 (continued)

the International Development Association (IDA) for concessional financing to the poorest countries, the International Finance Corporation (IFC) for equity investment in private enterprises, and the Multilateral Investment Guarantee Agency (MIGA) for insurance for private investment in developing economies. A Board of Governors makes the major policy decisions at its annual meeting; the Executive Board, which meets frequently, makes more routine decisions. A country must be a member of the IMF to be a member of the IBRD, which has 179 members and commands the largest resources of the World Bank group.

Regional Development Banks (RDBs)

Several development banks have been created at the regional level: the Inter-American Development Bank (IDB) in 1960, the Asian Development Bank (ADB) in 1966, the African Development Bank (AfDB) in 1966, and the European Bank for Reconstruction and Development (EBRD) in 1990. Like the World Bank, the IDB, ADB, and AfDB are clusters of institutions, including an ordinary lending facility and a concessional window. Borrowing countries may be more influential, to varying degrees, within the regional banks than within the World Bank. The IDB and ADB lend roughly the same amounts within their regions as does the World Bank. The regional banks and the World Bank are exploring ways to better coordinate their operations.

World Trade Organization (WTO)

The WTO was created in 1995 by the signatories to the Uruguay Round of the General Agreement on Tariffs and Trade (GATT). Although it facilitated extraordinarily successful multilateral trade liberalization over the postwar period, the GATT was provisional, with a limited international secretariat and no formal organization. The WTO does not replace the GATT but rather serves as an organizational and procedural structure for implementing the Uruguay Round agreements, which besides the GATT includes agreements on trade in services and intellectual property. The WTO has dispute settlement rules, a trade policy review mechanism, and plurilateral agreements. The WTO is based in Geneva and has 119 member countries.

and other crises throughout its existence. The G-7 coordinated national exchange-rate and macroeconomic policies for a brief time in the late 1970s. It coordinated currency and monetary policies extensively in the middle 1980s, helping to correct the enormous overvaluation of the dollar that threatened both the openness of the world trading system and international financial stability. It helped resolve the debt crisis of the developing countries in the 1980s and finance the Gulf War in 1991. It contributed to the growing consensus on the need to focus macroeconomic policy on fighting inflation and can thus take a modest part of the credit for the dramatic reduction in inflation over the past 20 years.

The G-7's effectiveness has declined sharply over the last decade, however. Indeed, it has totally failed to act on a wide range of issues in which global leadership was required. The world economy has been weak throughout the 1990s despite the ready availability of a coordinated growth strategy that the G-7 could have adopted throughout the early part of the decade. All G-7 countries (and many outside the group, notably Mexico) experienced severe currency crises that could have been prevented or at least handled much better once they erupted. Huge trade imbalances have been permitted to return: the American deficit and Japanese surplus soared to their highest levels ever, once again jeopardizing the global trading system.

We shall see in chapter 3 that this recent paralysis is the strongest indictment of the contemporary G-7. For reasons that will be analyzed in chapters 4 and 5, the group is no longer even attempting to lead on most occasions.

The G-7 has overcome its paralysis in several recent cases but it has often erred when it did attempt to act. It mishandled Russian economic reform in the crucial early years after the fall of the Soviet Union. It pushed the dollar up excessively in 1995, given the continued presence of large US trade deficits. The rest of the world, in a series of unprecedented rebukes to the G-7, rejected its proposal for an allocation of Special Drawing Rights at the IMF in 1994 and forced it to thoroughly overhaul its more recent initiative to expand the Fund's resources to finance "future Mexicos." All of these episodes will be recounted in chapter 3.

Part of the decline of the G-7 stems from traditional differences among the members on several key issues: the priorities to be accorded to growth versus price stability, the responsibilities of surplus versus deficit countries, the geographic scope (global versus regional) of the group's domain. The issue of geographic focus has become especially important with respect to the European members of the G-7. They have become increasingly preoccupied with their regional monetary arrangements, which they have sought to steer in a very different direction from the global regime.

These traditional differences have been particularly acute between the two main players—the United States and Germany. The rancor between the United States and Germany within the G-7 is paradoxical in light of the solid overall relationship between them. But it has occasionally reached the point where the United States has been afraid to ask for German cooperation—including in key instances such as the Mexican financial rescue and several episodes of intervention in the exchange markets—because it knew it would be rebuffed. The politics of the G-7 will be analyzed in chapter 4.

Some of these traditional differences have waned in recent years as, for example, the United States has itself become less inclined to espouse fiscal expansion programs for countercyclical purposes. But the impact of these differences on G-7 outcomes has probably increased with the decline in America's economic and security clout, which partly stems from the end of the Cold War, and with America's inconsistent policies and inept performance on a wide range of G-7 issues. The sharp growth in Germany's influence, as the increasingly dominant leader of an increasingly united Europe, also intensifies the effect of the traditional conflicts. Japan is the third most important member of the G-7, which has become a de facto "G-3" as the four other participants all play much smaller roles; it has increasingly sided with Germany and drifted away from its traditional alliance with the United States on monetary matters.

The main reason for the decline of the G-7, however, is not the traditional differences among the members but rather a growing consensus within the group that changes in global economic conditions make it impossible for them to pursue initiatives that were feasible as recently as a decade ago. Huge international flows of private capital are thought to preclude the monetary authorities from effectively influencing the currency markets. The existence of large budget deficits everywhere is seen as blunting the scope for macroeconomic policy coordination by sharply limiting any remaining flexibility for fiscal policy. In this view, fiscal inflexibility overburdens monetary policy with domestic objectives, rendering it incapable of responding to external objectives as well. Central banks have become vastly more important because of this primacy of monetary policy, and their jealous defense of their institutional independence in key countries (notably Germany and the United States) is seen as further dimming the prospects for international coordination. Disillusion with the perceived outcomes of past G-7 coordination efforts, especially in Germany and Japan, intensify the resistance to renewed activism.

The disagreements among G-7 countries, concerning the goals of policy coordination, have therefore been joined by a collapse of the group's confidence in its ability to pursue collective strategies even when it might wish to do so. This new consensus for inaction has led inter alia to a "nonaggression pact" among the G-7 members. The countries have decided to largely eschew criticism of each others' policies, especially in public, on the grounds that very little could be accomplished anyway. The result is ineffectual coordination among the G-7 members themselves, the most obvious responsibility of the group. These developments will be analyzed in chapter 5, and an alternative interpretation of the relevant structural changes in the world economy, which offers a much more optimistic picture of the prospects for cooperation, will be provided in chapter 6.

There was a similar period of prolonged G-7 inactivity in the early 1980s, caused by some of the same disagreements and loss of confidence that appear today. The group argued then that "sterilized intervention" in the exchange markets was ineffective, a view subsequently shown to be incorrect, just as it argues now that it is impotent in the face of the increased volume of international capital flows. It asserted in the 1980s that "convergence" of national economic policies and performance would obviate the need for international cooperation, a parallel to today's "nonaggression pact," but it had to explicitly disown that view in its own Plaza Agreement in 1985.

The "benign neglect" of the early 1980s subjected the world economy to serious risks. The international trading system was severely jeopardized because of American protectionism and the threat that it might escalate much further, triggered by massive dollar overvaluation and resultant trade deficits; thoughtful members of Congress feared that "the Smoot-Hawley tariff itself would pass overwhelmingly" had it come to a vote in 1985. There was a constant risk of financial instability; a "hard landing" almost occurred when the dollar tumbled and interest rates shot up in early 1987, and when stock markets crashed globally on Black Monday later that year. Japan was hit with recession due to the precipitate appreciation of the yen that was part of the necessary adjustment.

The world economy suffers to this day, and will for years or even decades to come, from the legacies of that period. America was transformed into the world's largest debtor country. National legislation that frays the trading system, such as America's "super 301," was adopted. Japan's "bubble economy" crashed into prolonged recession with an overhang of $500 billion or more of bad loans in the world's second largest national economy.

Many of these problems derived from domestic policies in the major countries, of course—Reaganomics in the United States in the early 1980s and reliance on monetary rather than fiscal expansion in Japan in the late 1980s. Effective international cooperation might have headed off some of these events, however, and certainly could have reduced the magnitude of the resulting costs. The interactions between "domestic" and "international" problems are addressed throughout this book.

The failures of the G-7 during the early 1980s provide the most compelling rationale for active cooperation now and in the future. But the failures of the 1990s, while less spectacular, greatly strengthen the case and give it urgency. Indeed, systemic leadership vacuums have almost always led to major disruptions in the world economy—because of a failure of the key countries to make needed changes in their own economic policies, because of their failures to respond effectively to systemic crises, and because of the erosion of institutional arrangements that contributes over time to a deterioration of economic outcomes, and even political relationships, around the globe.

The central economic problems facing the major countries today—sluggish wages and income levels in the United States, high unemployment in Europe, slow growth and an unsettled financial system in Japan—require primarily domestic responses. But effective international policy coordination could help deal with each, and international problems could deeply exacerbate these internal difficulties in the absence of global leadership. Just as uncoordinated expansion in previous periods produced global inflation, an uncoordinated reduction of budget deficits across the G-7 could push the world into recession. Sudden massive shifts in private capital—like those that triggered the European currency crises of 1992-93, the Mexican crisis of late 1994-95 and the plunge of the dollar against the yen and mark in early 1995—can reappear at any time, attacking ever larger numbers of countries with even more far-reaching "contagion effects," in the absence of a more structured policy framework and official reaction capability.

Moreover, the continuing sluggishness of the world economy clearly calls for a coordinated response—especially with real interest rates so high everywhere, including in countries with very high unemployment (Europe) or suffering from prolonged stagnation (Japan). There are new adjustment problems on the horizon, if not closer: the Europeans believe that the dollar is substantially undervalued but the United States continues to run large external deficits, implying a need to address currencies outside the G-7, just as the G-7 did with respect to East Asia in the late 1980s. The risks of trade protectionism remain strong and also call for G-7 attention, although the finance ministers and central bank governors do not exercise direct responsibility on those issues. There is likewise a need for creative and energetic efforts to tackle the structural and microeconomic problems that plague all G-7 economies, though most of these, too, lie outside the direct authority of the monetary officials.

Over the slightly longer run, the risk of a "hard landing" for the dollar—which many feared as recently as early 1995—could easily reappear, with the United States firmly entrenched as the world's largest debtor country and with its external debt growing by about $150 billion per year. Renewed growth of the Japanese trade surplus and American deficit, particularly if joined by economic slowdowns in key countries, could intensify protectionist pressures. The creation of a single European currency could prompt a sizable international portfolio adjustment from dollars into the new unit that would destabilize both economies and financial markets. The globalization of capital and financial markets requires more extensive international cooperation in supervising and perhaps regulating them, a process that has only proceeded part way with respect to commercial banks and has not even begun with respect to nonbank financial institutions.

All these issues require effective international cooperation. Global prosperity and stability will be jeopardized by continued abdication of G-7 leadership. History suggests that political and even security conflicts could also be triggered as a result.

Extensive reform of the G-7 is needed to enable it to respond to these needs. The depth of the problems besetting the group, however, suggests that such sweeping changes are unlikely over the short to medium term. Hence we advocate a more modest, largely evolutionary, series of steps that the group should take over the coming months and next few years. Most of these proposals, as laid out in chapter 7, are deliberately quite familiar; they should therefore require no further delays to achieve basic understanding or to conduct new, far-reaching debates over pros and cons.

On the financial side, our proposals will focus largely on modifying and implementing initiatives that have already been launched. The two key requirements are creation of an early warning system to head off Mexico-type crises and provision of adequate resources to deal with such crises when they do erupt. The G-7 summit at Halifax in June 1995 called for changes in both directions.

The current G-7 approach is inadequate, however, and needs to be augmented in four important ways. Its proposed early warning system correctly begins with a mandate to the IMF to closely monitor potential problem countries in the developing world and to convey policy advice to any that appear to be headed for trouble. The G-7 program also calls on all IMF members to publish, on a timely basis, a comprehensive set of economic data that will permit private capital markets to make more informed judgments on investment opportunities. These are the easy parts, however, and much more is needed.

First, the Fund should be authorized to "blow the whistle" on countries that do not accept advice that is intended to head off crises. This can be done subtly and judiciously by an escalating public release of data and analysis. Doing so admittedly risks triggering the crises that one seeks to forestall, but the threat of such pressure will add significantly to the prospect that countries will take preventive action. In any event, experience shows that a crisis is more manageable if it comes sooner rather than later and hence creates less dislocation and adjustment difficulty.

Second, the early warning system should apply to the G-7 countries themselves as well as to developing economies. These large industrial countries are, of course, the most important source of global economic activity. Hence their policies and performance have far greater impact than those in the developing world. Moreover, as indicated throughout this book, they, too, have frequently adopted policies that created large imbalances, which were extremely costly for their own people as well as the world as a whole. The crises that result sometimes take different forms than in developing countries but the economic effects are similar. They, too, should be subject to the new early warning system, both for substantive reasons and to legitimize the entire exercise in political terms.

Third, the amount of additional resources needed for the program is much greater than envisaged at Halifax and subsequently by the G-7 countries. They are aiming to double, from $27 billion to $54 billion, the line of credit that the G-7 (technically via the G-10) will be prepared to make available to the IMF through the General Arrangements to Borrow (GAB). But the Mexican rescue in early 1995 alone required about $50 billion. Mexico and Russia now have credit lines totaling nearly $30 billion directly from the Fund. To be sure, the IMF has a sizable stock of existing resources. But these resources need to be substantially increased, by augmenting the countries' regular contributions (quotas) and through additional GAB credit on the order of $100 billion—about double the level that is being pursued.

Fourth, the G-7 has had great difficulty in persuading nonmembers to contribute even the modest increase in GAB resources that it now envisages. This is mainly because it has been unwilling to share any real decision-making activity with the new donors, preferring to keep its cozy club intact rather than reaching out even to those countries whose increased economic capability qualifies them for a more active role in international economic leadership. The G-7 should instead regard the present fund-raising exercise as an opportunity to begin integrating such countries more effectively into the decision-making process, by expanding the membership of the G-10 to include the new donors and thereby creating a way station toward possible full membership in the inner steering committee at some later time. This would enhance the legitimacy of the entire G-7 process, a serious problem that we address in chapter 3.

On the adjustment side, there is neither possibility nor need for the G-7 countries to coordinate their macroeconomic policies *directly*. Nor should the group seek active countercyclical management of the world economy. Nor need it fundamentally alter the current regime of flexible exchange rates.

But the G-7's current ad hoc management of flexible rates could be substantially improved by setting and announcing broad target zones of plus or minus 10 percent around agreed midpoints, within which it would limit currency fluctuations. While leaving rates mostly free to float, target zones would avert the risk of large new misalignments, which will otherwise produce substantial economic dislocations, provide an impetus for trade controls, and generate future financial instability when the inevitable corrections occur in a disorderly manner. Target zones would convert the threat of destabilizing private capital flows, which the officials now fear so much, into stabilizing movements. They would transmit exchange rate signals that would improve rather than complicate the conduct of monetary (and occasionally fiscal) policy, even in terms of achieving its purely domestic objectives. These arguments are developed in chapter 6.

Like the Bretton Woods regime of adjustable parities prior to 1971 and the European Monetary System (EMS) now, such a currency commitment would also spur constructive policy coordination among the G-7 countries. It could thus pave the way for more extensive and more direct cooperation initiatives over time if the zones worked as expected and became accepted by the authorities and by the markets. To help achieve that longer-term goal, but more immediately to assure the successful and stable operation of a target zone scheme, all participants should be required to meet "G-7 cooperation criteria"—modeled on the European Union's Maastricht treaty criteria, though in a considerably modified form. All these proposals, on both the financial and adjustment issues, will be developed in chapters 6 and 7.

The G-7 also needs to undertake several institutional reforms. The members' central banks must participate fully in the process and in fact should be given complete authority to manage the proposed target zone system within the policy framework set by their governments. The G-7's current mistrust of the IMF must be replaced by conscious efforts to give the Fund a much more central role on virtually every issue discussed here, including implementation of the new early warning system and backstopping of the target zones.

Moreover, the G-7 should contemplate changes in its own composition. As Economic and Monetary Union (EMU) proceeds in Europe, the G-7 could well evolve into a more manageable G-3. This, in turn, would enable the group to enhance its legitimacy by expanding the membership over time to include major new economic powers, such as China and perhaps Russia, after the initial step of adding some of these countries to the G-10 described earlier. These institutional proposals are elaborated in chapter 7.

Political leadership from the G-7 summits will almost certainly be necessary to achieve the needed improvements in international economic and financial cooperation. Chapters 6 and 7 will show that the monetary authorities, for a variety of reasons, have never led such reforms themselves—and that they are particularly unlikely to move away from the current unstructured nonsystem of floating exchange rates, which serves their parochial bureaucratic purposes. The president of France and the chancellor of Germany had to launch the EMS. Likewise, the G-7 summits will probably have to lead the global reform process.

To their credit, some G-7 political leaders have noted the group's decline and have begun the effort to reverse it. The Clinton administration came into office in early 1993 citing the need "to revitalize the G-7" as one of the chief goals of its international economic policy. The G-7 summiteers in Naples in July 1994 reportedly agreed that the global economic and financial situation was far less satisfactory than their monetary officials depicted it; hence they recognized the need "to renew and revitalize" the international financial institutions and asked, "How can we adapt existing institutions and build new institutions to ensure the further prosperity and security of our people?" The Halifax summit in 1995 sought to avert "future Mexicos" by improving the IMF's capability to prevent such crises and by augmenting the resources with which it could respond when necessary. With economic issues now near the top of the global agenda, and with the G-7 countries still the dominant players in the world economy and hence clearly responsible for its prosperity and stability, there is a strong political as well as economic case for the summiteers to push their effort to a successful conclusion.

President Jacques Chirac of France, in preparing to host the 1996 summit in Lyon, has reportedly expressed interest in pursuing additional initiatives that would reassert effective G-7 leadership on international monetary issues. That meeting ought to build on the Halifax program by adopting the proposals made here to provide adequate systemic defenses against future financial crises. It should then move on to the adjustment problem and begin a process that would lead to the adoption of target zones, perhaps at the 1997 summit in the United States. The United States and Japan could begin the process by installing a "G-2" target zone for the dollar and yen, the most important of all the currency relationships in trade terms, as they in fact did in 1986 as a precursor to the G-7's Louvre Accord, which deployed target zones (then called "reference ranges") for a period in 1987.

This book traces the historical and recent record of the G-7 (chapters 2 and 3), analyzes the causes of its recent decline (chapters 4 and 5), and suggests how the group can be revived to exercise the leadership functions that are so critical for world stability and prosperity (chapters 6 and 7). A revival of the G-7 is both essential and urgent but will require important reforms in both the substance and structure of its activity. The analysis begins with a short description of the G-7 itself.

2

The Role and Record of the G-7

The G-7 as an Institution

International economic policy cooperation ranges far beyond the G-7, of course.[1] This cooperation manifests itself in the day-to-day operations of the International Monetary Fund (IMF), the World Trade Organization (WTO), the World Bank, and other global institutions. Regional groups, notably the European Union but a rising number of others as well, play important roles in many parts of the world. Bilateral negotiations, including those between such key pairs of countries as the United States and Japan, are often more important to the relationships of the countries involved—and, given their national weights, to the world economy as a whole—than the G-7 or other multilateral groups.

The G-7 is nevertheless of critical importance because it stands at the epicenter of the process. The group convenes government officials of the seven largest industrialized, market-oriented, democratic countries.

There are several conceptually distinct layers of the G-7. At the pinnacle is the annual gathering of the heads of state or government—the G-7

---

1. "Cooperation" refers to all collaborative activities among governments. "Coordination," which is the focus of this study, is an ambitious variant of cooperation involving the mutual adjustment of national economic policies (see appendix A for a full definition and explanation).

summits.[2] The president of the European Commission and the presidency of the Council of Ministers of the European Union also participate in this group (so it is really a G-8). They discuss political as well as economic issues, and in recent years the president of Russia has been invited to participate in a separate session devoted to political topics. Central bank governors do not attend the summits, however, so these meetings cannot address monetary policy.

The summits are supported by personal representatives of the summiteers known as "sherpas." The meetings of the sherpas, assistant sherpas ("sous-sherpas"), and deputy finance ministers have become a consultative mechanism in their own right. Their purpose is mainly to prepare the summits themselves and to monitor follow-up of decisions made there.

The next level comprises the ministers of finance and central bank governors. This group, which is the primary focus of this book, originated before the summit meetings and convened quite independently of them until the mid-1980s. Since then, there have been efforts to associate the ministers and governors more closely with the summit process, though they still operate largely on their own.

We use the phrase "the G-7" primarily to refer to the process that centers on the ministers of finance and central bank governors.[3] This encompasses the network of contacts among the ministers and governors themselves, among their deputies and officials, and the routine consultation among these agencies. We do not generally use the term to refer to the summits (exceptions will be explicitly noted) nor to the seven countries more broadly.

A major theme of this book is the increased role of central banks in international economic coordination. It is therefore important to note at the outset that they have their own consultative mechanisms. These center on the Bank for International Settlements (BIS) in Basel: the "central bank for central banks." The governors of the central banks of the G-10 (the G-7 plus Belgium, Holland, Sweden, and Switzerland—hence, 11 countries rather than 10) meet there monthly to discuss a wide range of issues. Some of these, such as payments and settlements systems and bank supervision, attract relatively little attention in the broader settings with ministers of finance. Some, however, such as the conduct of monetary policy and intervention in the exchange markets, are directly relevant. Some of the

---

2. The classic treatment of the summits is Putnam and Bayne (1987). For further treatments, see Smyser (1993), Ikenberry (1993), von Furstenberg and Daniels (1992), *Twenty G-7 Summits* (1994), *International Spectator* (1994), and Whyman (1995).

3. Other groups of G-7 ministers also meet from time to time. The trade ministers do so routinely, in an effort to steer world trade policy, as will be described in chapter 3. Other sessions, such as those of labor ministers in Detroit in 1994 and Lille, France, in 1996, have to date been wholly ad hoc.

central banks' institutional arrangements may be important for future efforts of the G-7.

The G-7 ministers and governors should serve as an informal caucus to provide leadership for the world economy, preferably within the international economic organizations but sometimes necessarily on their own. The IMF, the World Bank, and the WTO play an invaluable role and should be strengthened (as many of our proposals will seek to do). In practice, however, they must be led by a much smaller core group whose weight confers on them the responsibility for this leadership. There is simply no alternative management device that would work better.[4]

Throughout the modern era of the world economy—which dates from the late 1950s, with the initial advent of widespread currency convertibility and elimination of most postwar trading restrictions—a small group of industrialized countries has shouldered this responsibility: the G-10 in the 1960s, the G-5 in the 1970s and early 1980s, and the G-7 for the past 10 years (box 2.1). The rationale is simple: these countries account for the bulk of world economic activity (figure 2.1), their performance goes far to determine the success or failure of the global economy, they recognize the need for systemic leadership and are willing to provide it at least occasionally, and coordination is most effectively initiated—indeed, frequently can *only* by initiated—by a limited number of governments. These countries are also by far the largest shareholders of the global institutions that have weighted quotas; for example, the G-7 countries hold 46 percent of the votes in the IMF.

To be sure, questions have been raised in recent years about the legitimacy of the G-7 as the informal steering committee of the world economy in light of the rise in importance of a number of countries outside the group. These questions will be addressed in chapter 3, and several recommendations will be made for eventual reform of the G-7 as an institution. But the G-7 remains the responsible body today and, because there are no obvious additions to its membership at this time and because of the political difficulty of removing extraneous incumbents, it will probably maintain its position for the foreseeable future.[5]

The Responsibilities of the G-7

We have thus far discussed the G-7's place in the broad spectrum of international economic cooperation and the need for a small, core group

---

4. The management process can be conceptualized as encompassing three concentric circles of countries: the inner "steering committee," a middle group that includes the next most important countries that must be consulted on most issues, and the full membership of the global organizations (Bergsten, Berthoin, and Mushakoji 1976).

5. Some analysts believe that another alternative to the G-7 for exercising systemic leadership is a restoration of American domination or "hegemony." Active American leadership within the G-7 is certainly essential, as stressed throughout this book, but American domination

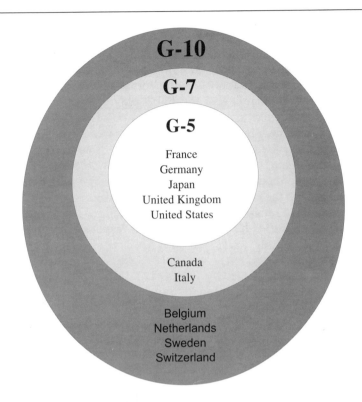

Box 2.1 The Three Groups

The Group of Five (G-5) comprises the finance ministers of the five largest industrial economies. It originated in April 1973 as a caucus on international monetary reform after the collapse of the Bretton Woods system. Central bank governors were later asked to join the meetings, originally on an occasional basis. The group served as a forum for private discussions among the ministers, was supported by a group of G-5 deputies, and issued no communiqués until its meeting at the Plaza Hotel in 1985. Since 1986, the G-5 has been progressively displaced by the Group of Seven.

The Group of Seven (G-7) comprises the finance ministers and central bank governors of the G-5 plus those of Italy and Canada. It was formed by a decision of the Tokyo summit of May 1986 to align the membership of the summit and the financial group. It met for the first time in the following September. The G-7 is now the main locus of monetary and financial cooperation among these countries. It supports the G-7 summits and is in turn supported by a group of G-7 deputies.

The Group of Ten (G-10) adds the ministers and governors of the Netherlands, Belgium, Sweden, and Switzerland to the G-7. Despite the name, therefore, 11 countries are represented. The membership of the OECD's Working Party 3, the main forum for discussing policy coordination and balance of payments adjustment in the 1960s, convened as the G-10 in 1962 to organize extraordinary lending to the IMF through the General Arrangements to Borrow. The G-10, like the G-7, meets on the margins of IMF meetings and occasionally elsewhere. The G-10 central bank governors hold separate monthly meetings at the BIS in Basel, Switzerland.

Figure 2.1 G-7 share of gross world output, 1960-94

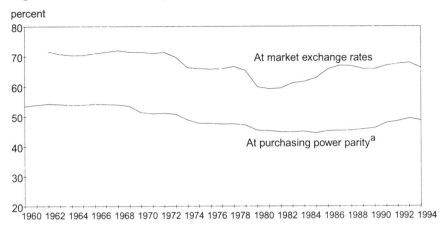

a. Purchasing power parity calculations include only countries for which estimates are available, and therefore overstate G-7 share by a few percent..

Sources: World Bank, *World Tables, World Atlas,* and *World Development Report;* National Bureau of Economic Research, *Penn World Tables;* IMF, *International Financial Statistics;* authors' calculations.

of key countries to take the lead role. But what should the G-7 do with this mantle of leadership? It is the premise of this book that there are five key areas of international economic policy for which the citizens of the G-7 countries, and people around the world, should hold the G-7 accountable: world growth and stability, exchange rates, current account imbalances, the stance of its members toward other countries (including developing countries and, recently, transition economies), and the design of the international economic system as a whole.

Some observers would expand this list. In particular, some would add trade policy, both because it is of such importance to the health of the world economy and because the present liberal regime is constantly threatened by protectionist pressures. Indeed, G-7 summits have frequently addressed the issue; they have provided political impetus for the successful conclusion of successive GATT rounds, for example, and had a decisive impact on at least the Tokyo Round of the late 1970s, according to one active participant. Then-US Special Trade Representative Robert Strauss stated at the time that the Tokyo Round would have never succeeded in the absence of the push from the Bonn summit in 1978.

The G-7 finance ministers and central bank governors are the focus of this book, however, and do not bear lead responsibility for trade policy in any of the member countries. Indeed, a parallel institution known as

like that of the early postwar period is now totally impractical (as well as undesirable from both an American and global perspective).

the Quad—a group that includes Canada, the European Commission (which represents the European Union on trade policy), Japan, and the United States—plays the role of informal steering committee for the world trading system. The members' trade ministers represent them in this forum, and, while subject to many of the problems addressed in this book on the macroeconomic and monetary issues, they have done a reasonably credible job in accomplishing their task in recent years. The relative success of the Quad in fact adds to the case for reforming the G-7 and suggests that doing so should be feasible. It also conveys a few lessons for the broader group, such as the merit of having Europe represented by a single spokesperson rather than by separate countries.

Other observers would add microeconomic issues, such as deregulation and labor markets, to the list of G-7 responsibilities. As with trade, the importance of the issues is undeniable; they lie at the heart of many of today's most intractable economic problems, especially in Europe and Japan. They, too, have been addressed from time to time at G-7 summits, and occasional meetings of the relevant G-7 ministers have been convened specifically to address some of them.

As with trade, however, most microeconomic issues lie outside the competence of the finance ministers and central bank governors. Labor market reforms and most regulatory policies, as well as crucial sectoral issues such as energy policy and farm policy, are largely determined elsewhere. Hence we will devote little attention to this set of topics as well.

One such issue that does lie within the purview of financial officials, and that the G-7 clearly needs to address, is the supervision and regulation of international capital and financial markets. These markets have become global in scope and massive in magnitude. National supervision and regulation are clearly inadequate. Banking crises have been frequent and usually costly affairs in both industrial and emerging markets over the past two decades (including, for example, the current bad loan problem in Japan). Moreover, such cases of financial fragility intensify many of the difficulties we address in this book, notably the ability of countries to avoid international financial crises (à la Mexico) and to adopt needed adjustment measures (such as raising interest rates).

The major countries, operating largely through their central banks, have recognized the problem for some time and attempted to address it. With respect to commercial banks, a "concordat" was in fact reached some time ago that sought to delineate authority between home and host countries for dealing with problems that crossed national boundaries. Agreement was also reached in the late 1980s on an international risk-weighted capital requirement for internationally active banks in the G-10 countries. G-10 central bank governors meet in Basel monthly to discuss issues of mutual concern, and the Basel Committee of G-10 bank supervisors continues to conduct studies and offer recommendations on how to reduce various elements of systemic risk.

But this process has only begun and many areas of potential systemic concern have yet to be addressed adequately, including the primitive nature of international coordination and even information sharing among supervisors of nonbanks (mutual funds, insurance companies, pension funds, securities houses, and futures exchanges); remaining settlement risk in the foreign exchange markets; various kinds of risks in the over-the-counter derivatives markets; weaknesses in some publicly run and some privately run payments systems; shortcomings in data disclosure and transparency for financial institutions, along with lack of a widely agreed and implemented international accounting standard; remaining uncertainties in the workout procedures for sovereign bond defaults; and serious drawbacks in the exercise of banking supervision in many emerging markets. The Institute for International Economics is conducting a major study of this topic (Garber and Goldstein, forthcoming), so we will not address it in detail here, but the G-7 should add this issue to its future agenda as an item of the highest priority.

There are also those who believe that the G-7's responsibilities should be much more modest.[6] Some would leave "international coordination" to market forces and avoid intergovernmental efforts that go beyond exchanges of information and informal consultation. Some believe that active intergovernmental cooperation can even be harmful, a view we address and reject in appendix A. Some would agree with at least some of the goals stated above but would differ with our choice of policy instruments to pursue them.

The remainder of this book attempts to make the case that active G-7 leadership is essential and that practical ways can be found for the major countries to exercise such leadership. The G-7 countries collectively carry extraordinary weight in the world economy. That power and influence confer a responsibility for managing not only their own affairs but also for the world as a whole. Moreover, with increasing economic interdependence, the ministers and central bank governors cannot effectively fulfill their domestic responsibilities without cooperating extensively with one another.

Indeed, the G-7 heads of government acknowledged their collective responsibility at the Tokyo summit in 1986. The leaders said there that there should be "close and continuous *coordination* [emphasis added] of

---

6. The present German finance deputy, Jürgen Stark, writes that the purpose of the G-7 summits is to "provide a forum for the informal exchange of views and the discussion of current world economic and general policy issues of fundamental significance." Cooperation among the G-7 finance ministers and central bank governors, in his view, "does not imply *coordination* much less joint decisions laying down specific interest rate or budgetary policies or even fixing exchange rates." On the other hand, he argues that "the foremost objective of G-7 cooperation is the *reconciliation* of national economic and fiscal policies" and that G-7 actions, moreover, can serve "to *reinforce* the economic policy adjustments needed in each individual country" [emphases added], (Stark 1995, 52–57).

economic policy among the seven Summit countries"; that "the purposes of improved *coordination* should explicitly include promoting non-inflationary economic growth, strengthening market-oriented incentives for employment and productive investment, opening the international trading and investment system, and fostering greater stability in exchange rates"; and that "the Finance Ministers and Central Bankers in coordinating multilateral surveillance [should] make their best efforts to reach an understanding on appropriate remedial measures whenever there is a deviation from an intended course"[7] (Tokyo summit communiqué, 1986). Although the G-7 ministers and governors have not always implemented this charge effectively, the objectives have never been repudiated.

Past Successes

Despite its recent record, the history of the G-7 suggests there is nothing inherent about its failure. In fact, the group's performance (and that of its predecessors, the G-10 and G-5) has fluctuated sharply. The original G-10 proved quite adept at firefighting, resolving the periodic crises that dotted the Bretton Woods period when international capital flows threatened to force currency devaluations (mainly of sterling and the dollar) or revaluations (mainly of the deutsche mark). It also worked out the two general realignments of parities that were required, the first via the Smithsonian Agreement, when the adjustable peg system of Bretton Woods collapsed in the early 1970s.

The G-10 also implemented modest systemic reforms with the creation of the General Arrangements to Borrow (box 2.2) to augment the resources of the IMF in 1962 and with the launch of Special Drawing Rights (SDRs) at the Fund in 1967.[8] Despite much discussion, however, the G-10 was unable to agree on needed changes in the international adjustment process—particularly an increase in exchange rate flexibility. Hence it failed to prevent the collapse of the Bretton Woods system in 1971-73, when the United States took unilateral steps to achieve dollar devaluation because it concluded that the system's excessive rigidity of exchange rates blocked needed correction of the American payments deficits and corresponding surpluses elsewhere.

The G-5/G-7 has experienced two periods of notable success since its creation in the middle 1970s. The first was the Bonn summit in 1978. The

---

7. The "intended course" presumably referred to the 10 economic variables included in the prior paragraph of the communiqué: "GNP growth rates, inflation rates, interest rates, unemployment rates, fiscal deficit ratios, current account and trade balances, monetary growth rates, reserves, and exchange rates."

8. The G-10 originally sought to create SDRs only for its own members. We will see that similar myopia still afflicts this group in its current effort to augment the resources that can be provided to the IMF.

impact of the outcome at Bonn was exceedingly controversial, both then and now,[9] but it represents the most far-reaching agreement ever achieved on international policy coordination and was clearly the most ambitious summit of all time. The G-7 adopted a coordinated global growth strategy with precise commitments for action by the largest member countries, all of which were faithfully implemented. That package in turn enabled President Jimmy Carter to win congressional acceptance of the expiration of American controls on domestic oil prices, and thus contribute substantially to a better global energy balance (which was of crucial importance at that time). Bonn also gave a decisive political push to the Tokyo Round of multilateral trade negotiations in the GATT.

The finance ministers, along with the responsible international organizations, prepared the macroeconomic components of the Bonn package. But the summiteers themselves, assisted by their sherpas, completed the package by bringing in broader issues such as energy and trade. They thus provided lasting evidence of the extensive policy coordination that can be achieved with political commitments at the highest level and trade-offs across issues that are typically handled by different ministries within each government (Putnam and Henning 1989).

An even more impressive period of G-5/G-7 success, this time conducted almost wholly by the financial officials, occurred in the mid-1980s (Tietmeyer 1988; Funabashi 1989). Through their Plaza Agreement of September 1985, the group played a central role in correcting the enormous overvaluation of the dollar that threatened both international financial stability and the global trading system. The Plaza process in fact produced a textbook correction in the external balances of the major countries: the American current account deficit fell from 3.8 percent of GDP in 1987 to about 1 percent in 1991-92,[10] and the Japanese surplus fell from 4.3 percent in 1986 to 1.2 percent in 1990 (Krugman 1991).[11]

The G-5 continued to operate successfully for a period after the Plaza. The central bank governors coordinated several interest rate reductions

---

9. Some observers believe that it contributed substantially to the subsequent jump in world inflation (see discussion below).

10. The US current account deficit actually fell to almost zero in 1991, but this outcome was distorted by receipts of over $40 billion from the allies for partial funding of the Gulf War (which count as inward "unilateral transfers" in the official statistics). The American recession of 1990-91 also contributed to the reduction in its current account deficit.

11. A few analysts (e.g., Feldstein 1994) argue that the dollar would have depreciated sufficiently without the Plaza and that the G-5 initiative was largely an exercise in public relations. No one can know, of course, but this view ignores the fact that the dollar continued to rise in 1984-85 without any conceivable justification from "the fundamentals" (Mussa 1994) and that, after beginning to decline in early 1985 with help from extensive European intervention, it rose again in the summer of 1985 before dropping again shortly before the G-5 met at the Plaza.

Box 2.2 The General Arrangements to Borrow

The General Arrangements to Borrow (GAB) originated in October 1962 to provide a mechanism for the G-10 to lend additional resources to the IMF. There was widespread concern then that the shift to capital account convertibility could create a need for large drawings on the IMF to fund balance of payments deficits, especially by the United States, which, contrary to all postwar expectations, had become a deficit country.

Under the GAB, each G-10 member undertook to lend to the Fund, beyond its Fund quota, specified amounts of its own currency. At its inception, amounts pledged under the GAB totaled $6 billion, of which the United States accounted for one-third. They now sum to SDR18.5 billion, or about $27 billion:

Participant	Amount (millions of SDR)
United States	4,250
Germany	2,380
Japan	2,125
France	1,700
Britain	1,700
Italy	1,105
Switzerland	1,020
Canada	892.5
Netherlands	850
Belgium	595
Sweden	382.5
Subtotal	17,000
Saudi Arabia (associated)	1,500
Total	18,500

Formation of the GAB represented a victory for the European members, who, having recovered from the postwar devastation, were now anxious to assert themselves in international monetary affairs. The influence of the European countries was reflected in the carving out of the GAB from the regular IMF decision-making processes. The Europeans regarded the IMF as dominated by the United States, which at the GAB's creation was expected to be the most likely borrower (R. Solomon 1982, 43). The European governments themselves, however, proved to be the more frequent GAB beneficiaries.

in 1986 to sustain global growth. The group made a major effort to institutionalize its cooperation, developing a set of "objective indicators" to guide the adjustment process that were adopted at the Tokyo summit in 1986 (but never implemented). That same summit sought to link the finance ministers more closely to its own political process, in part by aligning the membership of the two groups (and thus converting the finance group from its previous G-5 to a G-7).

Moreover, the Louvre Accord of February 1987 adopted a system of currency reference ranges, building on a US-Japan agreement of October

Box 2.2 (continued)

The GAB was activated for the first time in November 1964 for Britain, again for Britain in 1965, and for France in 1968. During the 1970s, the GAB was activated for Britain in 1976 and for Italy in 1977. The GAB has been activated for the United States only once, in 1978. It has not been activated since (Ainley 1984; de Vries 1985).

When a participating country wants to draw on the GAB, it first consults the managing director of the IMF and then the other participants. The managing director, after consultation with the Executive Board and GAB members, proposes activation of the arrangements. His proposal becomes effective when both the GAB participants and the Executive Board accept the proposal. Once funds are transferred to the IMF, they are re-lent to the borrowing country under an IMF program. The IMF therefore serves as intermediary between lender and borrower and as GAB administrator.

Originally, only GAB members could draw upon it. Thus, the GAB was controversial. Nonmembers argued that the borrowed funds should supplement the general resources of the IMF and be available to the full Fund membership. The G-10 argued that large drawings on their part would likely jeopardize the availability of IMF financing to IMF members outside the G-10 and that the arrangement would therefore help to protect the access of these nonmembers to IMF financing. The nonmembers acceded to the GAB.

An amendment to the GAB in 1983, triggered by the debt crisis, opened the arrangements for use by non-G-10 countries, but only in exceptional situations "associated with balance of payments problems of members of a character or aggregate size that could threaten the stability of the international monetary system." Activation for GAB members faces a somewhat easier test: ". . . in order to forestall or cope with an impairment of the international monetary system" (Edwards 1985, 290-91). In April 1992, the G-10 declared its willingness to use the GAB to finance a currency stabilization fund for Russia (G-10 communiqué 1992), although the GAB has not been activated for this purpose owing to the lack of a stabilization program deemed acceptable.

The IMF Executive Board, with the concurrence of GAB participants, has amended the GAB several times. Switzerland, which did not become a member of the IMF until 1992, became associated with the GAB in 1964 and a formal GAB member in 1983. Saudi Arabia, associated with the GAB, stands ready to lend SDR1.5 billion under the arrangement. Unanimous agreement of the GAB members and a decision of the IMF Executive Board would be required to make further enlargements in GAB participation, the subject of ongoing negotiations as of this writing.

1986 to stabilize the yen-dollar relationship. The accord was the most ambitious effort to restore global monetary stability since the breakdown of the Bretton Woods system.[12] The "telephone accord" of late 1987 led to the "bear squeeze" in the currency markets during the first week of 1988, which decisively ended the dollar's post-Plaza fall. There were a number of subsequent interludes of successful G-7 intervention in the

---

12. However, the ranges were adopted before the dollar had completed its correction and thus could not be maintained for very long (see discussion below).

currency markets even after the broader Plaza-Louvre framework had eroded (Dominguez and Frankel 1993; Catte, Galli, and Rebecchini 1994).

The Bonn summit agreement was more far-reaching than the Plaza process. It addressed a wide range of macroeconomic policies and outcomes, not just exchange rates, as well as several key issues that were even broader. Bonn's implementation and lasting impact were aborted by the second oil shock, however, and the summit could not address some highly relevant monetary policy issues because of the nonparticipation of the central bankers in summit meetings. Hence the Plaza-Louvre period represents the pinnacle of G-7 success to date.

There are several other successful episodes of international economic coordination that can be partially attributed to the G-7. One came in early 1991, when the finance ministers worked out and implemented the financial burden-sharing arrangements for the Gulf War. Just after the commencement of the allied aerial bombardment of Iraq and just before the ground offensive was launched, Treasury Secretary Nicholas F. Brady held bilateral meetings with his key counterparts to apportion the costs of the operation. A G-7 ministerial meeting provided the occasion for these discussions, and the G-7 process sustained working relationships among the ministers, as it always should. The regularized network of contacts among middle-level G-7 officials facilitated follow-through. The economic component of the war was thus handled efficiently, clearing the decks for the allies to pursue the military campaign to its successful conclusion.

Another success for which the group should get some credit was the rolling response throughout the 1980s to the debt crisis of the developing countries. Although the United States again took an active lead, the G-5 conducted part of the rescue of Mexico after its near-default in the summer of 1982. The group was involved in implementing the Baker Plan in 1985, when it became clear that the problem would last longer than had been initially believed, and the Brady Plan in 1989, when systemic debt relief became necessary. The evolving strategy bought time to enable American and other commercial banks to rebuild their balance sheets, to offset the losses on their lending to the developing countries, and thus to protect the international financial system. It also enabled the debtor countries to restore their creditworthiness (Cline 1995a). On the other hand, the G-7 was slow to recognize the need for debt reduction and thus may have contributed to weaker economic performance in the debtor countries, especially in Latin America, than was necessary.[13]

---

13. For a selection of major works on the debt crisis and its evolution, see Bergsten, Cline, and Williamson 1985; Cline 1983, 1995a; Cohen 1989, 1992; Dornbusch and Edwards 1991; Edwards and Larraín 1989; Eichengreen and Portes 1989; Frieden 1991; Kahler 1986; Kenen 1990; Fischer 1987; Husain and Diwan 1989; Kapstein 1994; Sachs 1989, 1990; Williamson 1988; Haggard and Kaufman 1992.

None of these initiatives worked perfectly. Indeed, disillusion with their results and unhappiness with the process that produced them have led some observers to question the entire concept of international economic coordination. This is especially true of some Japanese with respect to the Louvre Accord, many Germans with respect to the Bonn summit, and most of the independent central banks with respect to the coordination of monetary policies. These memories and interpretations of the past are clearly among the causes of the recent G-7 inaction. Moreover, changes in global economic conditions since the two periods of major G-7 success have engendered skepticism over the prospects for coordination today even from some who share the view that it is desirable in principle and that it worked well in earlier years.

This book evaluates these questions and concludes that, even though all of the "successful" G-7 efforts fell short of realizing their full objectives, they were clearly worthwhile. We argue that policy coordination remains quite feasible under contemporary circumstances, indeed that those circumstances *increase* the need for active G-7 leadership and, properly interpreted, provide a foundation for effective G-7 activity, albeit in a somewhat different manner from that of the past. The G-7 has experienced periods of effective cooperation; these successes are replicable and can be improved upon if the group will adopt reforms of the type proposed. The desultory record of the 1990s is anything but inevitable.

The rest of the book addresses these questions. Chapter 3 details the decline of the G-7. Chapter 4 assesses the causes of disagreement within the group that deter coordination. Chapter 5 analyzes the growing consensus within the G-7 that coordination is futile or dysfunctional, provoking inter alia a new "nonaggression pact" among the members. Chapter 6 presents the conceptual foundation for reviving the G-7, and chapter 7 proposes a specific action program to do so.

3

The Decline of the G-7

In the last chapter, we cited five areas in which the G-7 should exercise leadership responsibilities: world growth and stability, exchange rates, current account imbalances, the stance of its members toward other countries, and the design of the international economic system as a whole. Each of these five policy areas encompasses two central dimensions. First and foremost, the G-7 must try to prevent the emergence of major problems. Second, it must be ready to attempt to cure or at least contain such problems (or crises) when they arise—as they inevitably will.

There have been major failures, at the levels of both prevention and cure, in each of the five areas of G-7 responsibility in recent years. In this chapter, we first describe the decline of the G-7. We then assess whether global economic outcomes have suffered as a result—and thus whether the decline constitutes a major concern for the world economy as a whole.

World Growth and Stability

The chief failure of macroeconomic management in recent years has been high unemployment and/or income stagnation throughout the G-7, linked to the very slow recovery of the world economy from the recession of the early 1990s.[1] The main jobs problems lay in Europe and Japan, while the United States suffered from very slow increases in real standards of living. During this period, none of the large industrial countries have

---

1. A similar failure occurred in the early 1980s (Obstfeld 1995; Oudiz and Sachs 1984).

experienced a steady rise in the number of jobs that pay significantly higher wages.

Germany enjoyed a short-lived boom in 1990–91 as a result of its national unification while the rest of the world was stagnating. But the huge budget deficits that resulted from subsidizing the new eastern states without adequate tax increases, along with continuing structural problems and the absence of any substantial appreciation of the mark, produced inflationary pressures that forced the Bundesbank to raise interest rates sharply. Those high interest rates radiated out to the rest of the European Union—all of which (except Greece) at the time were members of the European Monetary System (EMS) with their exchange rates pegged to the mark—despite the fact that unemployment throughout the Union was already above 8 percent in 1991. The result was a Europe-wide recession that has left unemployment at about 11 percent. Another slowdown was already apparent in early 1996, even though there had been no substantial pickup after the earlier recession.

Japan, meanwhile, was entering its own recession in the early 1990s. Monetary policy had to be tightened substantially to burst the "bubble economy" brought on by excessively easy money in the late 1980s. But fiscal policy was also extremely restrictive throughout the early 1990s; the structural government budget was in surplus until 1993. The result was a prolonged recession, which, coupled with the sharp depreciation of the yen in 1989–90, led Japan's global current account to soar to record surpluses. This generated substantial pressure on the weak world economy and triggered strong attacks on Japanese trade policy from the United States and other countries.

The United States began to recover from its recession of 1990–91 shortly after the end of the Gulf War in early 1991. But its growth remained modest until 1994. In addition, its current account deficit, which had fallen to 1 percent of GDP in 1991–92, began rising again and reached a level in 1995 that was second in absolute terms only to the record deficit of 1987, importantly due to slow growth in the other industrial countries.

Unlike the other G-7 countries, the United States achieved full employment (as defined by most economists) by late 1994. But about half of the US labor force faced a real average wage that had been declining for two decades, and median family income stagnated over this extended period. Hence the United States also faced major economic problems. Slow productivity growth, rooted in domestic factors, was the chief culprit. Slow world growth exacerbated the problem, however, because it hindered the growth of the US export sector, where jobs pay up to 15 percent more than the national average (Richardson and Rindal 1996). Stronger growth abroad would have enabled the United States to further globalize its economy and thus deal at least partially with its income and wage problems.

We shall see shortly that the G-7's failure to manage its currency relationships effectively contributed substantially to these macroeconomic problems. The G-7's "benign neglect" of the yen after 1987 enabled Japan to rely on monetary rather than fiscal policy to stimulate domestic demand, and the result was the "bubble economy." The consequent sharp depreciation of the yen in 1989–90 triggered much of the huge Japanese surplus in the early 1990s that both exported unemployment to other countries and reduced pressure on Japan to undertake domestic stimulus measures. The subsequent sharp appreciation of the yen, in 1993 and especially in early 1995, prolonged the Japanese recession. In Europe, the failure to engineer an appreciation of the deutsche mark promptly after unification forced the Bundesbank to raise interest rates sharply to quell the resulting inflationary risks—and thus to export unemployment throughout the Continent. These recent episodes are a stark reminder of the crucial links among exchange rates, macroeconomic policies, and economic performance.

Whatever the cause of the global slowdown during the early 1990s, there was a strong case for a coordinated G-7 growth strategy at almost any point during that period. The G-7 had in fact worked out coordinated responses to very similar global configurations in the late 1970s and the mid-1980s but totally failed to provide the needed joint initiative on this occasion. The dimensions of such a strategy were clear:

- further reductions in the American budget deficit, to lower both world interest rates and the international imbalances;

- a substantial tightening of German fiscal policy, in essence paying for national unification, to permit lower German interest rates and thus lower interest rates throughout Europe;

- real Japanese fiscal expansion to restart the world's second largest economy and, along with substantial yen appreciation, to reduce its huge external surplus.

The United States in fact proposed elements of such a strategy during both the late Bush and early Clinton administrations. Germany and Japan refused to go along. The result included huge losses of world output, further rises in unemployment in Europe, the worst postwar recession in Japanese history, and continued wage and income sluggishness in the United States. There is no reason to believe that, given the extremely large amounts of unutilized capacity around the world, such a strategy would have reignited inflationary pressures.

Moreover, the world's two most important international imbalances— the American deficit and the Japanese surplus—rose to new highs. This confluence of economic developments again threatened the international trading system. The Uruguay Round nearly failed, which would have shattered confidence in the global trading rules and institutional arrangements. A close brush with trade war in mid-1995 was averted only when the United States decided not to make good on threats to retaliate against Japan, despite failing to achieve some of its goals in the negotiations over autos and auto parts. The G-7 failed to exercise one of its cardinal leadership responsibilities: the maintenance of global economic growth.

Exchange Rates

Management of the currency markets has two goals. One is to avoid "disorderly markets" and excessive currency volatility. The second, and far more important, is to avoid prolonged misalignments—discrepancies between market exchange rates and countries' underlying competitive positions—that create significant economic dislocations, including large current account imbalances and pressures for trade protection.

This is the area of greatest G-7 failure over the past decade. Virtually all observers agree that currency management represents the clearest responsibility of the group. It is the issue that led to the creation of the G-7's predecessors—the G-10 in the 1960s to stave off attacks on the dollar and sterling, and the G-5 in the 1970s to try to manage the new world of flexible exchange rates. It has been a goal of G-7 activity throughout its existence—except for the experiment with free floating in the early 1980s, which produced the largest currency misalignment of all time for the world's most important currency and thus demonstrated the folly of "benign neglect."

To be sure, some analysts and even officials question the effectiveness of G-7 efforts to affect the currency markets, at least for any prolonged period. That issue will be addressed in some detail in chapter 6. Suffice it to say here that it has been the revealed preference of governments to try to manage exchange rates throughout the history of the modern world economy (except for the disastrous interlude of 1981–84), most recently throughout 1995. Moreover, much recent research suggests that G-7 intervention can be quite effective when conducted properly (Dominguez and Frankel 1993; Catte, Galli, and Rebecchini 1994).

But every G-7 currency has experienced a major realignment during the last decade and none of them have been handled effectively. The most conspicuous failure relates to the yen. The Plaza-initiated adjustment was completed by the end of 1987, when the yen had appreciated to about 120:1 against the dollar. The exchange rate changes of 1985–87, along with some macroeconomic adjustment in both the United States (budget reduction) and Japan (domestic demand expansion), produced a sharp reduction in both countries' external balances, which we noted in chapter 2 as a G-7 success story. But the G-7 subsequently let the yen depreciate by one-third during the late 1980s despite the continued improvement in Japan's underlying competitive position (figure 3.1). Hence Japan's exter-

Figure 3.1 Yen per dollar,[a] 4 January 1988 through 22 April 1996

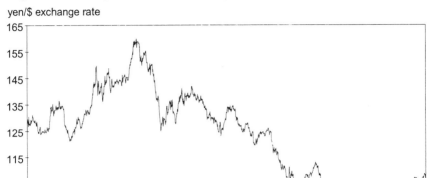

yen/$ exchange rate

a. New York noon buying rate.

Source: Chicago Federal Reserve Bank.

nal surplus, with the usual lag of two to three years and exacerbated by the onset of recession in Japan, soared to record levels in the early 1990s. The adverse effects on both the world economy and on Japan itself have already been described.

Another major failure of currency policy in recent years relates to the EMS crises of 1992 and 1993. The G-7 did not address these problems either, primarily because the Europeans viewed them as "their responsibility." The United States and Japan did not challenge this view, honoring the informal "nonaggression pact" that is described in chapter 5.

But the EMS crises had important global effects, so the G-7 (and the IMF) should have considered them. In particular, the failure of the EMS to engineer appreciation of the deutsche mark soon after German unification was decisive in leading Germany (and thus Europe as a whole) toward much higher interest rates, which prolonged the stagnation of their economies and the world economy throughout the early 1990s.[2]

---

2. More generally, the EMS comes under strain whenever the dollar goes through one of its periodic bouts of weakness. A large share of the conversions of dollars go into deutsche marks and thus push the mark up—against the weaker EMS currencies as well as against the dollar itself, hence stretching the margins within which the Europeans seek to maintain their exchange rates. The intensity of this problem has been reduced since the EMS sharply expanded the width of these margins in 1993 but it still exists, as revealed by European calls for further dollar appreciation—despite America's continuing large external deficit—into 1996. Hence the Europeans as well as non-Europeans should seek G-7 cooperation on this range of currency issues.

American and Japanese involvement in the contemporary discussion might have tilted the outcome in a more constructive direction.

The two European currency crises were quite different. In 1992, sterling and the lira were forced to depreciate sharply because they had become substantially overvalued—the pound because it had entered the EMS at an overvalued level in 1990 (Williamson 1991; Wren-Lewis et al. 1990) and the lira because Italian inflation had substantially exceeded German inflation since the prior realignment in 1987. The task for currency management was to prevent such large disequilibria; the two deficit countries were at fault, and the EMS should have maintained the practice of small, frequent realignments, which had been integral to its successful operation from 1979 until 1987. Postunification appreciation of the mark would have helped, though it would not have obviated the need for some depreciation of the two overvalued currencies. Coupled with this policy failure was the tendency to blame "the speculators" for causing a crisis that was patently due to governmental mismanagement, a charge that reflects the broader paralysis in G-7 attitudes about its own efficacy (which we discuss further in chapter 5).

In 1993 the French franc and several other European currencies were also attacked by huge capital outflows. On that occasion, the EMS responded by widening its exchange rate bands, and after temporary and modest depreciation the currencies in question moved back to near their original levels. The revealed shortcoming in this case was the absence of systemic currency arrangements—wider rather than narrower bands—that would have prevented such disturbances in the first place.

A potentially even more fundamental G-7 failure with respect to European monetary arrangements is the total absence of discussion of the implications of Economic and Monetary Union (EMU) for the world economy. Yet successful creation of the Euro would almost certainly produce the world's second key currency in a relatively short period. There could be a profound impact on the composition of world reserves, exchange rates, the dollar, and hence global financial arrangements—all of which should be central concerns of the G-7 (Henning 1996).

Another recent G-7 failure in the currency markets represents a case of misguided action rather than inaction. The G-7 began to call for a "stronger dollar" in early 1995 and launched a series of technically skillful joint interventions during the summer, with considerable success, to promote that outcome. The group was of course correct to reverse the excessive strengthening of the yen, which had overshot on the upside early in the year, soaring above 80:1. In addition, there was legitimate concern that the fragility of Japan's financial system posed a risk to the entire world economy and that an overvalued yen intensified that risk.

But with Japan's external surpluses at record levels, in absolute terms, far above those that represented even a generous definition of "equilibrium," there was no reason to start a bandwagon rolling in the opposite direction that weakened the yen well beyond 100:1. Moreover, in the face of large American external deficits, there was no need to push the dollar up against other major currencies if the goal was solely to engineer sufficient yen depreciation to alleviate the risk of a Japanese financial crisis. At a minimum, the G-7 should have agreed to a level at which it would intervene symmetrically to *stop* the appreciation of the dollar, especially against the yen, but there is no evidence that it did so.[3]

Several other recent episodes regarding the dollar are also noteworthy. In May 1994, with much effort, the United States induced the other G-7 countries (and some outside the group) to intervene strongly to stem a decline of the dollar (Federal Reserve Board 1994). That coordinated action worked effectively. But American trade officials shortly thereafter resumed their "Japan bashing," which the markets interpreted as indicating that the United States really wanted a *lower* dollar. The joint intervention was forgotten, and the dollar resumed its downward slide. America's G-7 partners, especially Germany, were furious over the "lack of commitment" by the United States to the agreed course of action—especially after they had invested heavily in an enterprise about which they were dubious in the first place. The real problem was a lack of policy coordination among government agencies in Washington, but the international damage was acute.

In November 1994, when the United States again decided that intervention was needed to defend the dollar, it was therefore forced to conduct operations without the participation of the European central banks. This was one of the cases where the United States knew that a request for help would be rejected and thus did not ask. After further depreciation of the dollar in early 1995, joint intervention resumed in the spring, but German policymakers undercut the effectiveness of the action with harshly critical statements about American fiscal policy. The disarray within the G-7, and

---

3. Cline (1995b) concludes that there will be no lasting reduction in the Japanese current account surplus with the yen at 100:1 or weaker, even on optimistic assumptions on the growth of Japanese domestic demand. At 85–90:1, by contrast, the surplus could be expected to drop below 2 percent of GDP and perhaps even meet the Framework Talks' target of $1\frac{1}{2}$ percent (as initially proposed in Bergsten and Noland 1993). Part of the reduction in Japan's surplus in late 1995 and early 1996 can be attributed to the short-term (J-curve) effects of the yen *depreciation* in that period and cannot be expected to last; most models, including those in Japan, predict renewed growth of the Japanese surplus by late 1996 or 1997 unless the yen appreciates again.

On the other hand, some Japanese now argue that the substantial "outsourcing" of production by Japanese firms, due to the prior appreciation of the yen, will lead to much sharper and more permanent declines in Japan's current account surplus even if the yen remains at weaker levels. Formal models would of course by unable to incorporate such parametric shifts for at least a couple of years. Our tentative judgment is that the equilibrium yen-dollar rate now lies somewhere between 90:1 and 100:1, and we advocate in chapter 7 that the two governments attempt to stabilize the rate within 10 percent on either side of 100:1.

particularly the sharp divergence of views between the United States and Germany, had become intense. The differences were overcome for a time later in 1995 to permit the successful (if excessive) intervention described above, but they remain sufficiently deep-seated that they cloud the prospects for meaningful cooperation.

The G-7 has thus consistently failed to exercise its responsibilities for currency management in recent years. Major problems have emerged in avoiding fundamental disequilibria, as with the yen and several European currencies; in actively pushing rates too far, as with the dollar and yen; and even in daily smoothing operations, as with the dollar more frequently. Every G-7 currency has experienced one or more severe problems or crises during the past decade; preventive action by the group has been conspicuous by its absence and the responses to the subsequent crises have often been ineffectual or even misguided.

International Imbalances

The avoidance of large current account imbalances is another obvious responsibility of the G-7 because current account positions are the most direct manifestation of the international economic relationships among the member countries. Its failures in this area are equally clear-cut and relate directly to its shortcomings with respect to economic growth and exchange rates.

The Japanese surplus, after falling to only 1.2 percent of GDP in 1990, largely as a result of the coordinated adjustment program launched at the Plaza in 1985, soared above 3 percent again in the early 1990s. This created several major problems. It exported unemployment because Japan was exploiting demand in other countries during a world recession rather than creating its own. It generated enormous pressure on the trading system because countries throughout the world concluded that Japan's continuing restrictions on market access were especially unacceptable in the face of such a surplus. It subsequently led to a sharp appreciation of the yen in 1993–95, such that the Japanese recession itself was prolonged and deepened, with further adverse effects on the world economy.

The American deficit, after falling to less than 1 percent of GDP by 1991–92, again rose sharply to between 2 and 2.5 percent (and to near-record highs in absolute terms) in both 1994 and 1995. These developments were an important source of the downward pressure on the dollar in 1994–95. In addition, they intensified aggressive American assaults on markets around the world. When the American economy weakens and unemployment rises again, they also are likely to produce renewed pressures for protectionist trade responses—as happened during the previous period of record US deficits in the mid-1980s (Grilli 1988).

The third large imbalance of the postwar period, the German surplus, was in fact the most persistent. It disappeared in the 1990s but solely because of the country's unification. The G-7 had nothing to do with the "solution" of this problem.

Hence the G-7 has also permitted the renewed onset of severe international imbalances. This failure is particularly discouraging because effective G-7 cooperation in the mid-1980s had resolved most of the previous imbalances that had caused such problems throughout that decade and was probably the group's greatest achievement. The Japanese surplus in the early 1990s was in fact very similar to the American deficit of the mid-1980s: an imbalance so large that almost every other country in the world, including the rest of the G-7, was on the other side of the ledger. Action by the country in question was clearly called for. If it were unwilling to act on its own, pressure from its G-7 peers should have been standard operating procedure. Even under such extreme circumstances, however, there was no major G-7 initiative and bilateral American efforts to elicit Japanese action were unsuccessful. The renewed soaring of the imbalances was closely related to the group's failure to promote more robust global growth and to avoid renewed currency misalignments.

External Relations

Relations with the rest of the world constitute a fourth area of G-7 responsibility. As part of its effort to steer the world economy, the group must coordinate its stance toward "external" problems such as the developing-world debt crisis in the 1980s and the transformation of the nonmarket economies in the 1990s. There has been some success in recent years but notable failures have occurred in at least three cases: Mexico, Russia, and allocations of Special Drawing Rights (SDRs) at the International Monetary Fund (IMF).

The rescue package for the 1994–95 Mexico crisis was ultimately successful in stopping both the Mexican financial panic itself and the "contagion effects" on other emerging-market currencies. This again revealed the capacity of the G-7 to contain international monetary crises. In addition, the IMF provided a vital component of the eventual program.

But the disarray of the G-7 was evident in at least three aspects of the crisis. First, the G-7 did nothing to prevent it. Numerous private economists pointed to the unsustainability of the Mexican current account deficits and the subsequent need for a large devaluation a year or even two before the events unfolded. Yet there is no evidence of any G-7 (or IMF or US) effort to urge Mexico to take preventive action, nor even of any recognition by the G-7 that a major crisis was brewing.

Second, the initial support package devised by the US administration— the proposal to Congress for legislation authorizing $40 billion of loan guarantees—had no meaningful international dimension. Despite the administration's forceful argument that the Mexican crisis was systemic in nature, the United States proposed to deal with it virtually alone.[4] The official American position was that the urgency of the situation required such a rapid response that there was no time to obtain foreign participation. Hence they did not ask for any.

But the administration had to know that congressional approval of its proposal would take far longer to obtain than would be necessary, under normal circumstances, to achieve international support. One of the cardinal purposes of G-7 cooperation is in fact to maintain close working relationships and consultations so that virtually instant responses to financial crises can be put together. By the administration's own admission, this central requirement of effective G-7 collaboration was absent when it was most needed.[5]

Moreover, the congressional reaction to the proposed support for Mexico could only have been undermined—as indeed it was, though much more powerfully for wholly separate reasons—by the absence of such burden sharing. Thus the administration's defense bears a strong resemblance to the case of exchange market intervention in the fall of 1994 described earlier: American unwillingness to ask for foreign help, especially from Germany, due to expectation of a negative reply. To be sure, it *would* have been worse to ask and be turned down than not to ask at all. But the implication once again is of severe disarray within the G-7.

Subsequent events confirmed the G-7 disarray over Mexico. The initial administration proposal attracted so much congressional opposition that it was forced to instead extend $20 billion of credit from the Treasury's own Exchange Stabilization Fund. But this halving of total support by the United States required an offsetting increase somewhere else, since the administration's earlier proposal had convinced the markets that the larger amount was needed. Hence it belatedly sought an unprecedented level of assistance from the IMF. In a third example of G-7 discord, two of its members—Germany and the United Kingdom, along with several other European countries—then abstained on the initial IMF vote on the US proposal. The plan still won enough support to succeed and the Europeans eventually went along, but the sharp disagreement among the key countries, in the face of a crisis that had become apparent to all, was starkly revealed.[6]

---

4. The Bank for International Settlements (BIS) was to provide a modest short-term line of credit but no longer-term money was to be provided by other G-7 countries.

5. Treasury Under Secretary for International Affairs Lawrence Summers recognized publicly that the G-7 partners "were not consulted in a timely fashion nor properly informed" (*Handelsblatt*, 25 April 1995, 39).

6. The Germans have also acknowledged publicly (Stark 1995, 54) that "cooperation in dealing with Mexico's problem at the start of the year was not as effective as it might have been."

The significance of the mishandling of the Mexican crisis for overall G-7 relations cannot be overstated, primarily because the Europeans saw it as a clear example of American ineptness. The original American plan was floated without prior consultation; one extremely influential European official "heard about it on the radio." Then the United States indicated that the rescue package would have to total $40 billion before US officials were sure they could assemble such an amount—and they were unable to do so on their own. Next came the announcement of the fallback support package without any agreement on a Mexican adjustment program, which took another three weeks to negotiate. Finally, the American argument that Mexico represented a "systemic threat"— justifying a record IMF program—shifted abruptly from stressing the risks to the financial markets to the threat to policy reform around the world if the "star pupil" were not defended. The episode shook foreign confidence in American leadership and has had a lasting impact on G-7 relations.

The decline of the G-7 has also been evident in the case of Russia, which has been a primary target of the group's attention throughout the 1990s. The end of the Cold War was a moment, if ever there was one, for the victorious coalition to jettison narrow, green-eyeshade calculations in favor of visionary, magnanimous treatment of the defeated power. The G-7, however, utterly failed to grasp the historic opportunity presented by the temporary ascendance of the reformers within the Russian government in late 1991 and early 1992. When a mini-Marshall Plan was called for, the G-7 sent their deputy ministers to Moscow to insist that the former Soviet republics accept joint and several liability for Soviet foreign debt (Armendariz de Aghion and Williamson 1993; Åslund 1995). The first large "assistance package," announced in April 1992, contained little new money and came too late; most of it remains undisbursed to this day. The G-7 spent considerable time working out a currency support program for the ruble, which the Russians have been unable to tap for more than three years, rather than assembling real assistance. The group's posture wholly failed to replicate the successful American posture toward Germany (and Europe as a whole) after 1945.

Assistance by the G-7 to Russia has of course been constrained by that government's wavering commitment to domestic economic stabilization. The group's second aid package, prepared in 1993 and amounting to $28 billion, was a distinct improvement; much of it, too, was not new money and has not been disbursed, but most of the package is committed and awaits Russia's meeting prespecified conditions. The engagement of the G-7 and IMF, and the availability of foreign resources, arguably nudged Prime Minister Victor Chernomyrdin toward reform in mid-1994. In April 1995 Russia reached a $6.8 billion stand-by agreement with the IMF, and disbursements were completed by early 1996. A new IMF loan of more than $10 billion was agreed upon in early 1996. The G-7 posture toward Russia has improved considerably, though its initial efforts were ineffectual and even counterproductive.[7]

The third case of external G-7 failure relates to its repudiation by the rest of the world at the annual meeting of the IMF in Madrid in September 1994. Fortunately, the substance involved was of secondary importance. It revolved around a new issue of SDRs, the international money invented by the Fund in 1967, which has remained moribund since its last distribution in 1981.

To help Russia and a few other countries build their international reserves, the G-7 proposed a "justice" allocation of SDRs limited to IMF members that had joined the organization since 1981 and thus had not participated in previous distributions. The group was unwilling to supplement this "special allocation" with a traditional allocation, as proposed by the Fund's managing director, that would benefit all member countries. The G-7 position apparently emerged at the behest primarily of Germany, which always seeks to avoid or sharply limit SDR allocations on the (highly dubious) grounds that they could fuel global inflation. The United States, which was desperately seeking devices to help Russia without having to tap its budget, agreed with the approach.[8]

In a stunning action never before witnessed in the collegial and normally nonconfrontational halls of the IMF, the rest of the world almost universally repudiated the G-7 proposal. Virtually all developing countries, and quite a few industrial countries, rejected the idea of allocating SDRs only to a limited share of the membership—fearing a precedent for future selective allocations that could leave many countries, notably developing countries, outside the scheme. The issue remained unresolved as of this writing.

---

7. The most recent G-7 strategy has properly relied primarily on the international financial institutions rather than the G-7 itself or bilateral channels for assistance to Russia. The G-7 also prodded the IMF to introduce the Systemic Transformation Facility, providing funds for worthy purposes in the absence of stabilization, and pushed IMF staff at several points to try to overcome technical obstacles to agreement with the Russian government.

8. Because the limited "justice" allocation would require amendment of the IMF Articles, however, it would require the administration to seek congressional approval—a step that the administration has rightly made every effort to avoid on all other international monetary issues of late. Moreover, amending the articles for this purpose would in turn open up the possibility of other amendments that would be distasteful to the United States, and even more unpopular in the Congress than a limited allocation of SDRs. Hence American support for the proposal may have been a cynical attempt by the Treasury to placate domestic supporters of aid to Russia while colluding with the German monetary authorities, whose help it needed on other issues, to ensure that nothing would happen. Then-Under Secretary of the Treasury for International Affairs Lawrence Summers indicated publicly that the United States "backed Bundesbank President Tietmeyer to the bitter end" on the issue (*Handelsblatt*, 25 April 1995, 39).

The decline of the G-7 can thus be observed in its external activities as well as in the internal relationships among its members. The group's efforts to deal with Mexico, Russia, and a key area of IMF policy have displayed both the fissures within the group that have prevented agreement and the serious errors that have resulted from its consensus positions. The G-7's failures of both omission and commission are again apparent.

The International Economic System

The fifth and final area of recent G-7 failure relates to the design of the international economic system itself. This responsibility has two aspects. One is the maintenance of an effective *adjustment* process to prevent and correct imbalances in national current account positions, including arrangements that induce constructive changes in national economic policies and exchange rates that will contribute to that outcome in a stable manner. The other is the provision of adequate *financial* resources to deal with crises that would otherwise both threaten domestic stability in affected countries and be unnecessarily costly to the world as a whole (à la Mexico in 1995). The G-7 has failed on both counts despite repeated evidence of the need for reform, the availability of sound proposals for achieving it, and, in the case of the liquidity issue, initiatives by the G-7 summiteers at Halifax to substantially expand the traditional but now inadequate approach.

The massive overvaluation of the dollar in the first half of the 1980s, the excessive fall of the yen in the late 1980s, the EMS crises of the early 1990s, and the problems of the dollar in 1994–95 all provide strong reminders of the inadequacies of present currency arrangements. The polar extremes of both fixed and flexible exchange rates have been tried and found wanting. Responsible proposals have been made for intermediate regimes that could achieve the virtues of both while avoiding their worst shortcomings (Bretton Woods Commission 1994; Volcker 1995).

But the finance ministers have displayed no interest in seriously considering any systemic adjustment alternatives. The call of the G-7 summit in Naples in July 1994 for a review of the international economic institutions can be interpreted as an expression of unhappiness over the inadequacies of existing arrangements, including the management of the G-7 financial group itself, by its own heads of state. The heads of state reportedly voiced such concerns explicitly. The ministers blocked any consideration of changes in exchange rate arrangements at the subsequent summit in Halifax, however, and nothing happened on that front.

The international adjustment process must address two types of problems: policy errors by governments and market errors induced by private capital flows.

Governments, of course, continually make errors across a wide variety of policies. For international economic purposes, the exchange rate is the variable that is most directly relevant. Here the main policy error is the maintenance of an overvalued currency. This error can incur substantial economic costs, trigger protectionist trade policies, and, in the extreme, bring on international financial crises.[9]

Two aspects of the problem are worthy of note. One is that currency overvaluations can now cause systemic problems whether they occur in industrial or developing countries. The sterling and lira misalignments of 1992 are the latest examples of the former, while Mexico is the clearest recent case of the latter. Systemic problems emanating from misalignments of G-7 currencies have traditionally caused sufficient spillover effects to be of global concern, but there are now probably a dozen other countries that can have significant international effects.

The second key point is that policy errors of this type can occur only under systems of fixed exchange rates. They happened frequently toward the end of the Bretton Woods period and eventually brought its downfall when sterling and then the dollar, the two key currencies of that era, succumbed to the overvaluation error. The more recent cases of this source of misalignment in the G-7, in view of the maintenance by the United States and Japan of flexible exchange rates since 1973, have come in Europe within the EMS. But the adoption of fixed rates by a number of developing countries, largely for "nominal anchor" purposes to fight inflation, have rendered them susceptible as well.[10]

The other G-7 countries, including the United States and Japan, have not avoided currency misalignments during this period. They have been hit by the second type of misalignment, that caused by market error. This variant results from markets' pushing currencies far from the long-run

---

9. It is, of course, possible for policy to maintain an undervalued currency as well, and the undervaluation of the mark after German unification in the early 1990s has already been described. In that case, however, some German officials *wanted* to revalue but were blocked by some of their EMS partners who did not want to accept even an implicit devaluation of their own currencies—replicating one of the traditional problems of overvaluations. There have also been occasional complaints about "competitive depreciation" or "exchange rate dumping" in the postwar period; Japan was a frequent target of such complaints in earlier years, and some other East Asian countries were accused of similar practices in the late 1980s, but of late most such charges have been directed at European countries such as Italy and Sweden.

10. To be sure, there is a degree of "market error" that can compound this type of "policy error." In both the southern European countries and Mexico, for example, huge inflows of private capital continued to suggest the possible sustainability of large current account deficits and an overvalued currency until shortly before the crisis broke. The authorities could have been genuinely misled long after the normal indicators suggested that trouble lay ahead. They nevertheless sought to maintain a position that was ultimately untenable by any objective reading of history and the contemporary indicators, so such problems do derive fundamentally from "policy error."

equilibrium levels needed to maintain sustainable national current account positions.

This "error" does not necessarily lead to financial losses for private participants in the markets and hence need not be irrational from their standpoint. "Rational speculative bubbles" occur when speculators ride a bandwagon that is moving away from equilibrium, and hence is destined to eventually reverse, but continues long enough for them to make money on the ride and get out in time (Frankel 1996, 2). Extrapolative expectations dominate, or as the traders put it, "the trend is your friend."

Market errors occur most clearly under flexible exchange rates. The dollar overvaluation of the early to middle 1980s and the yen undervaluation of the late 1980s are the most significant cases in recent years. It is noteworthy that the extent of those misalignments—at least 40 percent in the case of the dollar and perhaps as much in the case of the yen— was considerably greater than the recent misalignments of the fixed-rate European currencies or of any of the G-7 currencies during the Bretton Woods era. These market errors affected the currencies of the world's two largest national economies, currencies that are based in two of the world's largest financial markets. One could easily harbor doubts about whether these real-world approximations to "perfect markets" can produce sustainable results.

It might be argued that these "market errors" are simply a special case of policy error, transmitted through a different financial mechanism. To be sure, the excessive dollar appreciation of the 1980s occurred in response to the policy mix of Reaganomics—large and rapidly rising budget deficits accompanied by very high real interest rates. Likewise, the yen depreciation of the late 1980s flowed from Japanese reliance on expansionary monetary policy, in the face of restrictive fiscal policy, to expand domestic demand.

But the markets took the dollar far above any conceivably sustainable level despite constant warnings from many quarters for several years (Bergsten 1981a, 1981b; Marris 1983, 1985). All observers agree that at least the last 10 to 20 percent of that dollar appreciation was "pure bubble" and cannot be explained by any normal economic relationships. Similar warnings were issued about yen depreciation in the late 1980s (Cline 1989). In practice, we know that bubbles and bandwagons, including rational speculative bubbles, occur frequently. One cannot rely on markets any more than on governments to ensure equilibrium currency relationships.

An effective international monetary system would produce strong defenses against both policy error and market error. Of course, no system will ever completely deter either foolish governments or foolish investors. But the current system makes very little effort to address either. Fixed exchange rates induce policy error and freely flexible rates are demonstrably vulnerable to market error. The totally ad hoc approach of the G-7 has led it to miss some problems totally (the yen in the late 1980s, the EMS crises in 1992–93, and Mexico in 1994) or, to the contrary, to push rates too far (as with the dollar in late 1995). Far superior arrangements, as described in chapters 6 and 7, are available to deal with both types of error and thus enable the G-7 to carry out its stewardship of the adjustment process more effectively. One of the cardinal failures of the G-7 as the informal steering committee of the world economy is that it has erected no such system nor even made an effort in that direction.

In addition, the Mexico crisis revealed once again the absence of two essential systemic arrangements: an effective "early warning system" to head off such situations and a "rapid response facility" to deal with the crises that can easily result from the huge, volatile, and pervasive flows of private capital. The G-7 in fact recognized the need for such reforms at its Halifax summit in June 1995. On the recommendation of its finance ministers, who were responding to the call of the Naples summit for improvements in the international financial institutions, the heads of government called for the creation of both an early warning system to head off "future Mexicos" and an emergency financing mechanism to speed funding to them when required. As of this writing, however, the outlook for both initiatives is uncertain because of the G-7's unwillingness to share responsibility with anyone outside the group.

In the case of the early warning system, there are three key requirements (Goldstein 1995). One is close and continuous monitoring of all economies—including those of the G-7 itself—that are large enough to cause systemic disturbances. The second is effective transmittal of resulting policy advice to countries that appear headed for trouble. The third is increasing public revelation of the warnings of trouble if the target country does not respond adequately, in order to bring escalating market pressure to bear on it. (A fourth requirement, adequate provision of data by relevant countries, is essential but less important and controversial—and is the only element of the program that has been agreed to date.)

It is inconceivable that the G-7 could conduct such a program itself, due to the absence of any secretariat to do the work and the probability that the spotlight will on occasion have to be turned on some of its own members. Yet the group has been unwilling to cede adequate authority to the IMF, which is the logical repository of the function. Indeed, the G-7 does not permit a representative of the Fund even to participate in its discussion of exchange rate issues; its spokespeople hide behind irrelevant arguments such as "the IMF has no monopoly of wisdom."[11]

---

11. This is true, of course, and some of the IMF's positions run counter to the analysis in this book—such as its support for pushing the dollar up so far in 1995. But it has a critical mass of highly capable analysts, access to better data than anyone else, and a point of view that meets the two key criteria of objectivity and international orientation.

The G-7 is willing to let the IMF monitor non-G-7 economies but the obvious discrimination in this approach, along with its reluctance to support any Fund "whistle blowing" on pending problem countries, raises doubts about the whole strategy.

The Halifax initiative to obtain additional financial resources to deal with "future Mexicos" has stumbled even more badly and is even more telling with respect to the G-7 as an institution. The second decision of the 1995 summit was to seek a doubling of the $27 billion now available to the General Arrangements to Borrow (GAB), the mechanism through which the G-10 augments the resources of the IMF when needed to deal with a specific systemic threat—as determined separately by both the Fund and the G-10 itself (box 2.2). To do so, it decided to increase the contributions of its present members but also to invite countries currently outside the G-7/G-10—including some of the newly wealthy countries in East Asia—to contribute.

The problem, once again, has been the unwillingness of the G-7 (in this case, technically the G-10) to share its decision-making authority. It initially adopted the ludicrous position of asking nonmember countries (such as Australia, Austria, Korea, Singapore, and Spain) to contribute money but offering them no meaningful role in the group's decision-making, or even its consultative, process. The predictable result was flat rejection of the proposition—even by Austria to entreaties from its closest ally, Germany. The G-7/G-10 was then forced to modify its position to permit participants in a "parallel facility"—the New Arrangement to Borrow (NAB)—to vote on its use. But the initial efforts of the group to implement the Halifax initiatives again reveal their myopia and institutional shortcomings.

The Legitimacy of the G-7

These latest G-7 failures, which relate both to their external relations and to some of their systemic responsibilities, raise a much broader question: the legitimacy of the G-7 itself. There is little question about the propriety of the group's coordinating the activities of its own members, especially since the world economy as a whole benefits enormously when it does so effectively. There is relatively little resistance even to G-7 coordination of the group's positions toward external questions such as SDR allocations, although the rest of the world obviously now feels free to reject those entreaties when they disagree with them.

The real question is whether the G-7 can legitimately influence the policies of countries outside the group. Some spillovers to other countries are inevitable even when the G-7 members change their own policies. For instance, a G-7 decision to jointly tighten monetary policy would inevitably pull up interest rates around the world. But it would be much less palatable for the G-7 to push nonmembers to contribute to a common funding enterprise without their full participation in the decision-making process, as it has attempted recently, or to change their exchange rates to conform to a G-7 adjustment strategy, as was tried with several East Asian countries in the late 1980s.

The rise of new economic powers that are playing important global roles has underscored the legitimacy question. China is already the world's third largest economy and has become a key locomotive of Asian growth. The economies of China and India are now larger than those of two G-7 members, Canada and Italy, when measured on a market exchange rate basis; they are larger than all G-7 members except the United States and Japan when measured on a purchasing power parity basis. The G-7 has no membership at all from the developing world—including the most dynamically growing regions of Asia. It has no major oil-exporting country, despite the central role that product has played in global economic developments (including deliberations of the G-7 itself) during parts of the past two decades. Brazil and Indonesia are leaders in key international trade initiatives—the Free Trade Area of the Americas (FTAA) and the Asia Pacific Economic Cooperation (APEC) forum, respectively. Russia already participates in a separate political discussion at the G-7 summit meetings. Can the G-7 persist with its present membership? Does its failure to incorporate emerging economic powers doom it to continuing decline?

History is replete with cases in which the exclusion of rising powers ultimately undermined the existing international order (Gilpin 1981). Some observers have in fact likened the challenge of integrating China into the global system now with the challenge of integrating Germany in the late 19th century, which failed miserably with disastrous consequences (Kristof 1993). The bungled SDR allocation and the clumsy effort to expand the GAB represent recent, although fortunately not comparably important, examples of the G-7's inability to legitimize its activities. This failure adds to the list of G-7 shortcomings.

Evolutionary change in the makeup of the leadership caucus has occurred over the years. The G-10 was created in the early 1960s but was later deemed both too large and too Eurocentric. Hence it was superseded by the G-5 and then G-7 (box 2.1).

The G-7 does continue to comprise a large part of the world economy. On the basis of market exchange rates, the share of the G-7 has fallen modestly but remains at 66 percent of world output (figure 2.1). The group's share was slightly below 50 percent on the basis of purchasing power parities in 1994 but has not declined significantly over the entire postwar period. The G-7 countries accounted for about 50 percent of world trade in 1994 (tables 3.1a and b).

The dominance of the G-7 is even clearer on financial indicators, which weigh heavily in many of the issues it must address. The currencies of

Table 3.1a   G-7 share of world merchandise exports, 1950-94

Year	G-7	United States	Japan	Germany	United Kingdom	France	Canada	Italy
1950	44.0	16.6	1.4	3.3	10.5	5.1	5.0	2.0
1955	47.8	16.2	2.3	6.9	9.6	5.6	5.2	2.1
1960	51.9	16.4	3.4	9.6	8.9	5.7	4.9	3.1
1965	53.6	15.5	4.9	10.4	8.0	5.8	4.9	4.2
1970	56.3	14.7	6.7	11.8	6.7	6.2	5.8	4.5
1975	50.4	13.0	6.7	10.8	5.2	6.4	4.1	4.2
1980	48.2	11.8	6.8	10.1	5.8	6.1	3.5	4.1
1985	52.2	12.0	9.7	10.1	5.6	5.6	5.0	4.2
1990	53.8	11.8	8.6	12.3	5.6	6.5	3.8	5.1
1994	49.6	11.9	9.2	9.9	4.8	5.5	3.8	4.4

Table 3.1b   G-7 share of world merchandise imports, 1950-94

Year	G-7	United States	Japan	Germany	United Kingdom	France	Canada	Italy
1950	45.7	15.6	1.6	4.4	11.8	5.0	5.0	2.4
1955	46.7	13.2	2.6	6.2	11.5	5.1	5.3	2.9
1960	48.1	12.9	3.5	8.0	10.2	4.9	4.8	3.7
1965	49.9	12.7	4.5	9.6	8.8	5.6	4.7	4.0
1970	52.7	13.8	6.2	9.8	7.1	6.2	4.7	4.9
1975	49.9	12.6	6.9	8.9	6.3	6.4	4.3	4.6
1980	51.1	13.1	7.2	9.6	5.9	6.9	3.2	5.1
1985	54.4	18.7	6.9	8.4	5.8	5.7	4.3	4.6
1990	54.2	15.1	6.9	10.1	6.5	6.8	3.6	5.3
1994	50.2	16.3	6.5	9.0	5.4	5.4	3.7	4.0

Source: IMF, *International Financial Statistics* (series 70..d and 71..d).

the G-7 nations have consistently represented more than 90 percent of reserve currency holdings since the mid-1970s (table 3.2), as well as an overwhelming share of the currencies that denominate private international investment and trade (table 3.3). While their share has dropped since 1973, the G-7 nations still account for about 38 percent of world monetary reserves (with gold valued at market prices, table 3.4) and about 46 percent of the total quotas and thus voting power of the IMF (table 3.5).

Another key criterion for membership in the global steering committee is the extent to which a country thinks, and is prepared to act, in the interests of the system as a whole. Willingness to do so correlates highly with both the international orientation of a country's economy and, to a very important extent, with its global political and security interests. The prototypical historical cases were the United Kingdom during the 19th

Table 3.2 Share of G-5 currencies in world foreign exchange reserves, 1973-94[a]

Currency	1973	1978	1983	1988	1993	1994
US dollar	76.1	76.0	71.1	64.6	61.4	63.3
Pound sterling	5.6	1.7	2.5	2.7	3.4	3.8
Deutsche mark	7.1	10.9	11.7	15.5	16.1	15.5
French franc	1.1	1.2	0.8	1.0	2.2	2.1
Japanese yen	0.1	3.3	4.9	7.7	9.0	8.5
G-5 total	90.0	93.1	91.0	91.5	92.1	93.2
Non-G-5 total	10.0	6.9	9.0	8.5	7.9	6.8

Source: IMF Annual Report 1995 (appendix table 1.2) and previous annual reports.

a. For comparison purposes, ECU issued against dollars are treated as dollars. Other ECUs are ignored.

Table 3.3 Shares of major currencies in world private transactions

Currency	Foreign exchange trading in world markets[a]	External bank loans[b]	External bond issues[c]	Eurocurrency deposits[d]	Invoicing trade[e]
US dollar	41	81	36	48	38
Deutsche mark	20	3	12	17	21
Japanese yen	12	7	10	5	13
Pound sterling	7	2	11	3	10
French franc	2	n.a.	9	4	11
Canadian dollar	2	n.a.	6	n.a.	n.a.
G-6 total	84	93	84	77	93
Other	16	7	16	23	n.a.

n.a. = not available

Sources: Caves, Frankel, and Jones (1996, table 22.1); Black (1989, 512-26, table 2); George Tavlas, unpublished data.

a. Percent of transactions involving the currency, divided by two, so that the total adds to 100 percent. Figures pertain to trading in 21 financial centers in April 1992.
b. Data pertain to end-1993.
c. Data pertain to end-1993. (Includes international issues, foreign issues, and special placements.)
d. Data pertain to end-1993. ("Other" includes foreign currency position of US banks for which no currency breakdown is available.)
e. Calculations based on Black (1989, 512-26, table 2). Data pertain to 1987 and to trade undertaken by the six largest industrialized countries, plus OPEC.

Table 3.4 G-7 share of total international monetary reserves, 1973-95 (with gold measured at market prices)

	G7	United States	United Kingdom	France	Germany	Italy	Canada	Japan
1973	51.5	13.2	3.1	6.1	16.2	4.8	2.9	5.4
1978	49.5	12.5	3.8	5.8	13.6	5.4	1.5	6.8
1983	48.8	16.6	2.5	6.9	10.6	6.1	1.5	4.6
1988	48.6	12.9	4.6	5.3	8.7	5.5	2.0	9.5
1993	39.7	11.8	3.1	3.9	8.2	3.8	1.1	7.7
1994	38.4	10.7	3.1	3.8	7.4	3.8	0.9	8.8
1995	38.3	10.0	2.8	3.3	6.9	3.4	0.9	10.9

Source: IMF, *International Financial Statistics*. Data are for the end of the period. Market price of gold per ounce at end of each period was: 1973 - $112.25; 1978 - $226.00; 1983 - $381.50; 1988 - $410.25; 1933 - $390.65; 1994 - $383.25; 1995 - $386.75.

Table 3.5 G-7 share of total IMF quotas, 1950-95

Year	G-7	United States	United Kingdom	France	Germany	Italy	Canada	Japan
1950	62.9	34.2	16.2	6.5	0.0	2.2	3.7	0.0
1955	64.4	31.4	14.9	6.0	3.8	2.1	3.4	2.9
1960	60.9	28.0	13.2	5.3	5.3	1.8	3.7	3.4
1965	57.6	25.8	12.2	4.9	4.9	3.1	3.4	3.1
1970	55.9	23.6	9.8	5.3	5.6	3.5	3.9	4.2
1975	54.4	22.9	9.6	5.1	5.5	3.4	3.8	4.1
1980	49.5	21.2	7.4	4.8	5.4	3.1	3.4	4.2
1985	49.4	20.1	6.9	5.0	6.1	3.3	3.3	4.7
1990	48.4	19.7	6.8	4.9	5.9	3.2	3.2	4.6
1995	45.9	18.3	5.1	5.1	5.7	3.2	3.0	5.7

Source: IMF, *International Financial Statistics* (series .2f.s). Data are for the end of the period.

century and the United States during the first postwar generation. These were the periods of "hegemonic stability" in which those countries combined global interests, both political and economic, with capabilities that were sufficient to provide effective leadership (provided partly, in the latter case, through the G-10 and other international institutions).

As indicated throughout this book, no country—including the current membership of the G-7—scores very impressively in terms of global responsibility at the current time. Nevertheless, the United States retains enough of its traditional orientation to act systemically with at least reasonable frequency. The Europeans, while focused heavily on their regional activities, also have a long history of global involvement and periodically (if sometimes grudgingly) recognize the need to promote systemic rather than solely national goals. Japan has yet to exhibit much systemic thinking but had to be included in the leadership group as a result of the dramatic rise in its weight in the world economy.

None of the countries that are potential additions to the G-7 have begun to exhibit any significant element of systemic thinking. Like Japan a generation ago, China is the most likely addition because of its enormous economic weight. It has begun to think at least regionally, as evidenced by its recent activism in APEC and its support for cooperative financial arrangements in East Asia to protect against Mexico-type shocks. Moreover, membership in the G-7 would encourage systemic thinking in China and induce it to give greater weight to global considerations in setting its own policies.

But China's currency is not yet convertible, it is not yet a member of the World Trade Organization, and it maintains extensive barriers to trade and investment (as well as to market transactions internally). It remains a very poor country, with per capita incomes of around $1,000 or even lower. Some observers are unsure about the permanence of its economic reforms. There is another obvious difference from the other G-7 nations: China is not yet a democracy. It will eventually be a strong candidate for membership, but the time is not yet ripe.

A central issue for the future will be whether membership in the G-7 (or its successor) continues to be restricted to countries with democratic political systems. There has been no conflict to date: the world's strongest economies have all been functioning democracies. But conflicts are likely to arise in coming decades. China is the cardinal contemporary case. Russia may be another, depending on its political evolution.[12] Saudi Arabia could be another difficult case if energy issues were to resume their earlier importance for global economic management. The G-7 of the future will have to decide whether effective leadership of the world economy will require that it relax its political criteria, both to preserve its institutional role and to encourage any nondemocratic participants to open their regimes politically as well as economically.

---

12. The G-7 has invited Russia to recent summits on a meeting-by-meeting basis and for only the political portion of the talks. The Russians have pressed aggressively for permanent inclusion in the group and participation in the full summit meeting. The G-7 members have been correct to resist these requests: Russia has achieved neither the economic nor political maturity of the other G-7 countries and remains in a transformation stage of economic stabilization and political reform, the outcome of which is as yet unclear. Moreover, its role in the world economy is likely to remain less than that of China and several other nonmembers of the G-7, even if it successfully navigates all these current challenges. Accepting Russia into full membership in the G-7 without accepting China would represent a sharp slap at the latter that would add further to its suspicions that the West is trying to "contain" rather than "engage" it (Brzezinski 1996).

Figure 3.2 Monthly real trade-weighted dollar exchange rate against 101 trading partners, January 1988–December 1995

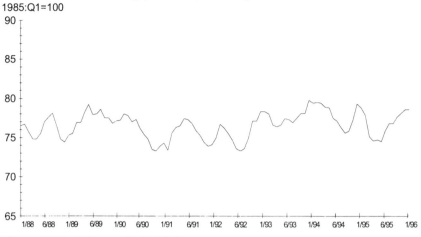

1985:Q1=100

Source: Federal Reserve Bank of Dallas.

Over the foreseeable future, however, the G-7—or possibly an even smaller G-3 (see chapter 7)—will almost certainly remain the appropriate group to provide leadership on global monetary and financial affairs. But the G-7 obviously cannot issue directives to the international organizations and the rest of the world. It must consider the views of other countries and modify its positions, substantially if necessary, to secure multilateral agreements. Restoring its political legitimacy is yet another reason that G-7 reform is essential.

The Bottom Line

In all of its major areas of responsibilities, and in its global political relationships as well, the G-7 has thus experienced a series of missed opportunities and outright failures in recent years. There have been a few offsetting successes but the contrast with the earlier episodes, described in chapter 2, is striking.

There remain two central questions, however. Has the world economy been made substantially worse off as a result of the policy failures of the G-7? Even if it has, how many of those problems can fairly be blamed on the G-7 as opposed to the member governments acting in a purely national capacity?

The world economy has certainly experienced some bright spots in the first half of the 1990s. Inflation has dropped substantially and seems likely to remain subdued. Despite the sharp and costly swings in the dollar-mark and dollar-yen bilateral rates, the trade-weighted exchange rate of the dollar, has been reasonably stable (figures 3.2 and 3.3). Trade policy,

**Figure 3.3 Monthly real trade-weighted dollar exchange rate
versus other G-7 countries,[a] January 1988-November 1995**

January 1988 = 100

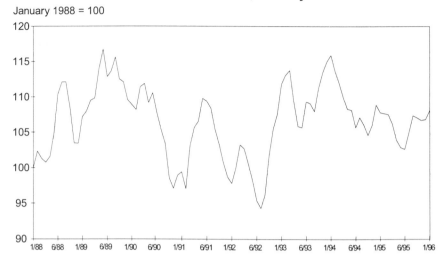

a. Weighting based on share of total trade with the United States in 1991 and adjusted for changes in CPI.

Sources: IMF, *International Financial Statistics* and *Direction of Trade Statistics.*

which relates closely to currency equilibria and current account imbalances, has made some notable forward strides: the successful conclusion of the Uruguay Round in the GATT, the creation of the World Trade Organization, and the launch of new regional liberalization initiatives in the Asia Pacific, Western Hemisphere, and several areas on the periphery of the European Union.[13] Market-based and outward-oriented economic strategies have been adopted throughout the world, including in the developing countries and the transforming economies of the former communist orbit. Full employment has been reached in the United States.

However, as already described, the bottom line is far from satisfactory. Growth in the industrial countries has been very modest throughout the 1990s. Unemployment remains far above traditional levels in every European country and, for the G-7 as a group, is much higher than in 1990. Average income levels have stagnated in the United States for over two decades and have fallen for about half the population. Unemployment has risen rapidly in Japan, which was just emerging from an unprecedented four-year recession in early 1996.

---

13. Over 60 percent of world trade now takes place within regional free trade arrangements, such as the European Union, or within groups that have made a political commitment to achieve free trade, such as APEC and the FTAA (Bergsten 1996).

The political fallout from these unsatisfactory economic conditions is reflected in the wholesale rejection of incumbents throughout the G-7. President George Bush in 1992 and then the Democratic Congress in 1994 were repudiated in the United States. The Liberal Democratic Party lost power after 45 years in Japan. Canadian Prime Minister Brian Mulroney was swept aside by the largest landslide against an incumbent government in modern history. The Socialists lost power in France. The Conservative government appears likely to be replaced after the next election in Britain. Only Chancellor Kohl in Germany has hung on, due to the ineptness of his opposition as well as the continuing glow from his successful political management of unification and the departure of Soviet troops. These political indicators hardly paint a picture of global economic success.

At a less macroeconomic and more directly international level, the bottom line is also unimpressive. Every G-7 country has experienced at least one major currency crisis during the past decade, and most of them were handled poorly. The Uruguay Round nearly failed, and American disputes with Japan and China, driven to an important extent by the reemergence of large currency and trade disequilibria, have shaken the trading system. Growth has been truncated in a number of developing countries, Mexico being the most notable but not the only example, with adverse effects on world growth. It is impossible to definitively link the early failures to provide external assistance to Russia with that country's continuing economic and political instability, but more decisive support from abroad might have made a considerable difference.

It would of course be incorrect to attribute all the shortcomings of the world economy in recent years to the failures of the G-7. Exogenous forces, such as the (highly desirable) fall of communism and thus (among other things) German unification, have been important as always. Internal political struggles have been a factor, as in Mexico with its Chiapas rebellion and political assassinations.

More importantly, some observers question whether the admitted policy failures of the period can be fairly blamed on the G-7 as opposed to the national governments themselves. It was the United States that chose Reaganomics in the early 1980s and thus transformed itself from world's largest creditor country to world's largest debtor country. It was Japan that chose to expand in the late 1980s via easy money and that failed to effectively supervise its financial system, thus bringing on "the bubble economy," renewed undervaluation of the yen, and the huge nonperforming loan problem. It was the United Kingdom that entered the EMS with an overvalued currency and other European countries that effectively vetoed appreciation of the mark when it was needed to head off high interest rates throughout the Continent. It was Mexico that hid its precipitate reserve decline and refused to devalue throughout most of 1994 despite numerous suggestions (from nonofficial sources) that it should do so.

Neither the G-7 nor any international economic mechanism can prevent governments from making such policy errors. But there are three vital things that the G-7, as the informal global steering committee, can do and has in fact done in the past. One, which it continues to do fairly well, is to respond to crises with sufficient speed and skill to keep them from engulfing the world economy.

The much more important responsibility of the G-7, however, is to make every feasible effort to avert crises and strengthen the underlying foundations of the world economy. One way to do this is through effective multilateral surveillance: the constant application of peer pressure to induce partner countries to adopt more sensible policies. The G-7 appears to have largely jettisoned this function in favor of a "mutual nonaggression pact" through which the members essentially agree not to criticize each other, whatever the folly of each others' policies. We will describe and analyze this new phenomenon in chapter 5.

Leadership also requires the steering committee to create and sustain an international economic system that induces countries to move in the right policy direction. This task has been largely accomplished in the trade area: the GATT and its successor, the WTO, encompass a series of international rules that deter countries from creating barriers that would violate their global commitments and subject them to retaliation. The international trade regime is, of course, implemented imperfectly, but most countries, including the largest among them, take their obligations seriously and the world economy is far better off as a result.

It should also be feasible to construct a set of international monetary rules and institutional arrangements that will similarly tilt the internal debates on economic policy within member countries in constructive directions. We will see in chapter 6 that more structured exchange rate commitments would have pushed the Japanese policy mix in a direction that could have avoided its "bubble economy" (as well as currency undervaluation) of the late 1980s. They might have even helped to head off the worst excesses of Reaganomics in the United States. Buttressed by a better early warning system, new surveillance arrangements could prevent future Mexico-type crises and limit the spillover effects whenever they do occur. New systemic arrangements, centered largely on exchange rate relationships, could even foster better coordination of national economic policies—as they did for extended periods under the gold standard, the Bretton Woods regime of adjustable parities in the 1960s, and the EMS more recently.

We should certainly not measure actual G-7 performance against a textbook standard of perfect policy coordination. Such a comparison would be totally unrealistic. It is legitimate, however, to charge the G-7 with failing to meet at least the minimum requirements of the world economy and to replicate its own past successes. It is striking that the failures of the 1990s mirror almost precisely the issues on which success was achieved, at least partially, in the past: currency disequilibria and international payments imbalances, crises outside the G-7, systemic reforms (such as the Louvre Accord), and even some coordination of the policies of G-7 members themselves and thus global macroeconomic outcomes.

In each of these areas, the substantial costs of G-7 failure include subpar world growth, repeated currency instability, renewed external imbalances, attendant protectionist pressures, and financial crises. These costs derive from the failure of both preventive actions and of decisive responses to crises. They encompass events in both the industrial countries and in the developing world.

The fragility of the world's economic and financial outlook underlines the urgent need for the G-7 to resume an effective leadership role. A renewed global recession is eminently possible, especially as all G-7 countries seek to reduce their budget deficits. Output losses would be substantial, unemployment would rise further, and the risk of financial crises would grow sharply. The renewed European clamor for a "stronger dollar" and similar desires in Japan, despite America's continued external deficits, portend the possibility of new clashes over exchange rates. The large external imbalances raise the specter of constant currency problems and unpredictable spillovers into other financial markets, including a possible "hard landing" for the dollar and the American economy. Those same imbalances could produce a new wave of trade protectionism. Mexico may be only the first financial crisis centered on an "emerging market economy."

Continued systemic inadequacies could also derail and even reverse reform movements in both the developing and transforming economies. Brazil as well as Mexico sharply increased trade barriers in early 1995 in response to the financial crisis in Mexico. Several countries have slowed, or even reversed, liberalization of their capital markets because there is no systemic machinery to protect them against the roller-coaster propensities of international money movements. Failure to erect both better defenses and effective response mechanisms could discourage, and even reverse, the healthy reform trend of the past decade.

The absence of effective G-7 cooperation raises the odds, in both tangible and intangible ways, that such events could occur. The recent failures of the G-7 to either prevent or quell crises increase the risks that future crises will erupt and that they could escalate out of control. A recognition by the markets of G-7 ineffectiveness would add considerably to those risks. The decline of the G-7 has had serious consequences for the world economy and could be even more costly in the future. It is both critical and urgent for the G-7 to get its act together.

4

The Sources of G-7 Decline:
Traditional Tensions

Two very different types of problem lie at the heart of the decline of the G-7. One is disagreement among the key countries, particularly the United States and Germany, over the proper roles and functions of the group. The other is a growing consensus across the group that the G-7 cannot, or should not, engage in some or all of the activities that characterized at least some periods of its past history. The second is much more important and we will address it in chapter 5. But the former helps to explain some of the recent disarray, and it is the subject of this chapter.

Three differences of view have traditionally existed within the G-7, creating tensions among its members and limiting its potential for decisive leadership: the relative importance attached to economic growth versus price stability, the respective roles of surplus and deficit countries in pursuing adjustment (or "burden sharing" more broadly), and the relative weight attached to global versus regional economic responsibilities. The chief proponents of these different approaches have been the United States and Germany, the two most influential members of the group.

Growth vs. Stability

The first of the differences, whose salience has recently diminished but is still quite relevant, is the relative emphasis to be placed on economic growth and price stability in the short term. For a variety of political, economic, and historical reasons, the United States has tended to opt for more expansionary economic policies while Germany has always leaned toward a more anti-inflationary stance.

The United States has therefore frequently pushed the G-7 to adopt "concerted growth programs." One of the clearest examples was the "locomotive strategy" promoted by the Carter administration from its outset in early 1977, which culminated in the Bonn summit agreement of 1978. That strategy sought (and won) the adoption by other G-7 countries of specific, quantified policy actions to promote growth and current account adjustment.

American administrations have pursued similar initiatives throughout the G-7's history. The second Reagan administration pushed both Japan and Germany to expand domestic demand to complete the adjustment of current account imbalances launched at the Plaza. The Bush administration repeatedly tried to get Germany and Japan to stimulate their economies to spur global recovery from the recession of the early 1990s. The early Clinton administration adopted similar initiatives toward Japan.

The conflict between US and German preferences arises partly from history, the lessons of which are embodied in national institutions and policymaking. The pivotal trauma for most Americans is the Great Depression of the 1930s, whereas most Germans' trauma is the hyperinflations that followed the two world wars. Events of the early postwar period reinforced the impact of those experiences: the United States saw repeated bouts of high unemployment through the 1950s and into the early 1960s, whereas the German postwar recovery eliminated unemployment for all practical purposes and even required the import of millions of workers.

The conflicting preferences also arise from different degrees of reliance on fiscal policy as a countercyclical remedy. Particularly during the 1960s and 1970s, American policymakers sought to manage aggregate demand through fiscal policy adjustments. The Reagan administration, which rejected this Keynesian approach rhetorically, adopted the largest fiscal stimulus in history with its massive tax cuts and budget deficits.

Germany experimented with countercyclical use of fiscal policy for a while, especially under its social-liberal coalition in the 1970s. But it has tended to stress supply conditions and to downplay the countercyclical application of fiscal policy to offset short-run changes in private activity. Governments in Bonn stress that their task is to provide macroeconomic stability as a framework within which the private sector can thrive. The Bundesbank, whose role in Germany is probably more salient to overall economic policy than that of any other G-7 central bank, advocates the primacy of consistency and stability even more strongly.[1]

The legacy of earlier G-7 coordination efforts has intensified this traditional disagreement over the proper approach to macroeconomic policy. In particular, very different interpretations linger on the effects of the 1978

---

1. This German consensus does not, of course, preclude an occasional excursion into more activist management in response to structural shocks, such as national unification in the early 1990s.

Bonn summit agreement. Many American analysts view the agreement as a prototype, perhaps even the zenith, of international policy cooperation: all countries faithfully implemented their commitments and the results were fully on course until derailed by a wholly exogenous event, the second oil shock. By contrast, most Germans (and some Japanese) view the agreement as a disaster that induced their governments to adopt excessively expansionary policies when an economic upswing was already under way and that helped trigger the inflationary excesses of the late 1970s and early 1980s.

Most scholarly analyses provide modest support for the sympathetic view (Putnam and Henning 1989; Holtham 1989). Given the impossibility of determining what would have happened in the absence of the second oil shock, however, no intellectual consensus has emerged. German officials and economists remain nearly unanimous in condemning the effort.[2]

In recent years, one might have expected the German and broader European view to converge toward that of the United States, as European growth slowed and unemployment soared to levels far above both their own historical experience and that of the United States. But the opposite has occurred: the international consensus has gravitated toward the German stance. Importantly, this shift is due to the growing consensus among economists throughout the world that there is little trade-off between unemployment and inflation over any extended period. In addition, most observers interpret the sharp rise in German (and overall European) unemployment after the early 1970s as due primarily to structural factors that should be attacked mainly via supply-side rather than macroeconomic stimulus efforts.

The immobilization of fiscal policy in most countries due to the onset of large structural deficits has in any event removed one of the chief instruments for pursuing expansionist strategies (see chapter 5). Germany has actually been running large budget deficits since unification, as a result of its huge transfers to the new Länder, and thus has little if any scope for further fiscal expansion in the foreseeable future—especially if it wants to meet the criteria of the Maastricht treaty. Despite high unemployment throughout Europe, all members of the European Union are seeking to *reduce* their fiscal deficits to qualify for Economic and Monetary Union (EMU). It would be particularly embarrassing for Ger-

---

2. Former Chancellor Helmut Schmidt, who chaired the Bonn summit in 1978 and committed Germany to its agreement, has added to the confusion by flip-flopping at least twice on the issue. After originally embracing it as the epitome of successful international cooperation, he reversed course before leaving office in 1982 and blamed it for many of the problems that subsequently beset the German and world economies. By the mid-1980s, however, the former chancellor was once again extolling the virtues of a concerted growth strategy and by the early 1990s was calling for a "new Bonn summit" to rescue the world from the slowdown of that period.

many, which has led the campaign for tough qualifying criteria, to miss the Maastricht budget target itself.

A number of events produced the shift of other members of the G-7 toward the German stance on this issue in recent years. Japan accepted American pressure to adopt expansionary fiscal policies in the late 1970s, including at the Bonn summit and in similar international compacts around the same time (such as the Strauss-Ushiba Agreement, centered on the countries' trade imbalances). But the large budget deficits and high government debt that resulted produced a sharp policy reversal in Japan around 1980. Thus, Japan has resisted similar efforts ever since—even when the result was an overemphasis on monetary policy to achieve domestic expansion, which produced the "bubble economy" of the late 1980s—until very late in the recessionary period of the early 1990s. Japanese policy has been largely determined by the conservative Ministry of Finance, whose overriding policy goal has been to avoid the deficit spending of the 1970s. It has often fought internal battles over this issue with more expansion-minded elements of the Japanese government but has generally prevailed.

France and the United Kingdom have undergone similar transformations. During the earlier postwar period, both were inclined to adopt expansionary domestic policies to promote faster growth and lower unemployment. Indeed, suffering from perennial current account deficits, the United Kingdom frequently joined the United States in pushing the other industrial countries to accelerate domestic demand and thereby contribute to both faster global growth and reduced international imbalances.

Since joining the European Monetary System (EMS), however, France has altered its policy preferences in the direction of promoting stability à la Germany. The *franc fort* policy, once adopted by the Socialist government in 1983 after the failure of its initial "dash for growth" strategy, has been maintained and reinforced by all governments since. The United Kingdom backed away from activist demand management when the Conservative Party came to power under Margaret Thatcher, and its ardor for concerted expansion programs has also diminished sharply. As European integration has progressed, the European members of the G-7 have increasingly sided with Germany in trans-Atlantic disputes over macroeconomic policy adjustments.

The traditional discord within the G-7 over whether global economic policy should tilt toward fighting unemployment or toward fighting inflation has thus diminished considerably. The balance within the group has clearly shifted in the latter direction over the past decade. The United States itself has recently reduced its traditional emphasis on the countercyclical use of fiscal policy—though this may simply be a temporary result of the achievement of "full employment" in 1995–96, the consequent focus on avoiding renewed inflationary pressures, and the immobilization of fiscal policy as a countercyclical tool in the United States as elsewhere.

Because this particular issue has been a much more important source of contention within the G-7 in the past, it cannot account for the recent decline in the group's effectiveness. Nevertheless, it could arise again. It is particularly easy to envisage the United States, with its economy increasingly dependent on trade, facing a serious recession in conjunction with a large trade deficit and again pressing its G-7 partners to adopt expansionary domestic policies. If unemployment remains high in Europe and Japan, receptivity there to entreaties for concerted growth could well revive (despite the acknowledged structural nature of much of the European problem and Europe's pursuit of EMU). But efforts to do so would surely rekindle the traditional tensions over the issue, and it cannot be ignored as a potential source of renewed G-7 conflict.

Surplus vs. Deficit Countries

The most perennial debate has arisen between countries running current account surpluses and deficits. The issue has been particularly important because the three largest and most influential members have tended to remain on a single side of this divide: the United States has been a chronic deficit country (figure 4.1) while Germany and Japan (figures 4.2 and 4.3) have been in chronic surplus, except for brief intervals after the two oil shocks and, in the German case, since unification. The United Kingdom also ran persistent deficits in the 1960s and early 1970s and, after a period of near balance in the late 1970s and early 1980s when North Sea oil first flowed, over the last decade (figure 4.4). France and Italy have traditionally run deficits but have shifted into substantial surplus during the past few years (figures 4.5 and 4.6).

The salience of this difference has also declined, however, as German unification has ended that country's surplus position for at least a time. Intra-German data on trade in goods and services show that the former West Germany is still the world's largest surplus "country" (Deutsche Bundesbank 1994, 25). Germany as a whole is still the world's second largest creditor country (after Japan), and most German officials still think and talk like creditors. But the unified Germany has run modest current account deficits since 1991. As a result, one no longer hears attacks on the external position of Germany, as emanated rather regularly from the United States over the previous three decades.

The deficit/surplus struggle has thus come to center on the United States and Japan. For several reasons, that struggle has tended to play

Figure 4.1   United States: current account and merchandise trade balance, 1970-95

percent of GDP

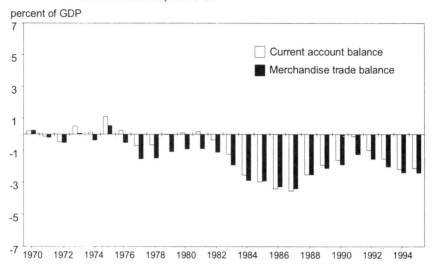

Source: US Council of Economic Advisers, *Economic Report of the President, 1996 Economic Indicators.*

Figure 4.2   Germany: current account and merchandise trade balance, 1970-95 [a]

percent of GDP

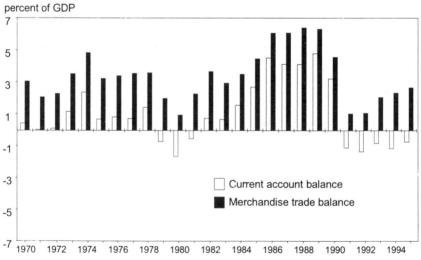

a. Beginning in mid-1991, data include former German Democratic Republic.

Sources: IMF, *International Financial Statistics,* and national sources.

Figure 4.3   Japan: current account and merchandise trade balance, 1970-95

percent of GDP

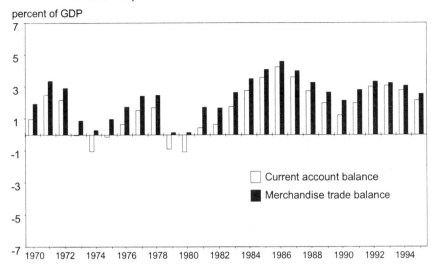

Sources: IMF, *International Financial Statistics,* and national sources.

Figure 4.4   United Kingdom: current account and merchandise trade balance, 1970-95

percent of GDP

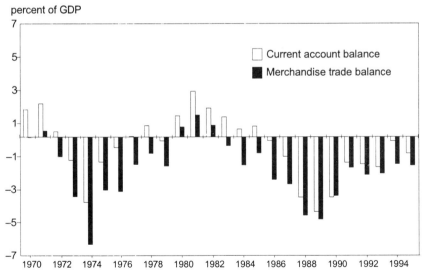

Sources: IMF, *International Financial Statistics,* and national sources.

Figure 4.5 France: current account and merchandise trade balance, 1970-95

percent of GDP

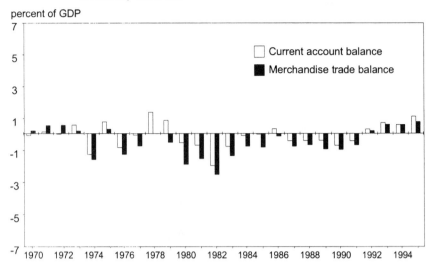

Sources: IMF, *International Financial Statistics,* and national sources.

Figure 4.6 Italy: current account and merchandise trade balance, 1970-95

percent of GDP

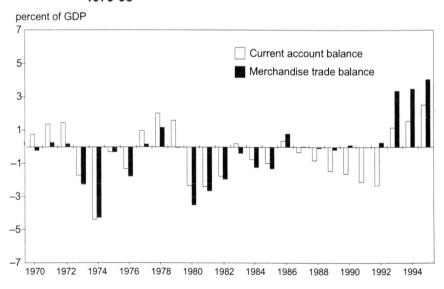

Sources: IMF, *International Financial Statistics,* and national sources.

out in bilateral negotiations between the two countries much more than in the G-7. One is that a large share of the two countries' global imbalances show up in their bilateral imbalance, a politically charged issue in the United States that pressures American governments to "go to the source." Another is the unique relationship between the two countries, which has led the United States to believe—at least until quite recently—that it maximizes its negotiating leverage by pursuing the bilateral channel. A third is the broader changes going on in the G-7, as described throughout this book, that have increasingly tilted the balance against US initiatives in general—and against activist governmental intervention in macroeconomic policy in particular.

Japan has in fact been a major beneficiary of the G-7's new aversion to activism. The Europeans, especially the Germans, have not wanted to attack Japan's surplus in the G-7 because they disliked "setting a precedent" that might next be turned on them. In practice, the Europeans have also tended to address their version of the "Japan problem" through bilateral devices, such as the quotas that they have imposed on Japanese automobiles throughout the 1990s.

This failure to address the Japanese surplus effectively and multilaterally, when it represented an international disequilibrium as clear-cut as the American deficit of the mid-1980s, represents one of the clearest indications of the decline of the G-7. It is also an indication of the G-7's asymmetrical treatment of surpluses and deficits, with much greater concern and policy attention addressed to the latter.

The traditional conflict between surplus and deficit countries appears obvious. Each wants the other to assume as much of the cost of adjustment as possible. In large part, however, this debate is specious. Any adjustment of an international imbalance, by definition, requires an equal reduction of the deficit *and* surplus. One cannot fall without a corresponding fall in the other.

Two distinctions are important, however. The first relates to the nature of the adjustment. Large economies that have relatively little exposure to international trade have an incentive to adjust via exchange rate changes rather than changes in domestic economic activity. This is because, in their circumstances, achievement of even modest external effects would require very large changes in domestic activity that would produce substantial unemployment or inflation. The United States, traditionally the largest and most self-sufficient of the major economies, has always opted for currency changes to reduce its external deficit (as in 1971–73, 1977–78, and 1985–87). By contrast, small economies that are heavily internationalized have an incentive to adjust domestic demand because exchange rate changes have very large effects on their economies, especially on the price level. These contrasting incentives do not lead to consistent patterns of actual adjustment behavior because of the impact of other variables (Hen-

Figure 4.7   EU, Japan, and US: trade in goods and services,[a] 1960-94

percentages of GDP in current prices

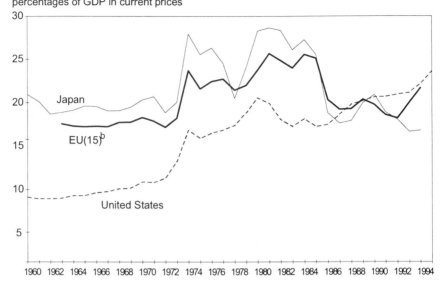

a. Trade is measured as exports plus imports at current prices.
b. Trade in services is apportioned between extra- and intra-EU(15) trade in the same proportion as trade in goods. EU(15) excludes eastern Germany prior to 1991.

Sources: IMF, *International Financial Statistics, European Economy, No. 59*; US Department of Commerce; IMF, *Direction of Trade Statistics.*

ning 1994) but can nonetheless become sources of conflicting national preferences in the G-7.

Significant convergence has occurred across this traditional cleavage, however. The individual European countries increasingly think of the European Union as a single entity for adjustment purposes and will have to do so to achieve their goal of creating a single currency. The resulting Europe-wide economy looks much more like the United States and Japan, with a much smaller share of trade to total GDP than in Germany or the others as separate nations. For its part, the United States has experienced more than a doubling of the share of trade in its economy over the past quarter century. The result is that trade shares are now quite similar in the United States, the European Union as a group, and Japan (figure 4.7). Germany and the other European countries continue to stress domestic adjustment within their region and would totally eliminate the exchange rate option by adopting a common currency, but they now seem quite willing to accept adjustment via alterations in exchange rates vis-à-vis the United States and Japan. Hence there could well be fewer differences among the three poles on this front in the future.

But a second distinction remains: whether it is up to surplus or deficit countries to *initiate* adjustment. In one sense, the perennial effort to get other countries to lead seems perverse since the country that initiates the adjustment action determines its nature and thus much of its distributional impact. But the question is extremely important in political terms because it goes far to determine which politicians will bear the onus for "causing the problem" and expose themselves to blame for the inevitable costs of the corrective action.

Hence surplus countries, traditionally Germany though especially Japan in recent years, call on the deficit countries (notably the United States) to initiate adjustment. The deficit countries, by contrast, insist that the surplus countries take parallel initiatives or even lead the way themselves. Standard economic analysis suggests that the allocation of adjustment initiatives should depend largely on the state of the world economy. If the chief global problem is recession and unemployment, surplus countries should expand demand and/or deficit countries should devalue. If the main international concern is inflation, deficit countries should contract and/or surplus countries should revalue.[3]

In practice, there are usually disagreements over the state of the global economy and, thus, which course is preferable. Moreover, different countries are frequently at different points in the cycle, so they do not want their policies determined by conditions elsewhere. The issue obviously intersects with that cited above concerning different preferences across the short-term trade-off between unemployment and inflation: Germany and the United States might draw very different conclusions from a genuinely uncertain international outlook, with Germany pressing the United States to contract to counter price pressures while the United States urged Germany to expand to limit the risks of higher unemployment.

This issue takes on moral overtones as well. Most people equate "surplus" and "creditor" positions with virtue and "deficit" and "debtor" positions with vice. But the deficit countries frequently use moral appeals as well, arguing that surplus countries must adopt expansionary domestic policies to avoid weakening world economic activity. Such considerations fuel the debate over adjustment and thus add to the tension over the issue within the G-7.

In two key senses, the "surplus versus deficit" problem has taken on a very different cast in recent years. As already noted, one element is the concentration of the "global surplus" in Japan (figure 4.8). With Germany's shift to deficit status due to unification, Japan has been the world's

---

3. Such guidelines for international adjustment are elaborated and formalized in Williamson and Miller (1987).

Figure 4.8 Current account surpluses by country share, 1994
(percentages)

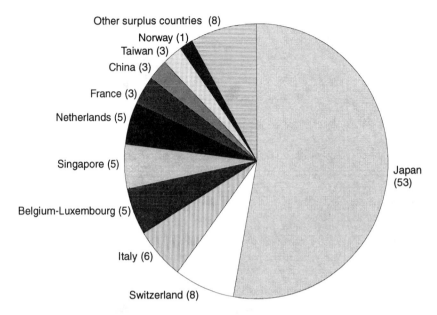

only large surplus country in the first half of the 1990s (despite some modest reductions in its level after 1994). Moreover, its inability or unwillingness to either effectively stimulate domestic demand or reduce its trade barriers throughout that period limited foreign sympathy with its concerns over the sharp appreciation of the yen that began in early 1993, or with its calls for help in reducing the imbalances.[4] The United States and to a lesser extent Europe did intervene to weaken the yen in mid-1995 but only after it had soared to a clearly overvalued level (80:1 against the dollar) and when it appeared that Japan's fragile financial system could be pushed into severe crisis as a result.[5]

---

4. There has also been skepticism in some quarters that the traditional adjustment tools, notably the exchange rate, are effective in the Japanese case. Casual observers often argue that "the Japanese surplus has remained in place and even increased further despite appreciation of the yen from 360:1 in 1971 to 100:1 today." In fact, the Japanese global current account position responds in virtually textbook fashion to changes in the trade-weighted real exchange rate of the yen, and its bilateral imbalance with the United States responds similarly to the dollar-yen rate (Bergsten and Noland 1993, figures 2.2 and 2.3; Cline 1995b).

5. Some analysts have argued that weakening the yen, at least in the circumstances of 1995 when its excessive appreciation had further weakened the Japanese economy, would help reduce Japan's external surplus because the favorable income effect of faster Japanese growth would overshadow the adverse price effect of a weaker yen. This is extremely dubious: Cline (1995b) shows that every fall of 1 percent in the real effective value of the yen strengthens Japan's current account balance by $3 billion to $4 billion, while every 1 percent rise in Japanese growth weakens it by only a like amount. It is, of course, inconceivable

On the other side of the issue, the American external deficit has grown to nearly record levels in absolute terms but is viewed very differently than at its previous peak in the mid-1980s. The deficit is now substantially smaller as a share of GDP. Its sharp rise in 1993–94, which was as rapid as its rise in 1983–84, was due largely to weakness in foreign economies rather than in the United States itself. The budget deficit, which is a key underlying cause of the external deficit and remains too high in light of the low private saving rate in the United States, has nevertheless been cut in half as a share of GDP and is the lowest in the G-7. More of the foreign borrowing has been used for investment than in the 1980s, when virtually all of it financed increased consumption. There is widespread consensus that American firms have regained much of their international competitiveness, and numerous surveys have even proclaimed that the United States is again "the most competitive economy in the world" (World Economic Forum and IMD 1995). In light of all this, no one, including American industry, views the dollar as being nearly as overvalued as it was a decade ago—if it is overvalued at all. So the responsibility directed at the chief deficit country is considerably less than in earlier periods. As a result, its deficit has proved relatively easy to finance through the private markets and with the Bank of Japan willingly providing the great bulk of whatever official intervention has been needed.

Some observers, especially in Europe, even argue that the dollar is undervalued. This judgment is based explicitly or implicitly on the purchasing power parity concept, which is irrelevant for market exchange rates except perhaps over the very long run, and it ignores the continued high level of America's external deficit. But as the European economies weaken again with unemployment already at very high levels, Europe is increasing calling for a "stronger dollar" to help it export some of its intensified difficulties. The problem may be that the yen has again become *undervalued* and that undervalued currencies exist outside the G-7, perhaps in China and other surplus countries in East Asia. A new conflict over the appropriate level of exchange rates may be brewing and may in fact have begun to surface at the G-7 meeting in Washington in April 1996.

But for now, the G-7's attention to the issue of current account imbalances has sharply receded. With the disappearance of the German surplus, and with the European Union as a whole near balance, the Europeans have displayed little interest in the whole question. As noted earlier, the United States and Japan have tended to address it primarily in their bilateral Framework Talks. Financing for the imbalances has been readily available, with the United States prepared to accept a continuing buildup

---

that Japanese growth could be accelerated by a full percentage point by a depreciation of only 1 percent in the exchange rate; the actual depreciation of 1995–96 amounted to 20 to 30 percent and almost certainly will substantially retard the decline of the Japanese surplus or even reverse it by 1997–98.

in its debtor position and Japan prepared to increase its dollar holdings despite the huge losses on its previous accumulations. Hence the "surplus versus deficit" issue, like the traditional "growth versus stability" debate, has become less prominent on the G-7 agenda.

The issue of burden sharing is sometimes posed in parallel to the deficit/surplus question, with surplus countries asked to contribute more of the funding for external G-7 activities such as the Gulf War in 1991. The deficit countries, primarily the United States, have used this argument to attempt to shift more of the costs of multilateral financing to the surplus nations.

There is widespread agreement, however, that international burden sharing should be based on the underlying size and strength of national economies rather than their immediate balance of payments positions. Hence the larger and richer economies should pay more, certainly in absolute terms and perhaps even on a relative basis (per the graduated income tax principle). This conclusion rests on the view that international imbalances are inherently temporary and tend to fluctuate (although this has not been borne out in the performance of any of the three largest national economies over most of the past quarter century). The burden-sharing issue also relates directly to our next topic, the proper geographic scope of responsibility for both the G-7 as a group and its individual members.

Globalism vs. Regionalism

The third issue that has traditionally divided the G-7 is the relative weight to be attached to global versus regional concerns. The United States, despite the rhetoric of a few neoisolationist politicians, remains the only global power with active interests in all parts of the world. In the economic sphere, its global activism may even be increasing, as evidenced by its leadership of new trade initiatives in the Asia Pacific region (the Asia Pacific Economic Cooperation forum, or APEC), as well as in the Western Hemisphere (the Free Trade Area of the Americas), and in its aggressive effort to expand commercial ties with "Big Emerging Markets" on all continents (including India, Poland, South Africa, and large Asian as well as Latin American nations).

All other G-7 countries have a narrower geographic focus. Japan is increasingly oriented toward Asia, while maintaining its traditional priority on relations with the United States, but cannot yet be viewed as adopting a global posture. All four European members have focused increasingly on Europe as its regional integration has proceeded, especially in the monetary and macroeconomic areas.

Indeed, the overwhelmingly regional focus of the European members of the G-7 since the late 1980s or early 1990s is one of the key reasons for the decline of the G-7. This shift had both economic and political roots.

A major political consideration in Europe's shift toward a regional focus was the collapse of the Soviet Union in 1990–91 and, with it, the end of the Cold War and the unification of Germany. These events had several major effects of interest here. First, German unification raised the specter of a dominant, assertive Germany that would be uninterested in the rest of Europe and thus heightened the emphasis of the other Europeans (as well as many Germans themselves) on accelerating the integration of Europe. EMU, rightly or wrongly, became the chosen means to do so.

Second, the events of 1990–91 radically changed the global political environment. The Central and Eastern European countries and the new republics of the former Soviet Union were suddenly independent and in need of outside help—which inevitably would come mostly from their neighbors in Western Europe.[6] Germany had a particular responsibility for the former East Germany. American protection was no longer as vital, and American clout dropped sharply as a result. All these changes added further to the regional focus of the Europeans.

Within this new political environment, two economic developments coalesced in the early 1990s to redirect Europe almost solely to regional affairs: the negotiation of the Maastricht treaty in 1991, which ordained the creation of a single European currency, and the turbulent EMS crises of 1992–93.

The original EMS was reasonably compatible with the global monetary system. From its creation in 1979 to early 1987, the EMS quite successfully carried out frequent, small currency realignments. It was an adjustable peg system, but unlike the global Bretton Woods regime of the 1960s it had enough adjustment of the pegs to avoid major disequilibria. This compatibility was particularly clear after the Plaza Agreement in late 1985 rejected the free floating of the early 1980s and restored active G-7 intervention in the exchange markets.

After 1987, however, the Europeans terminated their pattern of small, frequent realignments in favor of maintaining fixed rates for prolonged periods. This stance was reinforced in 1991 by the Maastricht treaty, with its goal of achieving a single European currency, and placed Europe increasingly at odds with the currency flexibility practiced by the other G-7 countries. The world's two key monetary systems were being structured and managed in very different ways.

One key participant in the G-7 process during this period, Under Secretary of the Treasury for International Affairs David Mulford, has characterized the resulting European attitudes as "schizophrenic." The same countries that pledged fealty to a common currency within Europe, and thus were willing to totally abandon national exchange rates and monetary

---

6. Collins and Rodrik (1992) show that the natural trade patterns of the Central and Eastern European countries, and of the former Soviet Union, focus overwhelmingly on Western Europe in general and Germany in particular.

autonomy, opposed currency and monetary cooperation with the rest of the G-7 that was far weaker (such as Louvre-type reference ranges). Paradoxically, inflation differentials have been far smaller among the three global poles, whether Germany alone or the European average is compared with the United States and Japan, than within Europe. Hence one of the key foundations for currency stability has been considerably stronger across the G-7 than for the EMS/EMU.

The key reason for this Janus-like policy in Europe was Germany's willingness to pursue monetary cooperation only where it could dominate the process. Germany was the dominant player within Europe on monetary matters but only a secondary power at the global level. The German government and Bundesbank were increasingly successful over the 1980s and into the 1990s in persuading their European partners to pursue low-inflation monetary policy as the basis for currency stabilization. German officials, in contrast, were keenly aware of their vulnerability to American policy shocks historically and their lack of influence over US monetary and fiscal policy.

German concerns have been accentuated by American pressure for expansionary monetary and fiscal policies during periods of large US current account imbalances. The Germans thus hold an abiding suspicion of entering into exchange rate agreements with the United States. We sympathize with some of these concerns and address them at length in the concluding chapter of the book.

In addition to these serious substantive implications of the Europeans' focus on regional integration, there have been several direct effects of that development on the G-7. As noted above, the EMS countries have opposed any G-7 (or IMF) consideration of "their issues," despite the obvious impact of those issues on the world economy and financial system—as the currency crises of 1992–93 so clearly demonstrated. This impact would be even greater if the Euro were to become a leading reserve currency. But the deflection of Europe from the G-7 also derives simply from the enormous expenditure of time on the European projects that is required of the same officials who represent their countries in the G-7 and other global forums. The regionalization of Europe is clearly an important factor in the decline of the G-7.

Another contrast in geographic perspectives is apparent in G-7 views concerning the proper assignment of responsibilities for economic and financial problems outside their own borders. The Americans generally believe that the group as a whole should accept responsibility for any situation, anywhere in the world, that is large enough to have systemic consequences. The Europeans and Japanese, by contrast, have tended toward a "financial spheres of influence" approach under which each of the three industrial regions (Europe, Japan, North America) is primarily or even solely responsible for problems "in its own backyard."

The American attitude was clearly manifested in its responses to the Gulf War, the recurrent debt problems of Mexico and others, and Russia. Though some might view the Gulf as an American sphere of influence, in light of its traditional military and commercial ties there, the United States insisted that other industrial countries—especially Japan and Germany—share a large part of the financial costs of the Gulf War of 1990–91. The systemic nature of that threat, with respect to both energy markets and financial markets, was widely agreed. Hence the United States was on strong ground and, despite grumbling about the lack of full consultation, prevailed in obtaining extensive burden sharing.

Mexico is much more clearly in the American sphere of influence. Nevertheless, the United States took the view that both the country's debt problem of 1982 and the currency crisis of 1995 called for substantial contributions from others (but, in the latter case, only after its initial failure to seek such support; see discussion in chapter 3). The argument was again that a failure to respond promptly and effectively would create major systemic problems—for the global banking system in 1982, for financial markets more broadly and for continued policy reform in 1995. Success was obtained on the first of these occasions but very imperfectly on the second.[7]

Russia is perhaps the clearest case in point. No one would argue that it lies in America's "sphere of influence." It is obviously much closer to Europe and Japan. Yet the United States has been willing to play an extremely active role in providing economic support and advice there (and to a number of other republics of the former Soviet Union as well). The United States has, of course, been motivated largely by its post-Cold War security concerns, including the continuing status of Russia (and Ukraine and Kazakhstan) as a nuclear power. But it could have tried to "assign" Russia and the rest of the former Soviet Union to Europe and perhaps its Siberian component to Japan, whereas it chose instead to remain heavily involved and has tried to exercise an active leadership role.

It should be noted that the United States has not always pursued its global focus with perfect fidelity. When the Polish debt crises broke out in the early 1980s and again in the early 1990s, for example, the United States essentially left the solution to the Europeans. The United States has been content to let Germany and others in Western Europe bear a

---

7. The difference in Japanese and especially European responsiveness to Mexico in 1995 compared with 1982 may be another reflection of the impact of the end of the Cold War. It also reflects honest differences, however, over the severity of the threat. The 1982 crisis clearly jeopardized the global financial system, via its impact on the largest American banks, and quickly spread to a number of developing countries in other parts of the world. By contrast, the 1994–95 crisis generated a much more diffused financial impact because of the broad range of investors in Mexico and other countries sideswiped by the "tequila effect." It thus generated real disagreements over the breadth and severity of the contagion effects themselves.

disproportionate share of the costs required in Eastern Europe. But America has generally espoused, and itself pursued, a global rather than a regional approach.

Although all the other G-7 countries have revealed a proclivity toward "financial spheres of influence," the European Union has been the strongest adherent of this view, particularly with respect to its own regional initiatives. The EU has rejected any G-7 (or IMF) involvement in EMS issues, as discussed above. In addition, the Europeans have apparently accepted primary responsibility for the problems in Eastern Europe and even to an extent in the former Soviet Union (despite its much greater size and the continued American involvement). Germany in particular has assumed a disproportionate share of the financial costs in both areas.

For its part, Japan has been willing (or even eager) to respond bilaterally to China's periodic requests for outside assistance rather than referring them to the G-7 or any broader body. It has also become the largest aid donor by far to Indonesia, Thailand, and other Asian nations. But both Japan and Europe have hesitated to become extensively engaged in Latin America, including in the Mexican crisis of 1995.

It would be easy to dismiss the European and Japanese preference for "financial spheres of influence" as a transparent excuse to avoid burden sharing if that preference were revealed solely, or even mainly, through efforts to avoid "out of area" engagements. The Europeans, to be sure, have supported active engagement by the multilateral financial institutions, and thus a degree of international burden sharing, in Central and Eastern Europe and the former Soviet Union. But neither Europe nor Japan has shirked active engagement themselves—or paying the substantial bills that have accrued—in response to problems in their own "near abroads."

The United States could likewise be viewed as simply trying to shift some of the costs for defending its priority interests. But it has been almost as willing to contribute to distant areas (such as Russia and the Middle East) as to seek help in responding to difficulties nearby, so a broader and more consistent view on burden sharing is apparent as well. The United States has in fact been much more willing to help Russia and the Middle East than the Europeans or Japan have been willing to help Mexico, clearly suggesting a much broader sense of burden sharing on the part of the United States.

However, the share of American funding for international (including G-7) activities, both in the aggregate and in specific cases, has fallen considerably in recent years for both budgetary and broad foreign policy reasons. With some justification, the United States has been increasingly charged with seeking to "run the world with other peoples' money." This growing contrast between American policy and American performance is another source of tension within the G-7. It undermines American influence and further erodes its leadership capacity within the group.

Unlike the other two traditional sources of G-7 tension discussed above, the disagreement within the group over the proper geographic scope of its responsibilities has probably increased. This is due partly to the end of the Cold War and the resultant decline in global security concerns in general. It is due partly to the related reduction in the clout of the United States, with its stronger preference for globalizing the response to problems that Europe and Japan may view as nonsystemic in nature, and its growing inability to pay its way even in generally agreed operations—let alone the more ambitious initiatives that it sometimes advocates. But the G-7 disagreement also relates to the broader penchant for inactivity on the part of key members, an apparent paradox in light of the undeniable increase in the globalization of markets—especially in the financial arena, where G-7 responsibility is greatest.

The Politics of the G-7

The United States and Germany have been the chief protagonists, as the previous sections reveal, in all of the traditional G-7 debates.[8] This pervasive conflict has been manifested most dramatically in American demands, levied in every decade, that Germany undertake expansionary domestic policies to simultaneously boost world growth and help reduce the American external deficit. But Germany has likewise been consistently critical of American external and internal deficits, periodic "benign neglect" of its own currency, and—especially in recent years—its alleged desire "to run the world with other peoples' money." In recent years, Germany has openly criticized America's failure to follow through effectively on agreed intervention policies and abstained on the initial IMF vote to support the American effort in Mexico.[9]

---

8. For one of the rare public revelations of this clash in recent years, see the two articles in the 25 April 1995 *Handelsblatt* based on an interview with Under Secretary of the Treasury for International Affairs Lawrence Summers. One is entitled "Germans Are the World's Top Nay-Sayers" (1), and the other (39) "The Germans Should Not Always Say No and Step on the Brakes." Summers is quoted as "perceiving a number of weak points in German-American cooperation in the G-7 which cause him concern."

9. As noted in chapter 1, the sharp differences between the United States and Germany over financial issues are ironic because overall relations between the two countries are quite good. Despite the reduced imperative to cooperate that accompanied the end of the Cold War, the United States and Germany have worked smoothly together on a wide range of central foreign policy issues, including American support of unification, German support for the American effort in the Gulf War, plans for the expansion of NATO, and policy toward Russia and other parts of the former Soviet Union. The strength of the overall bilateral relationship should be able to withstand the countries' continued difficulties on macroeconomic and monetary topics but does not seem to have much effect in blunting them—perhaps because the American monetary authorities have become less skillful in mobilizing the strengths of the overall relationship.

Four developments in the 1990s have intensified the salience of the German-American conflict: the declining relative role of the United States; the increasing relative role of Germany; the growing alignment of the other European countries, especially France, with Germany in the G-7 due to European integration; and the failure of Japan to play a role commensurate with its economic strength.

The pace and extent of the relative decline of the United States have been debated extensively elsewhere, but two aspects of American influence are particularly relevant for our purposes. One is the reduced importance of America's military presence in Europe. During the Cold War, the security situation was paramount in American relations with Germany, which the United States defended against the threat of Soviet invasion. The United States could thus force economic concessions on Germany, such as the military offset purchases that contributed to bringing down a German government in 1966 and the pledge, conveyed by the "Blessing letter" in 1967, to refrain from buying American gold (Bergsten 1975). It is inconceivable that the United States could force such German actions today.

The second American development was its shift from world's largest creditor to world's largest debtor country in the 1980s and the rapid, continuing growth of that debtor position. The shift has had limited tangible effects so far but represents a proxy for the decline in America's world economic leadership, which in turn hamstrings its ability to win German (and other G-7) acceptance of its initiatives. It would also now be inconceivable for the United States to force the rest of the world to accept its monetary positions, as it did with the adoption of the two-tiered gold regime in the late 1960s and the abandonment of fixed exchange rates in the early 1970s. The fact that the United States has now backed away from much of its traditional proactive stance in the G-7 itself provides further evidence of this declining clout.

Even more important for the relative position of the United States on monetary and financial affairs is the ascendance of Germany. Unification of the country of course increased its size and economic weight (albeit saddling it with a significant problem of assimilation during the transition period). Much more central, however, is the evolution of European monetary integration centered on Germany. Despite the periodic crises and setbacks, and doubts over when or even whether the Maastricht treaty will produce full Economic and Monetary Union, it is clear that Germany has come to dominate a European-wide economy that is larger than that of the United States. Hence Germany's global clout on monetary and macroeconomic issues has risen enormously. It will continue to grow if EMU proceeds, even if initially through only an initial "core group" of half a dozen countries (including France) clustered around Germany but especially if it ultimately includes most of the Continent. If a truly European currency that unifies the Continent economically does emerge, the negotiating clout of the group could come to fully equal, or even exceed, that of the United States—and Germany would continue to be the dominant voice within the group.

An important element of the evolution of German economic power has been the rise of the Bundesbank. Its successful pursuit of monetary stability over a prolonged period has been the key factor in other countries' acceptance of German economic leadership and EMU. The German government has given its central bank wide latitude in conducting the country's exchange market activities, both in the EMS and vis-à-vis non-European currencies, including the dollar. The Bundesbank has thus moved up alongside the US Treasury and Federal Reserve as one of the most powerful international financial institutions in the world. The sharp differences between the Bundesbank and Treasury over a series of recent issues, including currency intervention and Mexico, augur poorly for early resolution of the German-American split and restoration of effective G-7 cooperation.[10]

A third feature of the G-7 political dynamic is the fading role of France and the United Kingdom. France has traditionally been a major independent player in world finance—sometimes destructively, as with its gold purchases in the 1920s, which forced sterling to devalue, and its attempts in the 1960s under President Charles de Gaulle to "dethrone the dollar." But it became the United States' main partner in working out the Second Amendment to the IMF Articles of Agreement in 1975–76, legitimizing floating exchange rates, and winning G-6 consensus on reference ranges at the Louvre.[11]

Over the past 15 years, the French have shifted to full and faithful participation in the EMS, partly because of their conviction that achievement of German-type stability is the best course for France economically. But, as already noted, they also view monetary union as essential politically—especially since unification—to prevent Germany from abandoning the rest of Europe and thus risking a revival of historic antagonisms. Many in France also believe that its only route to increased international economic influence is via the creation of an EMU in which it can have greater impact on German policy and thus a greater role in overall European leadership.

France has therefore adopted most German views on international monetary issues, dropping its traditional penchant for more activist domestic

---

10. The Bundesbank and the Federal Reserve have maintained close cooperation throughout this period, however. An enhanced role for the central banks in the G-7 coordination process, as proposed in chapters 6 and 7, should thus help overcome the broader American-German conflict.

11. Italy refused to participate in the Louvre Accord because the G-5 had caucused without it (and Canada) prior to meeting with the broader group. Hence the accord was a G-6 arrangement.

management and currency intervention. For example, it no longer champions target zones for currency management, as it did less than a decade ago (although President Jacques Chirac has reportedly expressed renewed interest in the exchange rate issue). France has in fact largely ceased to be an independent participant in the G-7, further strengthening Germany's position.

The United Kingdom has remained more independent from Germany than France and has sometimes sided with the United States on G-7 issues, but it has become a minor player at most times. Sterling was, of course, the world's second key currency as late as the 1960s, and the United States regarded it as "the first line of defense of the dollar" throughout that period. But the pound was also the main target of market attacks and thus G-10 rescue packages at that time, and the country's economic decline relative to the rest of the G-7 has marginalized its ability to affect important decisions in the group. Its reticence to participate in Europe's monetary arrangements has also alienated it from the Continental countries while its membership in the European Union has necessarily weakened its traditional ties with the United States.

A fourth feature of G-7 politics is Japan's failure to play a role even remotely commensurate with its economic weight. As the world's most dynamic economy for the first three decades of the modern era and the world's largest creditor country by far, Japan could and should play a leading role in the G-7. There have been brief periods when it tried to do so, such as Finance Minister Kiichi Miyazawa's close cooperation with Treasury Secretary James Baker in October 1986 in devising a yen-dollar reference range that was the forerunner to the Louvre Accord and his initial proposal for a new G-7 strategy on developing-world debt. Nonetheless, Japan has never achieved a leadership role in the group.

There has been a subtle but important shift in Japan's stance within the G-7 in recent years, however.[12] Through the 1980s, Japan largely sided with the United States in G-7 debates despite the similarity of its views and those of Germany on such key issues as the relative roles of surplus and deficit countries and responsibility for regional as opposed to global developments. The overriding importance to Japan of its bilateral relationship with the United States simply overwhelmed these other factors. But Japan has moved away from its traditional, virtually automatic, support for American positions within the G-7 and become more independent.

There are several reasons for this shift. One centered on the Gulf War in 1991. The United States sought sizable Japanese financing (eventually $13 billion) but largely ignored Japan in consultations over basic policy on the issue. The United States also evinced little gratitude after Japan provided the funding. The Japanese resented America viewing it as an "automatic teller machine," and this resentment has persisted.

---

12. The authors are indebted to Yoichi Funabashi for some of these insights.

A second issue concerned aid to Russia. The United States led the effort and placed heavy pressure on Japan to contribute substantially, which it eventually did. But there was little public support in Japan for such largesse, and in fact the dominant domestic view was to resist any significant financing for Russia until it resolved the problem of the Kuril Islands. Resentment against foreign, especially American, pressure intensified. As in the Gulf War, the United States insisted that Japan pay for a large part of what was an essentially American initiative.

The Framework Talks of 1993–95 added further to that resentment. The Japanese viewed themselves as the defenders of "free trade" against the American push for "managed trade."[13] Trade issues clearly came to overshadow macroeconomic and monetary topics in the discourse between the two countries, despite their explicit equality at the outset of the talks. Worse yet, from a Japanese perspective, the US government was conniving to push the yen up to elicit Japanese trade concessions[14]— a view that gathered support when the United States refused to intervene to weaken the yen until the conclusion of the auto talks in mid-1995.

Perhaps the most serious reason that Japan has tempered its support for American initiatives in the G-7, especially with respect to policy coordination to support global growth, is its disillusion with the results of past coordination exercises. Japan fears that any "global growth strategy" would call for it to again undertake sizable fiscal expansions, as it did in the 1970s, and thus run directly counter to its antipathy for budget deficits. But Japan does not want to be pressured to ease monetary policy either. Many Japanese, including those in the powerful Ministry of Finance, believe or at least argue that the G-7 (especially the United States) forced on them the loose monetary policy of the late 1980s that brought on the "bubble economy," as part of the Plaza-Louvre strategy to strengthen (or

---

13. We disagree with the substance of this Japanese view. It is clear that Japanese trade barriers remain extremely high (Sazanami, Urata, and Kawai 1995) and that even the American use of "numerical targets" aimed to "unmanage" rather than manage trade (Bergsten 1993). It is equally clear, however, that most of the world (including many Americans) sided with Japan in this debate and thereby encouraged it to resist most of the American demands— which it did.

14. Treasury Secretary Lloyd Bentsen, when asked in February 1993 if he advocated a weaker dollar, did reply that he wanted to see "a stronger yen." But this view was wholly justified by the macroeconomic situation at the time, and the new Clinton administration had not yet even formulated its trade policy toward Japan. The comments of US Trade Representative Mickey Kantor and other American trade officials that pushed the yen up later in 1993 and in early 1994 were, as noted above, inadvertent and even inept rather than part of any coherent strategy. And even these officials maintained a studious silence on the issue after mid-1994 and said nothing that could be blamed for the appreciation of the yen to 80:1 in early 1995. The markets nevertheless believed that the United States continued to seek a stronger yen until it intervened to weaken it in mid-1995 after the conclusion of the auto talks, which at least for a time brought to a close a series of high-profile trade conflicts dating from the middle of 1993.

at least stabilize) the dollar after its sharp fall to a postwar low in early 1987 and again at the end of that year.

There are two obvious flaws in the latter argument. The first is that Japan's need to expand domestic demand as a result of Plaza-Louvre coordination could (and should) have been exercised via fiscal rather than monetary policy. Thus, the Louvre Accord is a convenient excuse for a huge policy error—an error that can be blamed squarely on the Ministry of Finance, which refused to accept budget deficits and pressed the Bank of Japan to pursue monetary ease.

Second, Japan vastly overdid any obligation it might have had to support the dollar by permitting a depreciation of the yen by fully one-third during the late 1980s.[15] It was Japan's *failure* to conform its policy mix to the needs of the world economy during this period that brought on both its domestic "bubble" and the renewed surge in its external surplus that created huge problems—including for Japan itself—in the 1990s. Indeed, we have cited this episode as one of the key instances of recent G-7 failure. Many Japanese nevertheless harbor bad memories of the Plaza-Louvre effort, just as many Germans harbor ill feelings toward the Bonn agreement of 1978, adding to their resistance to renewed G-7 coordination efforts now.

The United States' increasing isolation within the G-7 is also the result of its own inept performance. Frequent public criticism of other G-7 members generated considerable foreign resentment of American tactics. Such criticisms reached their zenith with Treasury Secretary Baker's denunciation of German policy, which helped trigger Black Monday in 1987, but continued throughout the Bush administration.[16] Even the Brady Plan for developing-world debt and the burden-sharing agreement of the Gulf War, which were substantively successful, left lasting scars because of the peremptory manner in which the United States handled them, and its failure to include the main contributors, especially Japan but Germany as well, in the decision making. The failure of the Clinton administration to internally coordinate its dollar intervention policy in May 1994 drew sharp criticism abroad, especially from Germany. As described in chapter 3, most of the G-7 countries regarded the American effort on Mexico in early 1995 as incompetent from its inception to its conclusion.

The consultative aspects of these issues are extremely important because G-7 cooperation is informal and voluntary, and rests largely on personal relationships among the key officials of the key countries. It was no

---

15. The Japanese in essence recognized and admitted they were overdoing it by intervening heavily in the currency markets in 1989–90 to keep the yen from falling even further.

16. The Clinton administration has consciously and consistently avoided public criticism of other G-7 countries. This has the virtue of reducing adverse reactions from others but the shortcoming of removing a potential tool for inducing foreign cooperation. It has had the net effect of reinforcing the proclivity toward inaction that is addressed in chapter 5.

coincidence that the G-7 achieved its greatest successes during a period of close personal ties between the key finance ministers—Baker in the United States, Gerhard Stoltenberg in Germany, and Noboru Takeshita and then Miyazawa in Japan. This reliance on personalities is one of the great weaknesses of the G-7, and one of the reasons we will recommend in chapter 7 both a larger role for the institutionalized IMF and systemic reforms that will provide permanent incentives for more cooperative behavior in the G-7 itself. But failures to consult effectively and to bring one's own government along in a cohesive fashion violate the informal but powerful "rules of the game." American failure to play by those rules in recent years has often soured the prospects for effective collaboration even when the substantive bases for such cooperation have been in place.

The most conspicuous shortcoming of American policy toward the G-7, however, has been its substantive inconsistency. US international economic policy has fluctuated wildly between the extremes of "benign neglect" and hyperactivism (Bergsten 1986). The United States has ignored the dollar for prolonged periods—as in the late 1960s, mid-1970s, first half of the 1980s, late 1980s, and mid-1990s—and then sought extensive foreign help to either defend it (as in 1978–79, 1987, and 1994–95) or to engineer its depreciation (as in 1971–73 and 1985–86). It rejected any forgiveness of Third World debt through 1988 and then suddenly espoused substantial debt relief in 1989. With respect to the G-7 itself, the United States reversed course—from extreme activism in 1985–87 back to virtual neglect of the entire process at the end of the Reagan administration and throughout the Bush period.

The Clinton administration came into office vowing publicly "to revitalize the G-7" but subsequently slipped back to acceptance of, or even complicity with, the passivity of most of the other members. It, too, flip-flopped on the dollar—accepting or even encouraging its depreciation in 1993–94, at least against the yen and mark, and then seeking to strengthen it throughout 1995.[17]

This American inconstancy has been a recurrent stumbling block for effective international management over the past three decades. For much of that period, America's security and economic dominance induced the other countries to defer to American policy despite its erratic behavior. Coupled with the recent decline in American authority that derives from the structural changes in both the security and economic spheres, America's inconsistent policy pattern has further weakened the clout of the United States and contributed to the paralysis of the G-7.

To be sure, even with the clearest and most consistent American strategy, it would have been more difficult for the G-7 to navigate the rapidly

---

17. These sharp swings in American international monetary policy are made possible by the absence of a private-sector consensus on exchange rate policy and by the ability of the Treasury and Federal Reserve to effectively veto each other's initiatives (Henning 1994).

changing circumstances of the past decade: the end of the Cold War, German unification, European integration, and the pluralization of economic power. Yet it is also true that, because of the regional preoccupation of Europe and the continued insularity of Japan, American leadership remains essential for the G-7 to function effectively. Its absence has been an important cause of the decline of the G-7, and the gyrations of American policy have produced similar ups and downs for the G-7.

A Summing Up

The erosion of American power and influence does not necessarily doom the G-7, however. It is true that the prospects for international cooperation, on terms consistent with the interests of the dominant power, are better under hegemony than without it. The changes in the world political economy that have shifted power away from the United States and toward the European Union and Japan have made G-7 cooperation more complicated.

But hegemony is neither necessary nor sufficient for international cooperation. Even in the presence of a hegemonic power, such as the United States at the end of World War II, international economic cooperation depended upon the voluntary adherence of other important countries. The US government offered Europe and Japan inducements to adhere to open multilateral trade, money, and investment regimes in the form of financing and access to the US market. Ultimately, however, it was not so much American power as the preferences of European and Japanese governments and entrepreneurial American diplomacy that enabled open multilateralism to survive (Eichengreen 1989; Keohane 1984). Nye (1990) contends that American predominance after World War II, and its subsequent decline, have been exaggerated by many analysts, who therefore also exaggerate the importance of the power structure for international economic cooperation.[18]

Even in the absence of a hegemon, dilemmas of collective action that arise in constructing and maintaining a regime can be overcome. For example, Eichengreen (1989) argues that, although British dominance declined dramatically as a result of World War I, substantial international cooperation was restored in the 1920s. Moreover, although the United States was dominant in 1933, 1936, and 1944, on objective measures of

18. Much of the relevant literature has arisen in reaction to the "hegemonic stability thesis," which argues that the presence of a hegemonic state is a necessary (but not sufficient) condition for an open, multilateral international economic system. As a corollary, changes in the underlying distribution of economic power among countries presage changes in international arrangements, institutions, and regimes (Kindleberger 1973; Gilpin 1981; see also Keohane 1984; Gilpin 1987; Eichengreen 1989; Nye 1990; Nau 1990).

output and trade, the outcomes of international monetary bargaining varied greatly (Odell 1988; Oye 1993). That both economic conflict and cooperation existed under the same power structure indicates that power configuration alone does not determine the outcomes of cooperation.

The continued split between the United States and its partners over the appropriate geographical scope of G-7 actions (global versus regional) remains a major hurdle to effective cooperation. But the decline in the importance of several of the traditional differences addressed earlier in this chapter should buoy its prospects. The enthusiasm of the United States for countercyclical policy initiatives in general, and Keynesian stimulus programs in particular, has clearly waned. Most of the other G-7 members, including those that advocated (or at least accepted) such strategies in the past, have undergone a similar transformation. Thus this particular set of distinctions is no longer such a crucial barrier to G-7 cooperation.

The conflicts between surplus/creditor and deficit/debtor countries remain more acute and continue to arise. Their salience has diminished for the moment, however, with reduced international (and domestic) concern about the American external deficit, with the "global surplus" concentrated in Japan and addressed largely in its bilateral negotiations with the United States, and with the relative ease of financing the imbalances in recent years. The recent maintenance of rough equilibrium in the German (and overall European) external position has limited the interest in this issue in four of the G-7 countries.

The reduction in intensity of these two traditional causes of conflict within the G-7, particularly between the United States and Germany, should augur well for a revival of effective cooperation. This should be especially true with respect to policy coordination *within* the group, since these two issues relate directly to the purposes and methods of achieving international adjustment. Yet, as we have already seen, the decline of the G-7 is most pronounced with respect to precisely these adjustment issues. This is also the most serious aspect of the G-7's recent failures, in light of its members' continued dominance in the world economy.

Hence, the chief explanation for the decline of the G-7, at least on the most important issues it must address, does not lie primarily with the traditional conflicts within the group. It springs rather from its new consensus for inaction. We turn now to a more extensive examination of that phenomenon and how it has come to dominate the process.

5

The Sources of G-7 Decline:
The New Consensus

The G-7's new consensus for inaction takes two forms. One is a nonaggression pact among the members of the group. They no longer seek to influence each others' policies in any major or consistent way. They have largely decided on a "live and let live" philosophy.

There are, of course, occasional exceptions to this new rule. As we note at several points, the Bush and early Clinton administrations did push Europe and Japan to participate in a global growth strategy. Top German officials briefly renewed their traditional criticism of American budget deficits in early 1995. American officials again urged Europe to stimulate growth in early 1996. But there has been a dramatic reduction in the propensity of G-7 countries to attack each others' policies, publicly or even privately.[1]

The second dimension of the new consensus is the group's self-imposed limitation on efforts in the rest of the world. They are making no effort to improve the functioning of the international adjustment process, despite its evident shortcomings and its great importance for the world economy, including through its impact on the trading system. Burned by their experiences with Russia and Mexico, they are unlikely to launch many future rescue missions.

---

1. The G-7 has successfully kept most of its problems out of the public eye. This is fortunate because public attention to the group's decline would have unsettled markets and further increased the adverse impact of its ineffectiveness. But the "conspiracy of silence" among the members has also reduced public awareness of the need for remedial action and has thus permitted the group to perpetuate its shortcomings.

The G-7 has not come to this passivity for doctrinaire reasons as it did in the early 1980s, when the first Reagan administration genuinely believed that international economic cooperation was unnecessary and even undesirable. Nor does the group come to it idiosyncratically, though the personalities of some of the key players have undoubtedly rendered cooperation more difficult in recent years.

Rather, there are several underlying developments of major importance that have pushed the G-7 in this direction. At the broadest level, the G-7 is suffering from two fundamental historic transitions—the end of the Cold War and the advent of multipolarity.

The world, including the world of international economics, is thus in a transition period—one would hope to a new regime of effective multilateral cooperation led by two or three near-equals. The problem, as historians and political scientists frequently observe, is that collective management demands considerably more brokering, negotiation, and policy entrepreneurship than hegemonic leadership. Collective management will therefore be more complex and difficult.

The strong interests of all three of the major economic powers—the United States, the European Union, and Japan—should eventually induce them to develop such a cooperative regime. Such an outcome is by no means assured, however, and historic rivalries and even conflict could reappear. Transition periods such as the present are inherently dangerous, and the specter of such dangers should enhance the resolve of the G-7 countries to revitalize their cooperation.

It is unlikely that any new steady state, whether benign or dangerous, will emerge in the near future. The evolution of the preferred outcome will require major developments within each of the three economic superpowers. The United States will have to accept the end of its dominance without becoming unilateralist or isolationist. For their part, Europe and Japan will have to accept greater responsibility.

In addition, there are a number of specific developments in recent years that have pushed the G-7 toward inaction. The advent of large structural budget deficits in all the member nations has deprived their governments of a major tool of traditional macroeconomic policy, thus limiting the scope for international policy coordination as well as domestic management. The related ascendance of central banks, which are independent of governments in the two most important G-7 countries and fiercely resist being coordinated by anybody, is another problem for G-7 activism on macroeconomic policy. The enormous growth of international capital movements has instilled a deep conviction in most G-7 officials that they could not win a battle with the markets even if they tried. Taken together, and within the broader geopolitical context sketched above, these factors have immobilized the G-7 on most issues—and have produced a consensus in the group that this is the right, or at least the only feasible, course.

This chapter will analyze each of the elements that underlies the current position of the G-7. In each case, we will ask whether the group has drawn the proper conclusions from those developments. We will conclude that, while present and foreseeable conditions do preclude some types of initiatives that the G-7 undertook in the past, other and sometimes more promising efforts can and should be pursued. In one or two central areas, we will in fact argue that modern conditions provide important new opportunities for active G-7 initiatives that would go far to restore the group's leadership in promoting global prosperity and stability.

Before analyzing the "legitimate" sources of the G-7's tendency to inactivism, two false "explanations" need to be addressed. The G-7 often justifies its inaction by arguing that the political weaknesses of its governments preclude such collaboration. All G-7 governments are indeed quite fragile, as revealed by the latest election results and polls. But this is a peculiar argument, because their domestic political problems derive at least partly from the weakness of their economies, which in turn relates directly to the shortcomings of the world economy itself. The Baker-Stoltenberg-Miyazawa triumvirate in the middle 1980s understood that they could *help* each others' political fortunes by active cooperation that promoted better performance of their individual economies. Their successors ignore the benefits of cooperation at their peril.

A second false explanation for the new consensus is "reassertion of the primacy of domestic over international goals." G-7 spokespeople will often justify their failure to cooperate more effectively in these terms. Indeed, the desire of several of the key G-7 members to avoid foreign criticism of their domestic policies is one of the most obvious explanations for their adoption of a de facto nonaggression pact.

As elaborated in appendix A, however, this formulation misspecifies the issue. Countries have never "given primacy to international objectives," nor would anyone reasonably ask them to do so. The issue is rather whether pursuing internationally sustainable policies, and even occasionally changing policy in response to external signals such as the exchange rate, is likely to promote better economic outcomes within countries. This is a complex question that will be addressed in some detail in chapter 6. But the simplistic contrasts between "domestic versus international goals" and "foreign versus national interests" introduces red herrings that should not be permitted to sidetrack the debate.[2] We turn now

---

2. To be sure, any *appearance* of "placing priority on international goals" is distinctly unpopular in most countries. In the United States, the strong attack on the administration's Mexican support package by the Congress has sharply reduced, for at least the foreseeable future, the administration's propensity to participate in (let alone lead) similar efforts.

to genuine problems that have produced the G-7's rejection of active policy coordination.

The Immobilization of Fiscal Policy

One of the elements driving the new consensus has been the onset of large budget deficits in all of the G-7 countries. The circumstances and timing have been different in the different countries. Japan got into trouble in the late 1970s as it tried to reverse the adverse effects of the oil shocks and cut its external surpluses, including through participation in international coordination programs such as the Bonn summit. The United States succumbed in the 1980s through Reaganomics. Germany diverged from its normal rectitude to finance national unification in the early 1990s. The resultant sharp decline in the ability to use fiscal policy as a discretionary policy tool explains much of the waning of the earlier propensities, especially in the United States, to pursue expansionary policies at both the national and international levels.[3]

Fiscal policy has not, of course, been totally immobilized. The automatic stabilizers still work in every country (although some Europeans are trying to blunt them to meet the Maastricht criteria). Extraordinary circumstances, such as German unification or earthquakes and prolonged recession in Japan, do produce fiscal responses. But fiscal policy was already very difficult to adjust quickly in all the major countries—due among other reasons to the congressional system in the United States, the key role of the Länder in Germany, and the dominance of the conservative Ministry of Finance in Japan. The onset of large deficits has rendered the instrument even less flexible and sharply reduced its utility for discretionary countercyclical purposes.

This relative immobilization of fiscal policy has sharply increased the reliance of all countries on monetary policy. One result is that most countries now rely on it to promote an optimal trade-off between employment and price stability—an exceedingly difficult task even before external considerations are factored in. This in turn reduces their proclivity to adopt international policy coordination initiatives, addressed either to a specific circumstance or more systemically, that could require diversion

---

3. The behavior of the Clinton administration provides persuasive evidence in the case of the United States. It came to office in 1993 pledging to strengthen the economy. The fiscal outlook was tight, however, so its proposed stimulus package was so small (less than $20 billion in a $6 trillion economy) that the Congress rejected it as irrelevant. The administration then turned unambiguously toward deficit reduction, arguing inter alia that the effect would be expansionary because of the lower interest rates that would result—a "reverse Keynesian" view that turned out to be largely correct. The possibility that fiscal contraction can be expansionary for the economy in some circumstances has added further to G-7 doubts about attempting to deploy it actively in international coordination efforts.

of monetary policy from domestic goals.[4] The reduction in the number of effective policy instruments makes it more difficult to coordinate policies internationally (just as it does internally).

The Primacy of the Central Banks

The immobilization of fiscal policy and the consequent rise in the role of monetary policy has strengthened the hand of central banks in all G-7 countries. Because the central banks rightly focus on price stability, this change biases economic policy in an anti-inflationary direction. Combined with the incapacity of fiscal policy, this economic orientation helps explain the slow growth of the 1990s as well as the (related) decline of the G-7.

There is a substantial difference in the independence of central banks across the G-7—from the high degree of autonomy the Bundesbank and Federal Reserve enjoy, through the new but untested independence of the Banque de France, to the continuing subordination of the Bank of England and the Bank of Japan to their governments (Henning 1994). But the central banks in the two key countries, Germany and the United States, jealously guard their independence and thus would make it extremely difficult for their governments to conduct a coordinated economic strategy even if they wanted to.[5]

It is true that governors of the G-7 central banks attend most meetings of the group's finance ministers. Their deputies now also attend the meetings of G-7 deputies that are held prior to, and for the purpose of preparing, those ministerials. And the central banks did in fact implement several coordinated reductions in interest rates during 1986 (Funabashi 1989).

But that experience, along with the subsequent G-7 efforts to manage exchange rates through the Louvre Accord in 1987, which could have carried substantial commitments for monetary policy, led the monetary authorities to fiercely resist any further agreements that would have similar implications. They believe that such programs weaken their independent status, thus dampening their credibility and hence their effectiveness in exercising their primary responsibilities—especially in combatting inflation. The central bankers sometimes even urge their foreign counterparts, and the international economic organizations, not to issue recommendations with which they agree on the grounds that it will then be *harder* for them to take the actions being urged.

---

4. France is the only current exception in the G-7, determining its monetary policy largely by the goal of maintaining close links to the deutsche mark.

5. The literature on central bank independence is vast (see, e.g., Alesina and Summers 1990; Grilli, Masciandaro, and Tabellini 1991; Lohmann 1992; Posen 1993; Goodman 1991, 1992; Binaian, Laney, and Willett 1986; Woolley 1985; Eijffinger and Schaling 1993, 1995; Eijffinger and de Haan 1995; Cukierman, Webb, and Neyapti 1992).

It appears that the central banks have resisted coordinating their actions even when they have independently decided to take steps that would have been natural candidates for coordination, and despite the clear lesson of history that coordinated packages have a much stronger impact on market psychology than parallel but independent steps. For example, in May–June 1994 the G-7 intervened to resist a sharp decline of the dollar, and their central banks subsequently moved in the appropriate directions—to reduce interest rates in Germany and Japan and to raise them in the United States—but without linking the several steps together. They thus dissipated much of the potential market payoff.

The leading central banks clearly prefer to cooperate closely among themselves rather than as part of broader programs with their governments.[6] The G-10 central bankers meet monthly at the Bank for International Settlement (BIS) in Basel and hence are in much more frequent formal contact than their counterparts in the finance ministries. The central banks, of course, cooperate in ways that are fully sensitive to the institutional requirements of each and may thus be coordinating more extensively than is acknowledged or even perceived publicly.

Some proposals to strengthen international coordination through greater involvement of central banks have foundered as much on the unwillingness of the central banks themselves to become more involved, in a process they see as dominated by finance ministries, as on the unwillingness of the finance ministries to bring them more frontally into the picture. In light of their importance, however, the central banks should be integrated into the operations of the G-7 as a whole. How this might be achieved is discussed in chapter 7.

The flip side of the increased power of the central banks is the reduced power of finance ministers. Since the ministers represent their countries in the G-7 and are the political driving force behind the group, the decline in their effective authority weakens the institution still further.

The authority of its finance minister has always been a particular problem for the United States in the G-7. Under the unique American political system, no executive official below the president can speak with full authority on overall economic policy, and on fiscal policy in particular. Within the administration, the Treasury secretary must share authority with other key officials of similar rank—notably, the director of the Office of Management and Budget, the chair of the Council of Economic Advisers, and other top officials in the White House, including, under the Clinton administration, the leadership of the National Economic Council.

---

6. That central banks prefer to cooperate among themselves rather than with their own governments is an example of the importance of transnational and transgovernmental coalitions, as initially identified by Keohane and Nye (1971), in which nonstate actors and state bureaucracies join forces across borders to advance common interests over the opposition of other international actors and sometimes competing domestic actors.

The executive branch as a whole, of course, shares authority over budgets and taxes with the Congress. Hence the secretary has never been able to bargain credibly with his G-7 peers on fiscal policy, further weakening the American stance in the G-7 even before the increased role of the Federal Reserve in recent years exacerbated that problem.[7]

The G-7 in fact suffers institutionally from the different competencies of its participants. As noted, the American Treasury secretary speaks with less authority than many of the other ministers of finance. We have already seen the sharp differences in the independence, and hence authority, of central banks across the G-7. There is thus a considerable mismatch in the clout of the individuals sitting around the G-7 table, as well as the clout of their countries. This has been a perennial problem of the G-7 from its inception, however, and does not explain the group's decline in recent years. It must simply be accepted and accommodated as the group goes about its business.

The Growth and Spread of Private Capital Flows

The enormous increase in international flows of private capital has been another deterrent to G-7 activism. The latest estimates suggest that well over $1 trillion flows through the currency markets daily. Though most of these flows have no net effect on exchange rates and other markets, as will be explained in chapter 6, most officials believe their reserves are grossly inadequate to counter such large amounts. This calculation relates directly to two types of G-7 activities: intervention in the exchange markets and support programs for beleaguered countries.

Intervention, of course, pits the officials directly against the private markets. Most officials appear to doubt their ability to win such a confrontation. They point to the "successful speculative attacks" that forced sterling and the lira to leave the Exchange Rate Mechanism (ERM) in 1992, for example, and the subsequent attacks on the French franc and other currencies a year later that forced the ERM to convert its narrow bands (formerly $\pm 2\frac{1}{4}$ percent) into much broader target zones (± 15 percent). Reinforcing such concerns was the private selling of the Mexican peso after its devaluation in December 1994, which greatly intensified that country's crisis and spilled over to numerous other economies.

There has thus developed a fairly widespread view, including in academic circles, that the only two viable exchange rate regimes are freely

---

7. This is a key reason why G-7 summits are particularly important from the standpoint of American participation in international economic coordination. The president cannot speak for the Congress either, a problem that is sometimes less serious in one-party parliamentary governments, but he can at least present a unified view for the executive branch.

floating rates and a currency union à la EMU—the two polar extremes (Eichengreen 1995 and Wyplosz 1995, but see Garber and Svensson 1995 for a rebuttal).[8] Virtually all G-7 countries, even the Europeans in their intraregional arrangements and despite their desire to move soon to currency union, are now afraid to set fixed rates or even narrow margins. Indeed, many Europeans even resist narrowing the very wide 15 percent bands now in place in the European Monetary System (EMS) on the grounds that the limits could be attacked and defeated by the far greater resources of private investors. There is growing reluctance to intervene in the markets for currencies that are floating as well. Hence doubts about the practicability of active exchange rate policy have contributed to sharply reduced activity by the G-7 in one of the areas where it has traditionally played a major role.

The other aspect of this phenomenon is closely related but operationally different: support packages to countries whose economies are in severe difficulty. Substantively, such packages provide resources to the target country to enable it to defend its currency. Like the Mexico package of early 1995 and its many predecessors over the years, their magnitudes and nature are usually quite precise, so they, too, represent a target for the speculators to shoot at. Hence many G-7 officials also now view these programs with some suspicion.

The number of countries that participate actively in the international capital markets has increased sharply in recent years. Many more countries have become vulnerable to the volatility of such flows. The international financial system as a whole can be affected by a much wider range of nations. Mexico had become the single largest recipient of portfolio inflows among the developing countries, but a dozen or so others are, or could soon become, large enough participants in those markets to carry systemic implications.

G-7 officials therefore confront an increase not only in the volume of private capital flows across borders but in the number of countries that are involved. This adds to the complexity and daunting nature of their problems and increases their misgivings as to whether their governments can cope. In the case of Mexico alone, for example, the United States committed $20 billion from an Exchange Stabilization Fund whose total holdings were less than $40 billion—immediately raising questions in the markets of whether the United States could defend its own currency effectively, and thus probably adding at least a bit to subsequent selling pressures on the dollar.[9]

---

8. Such analyses would admit exceptions only for countries that are very small and dependent on trade or for temporary periods for countries that peg to a stronger currency as part of a stabilization program designed to end hyperinflation.

9. This concern is unfounded, because the Federal Reserve can augment US intervention resources enormously by activating swap networks with other central banks and the Bank for International Settlements; these agreements now amount to $35.4 billion and can be

Doubts have thus become widespread about the likelihood of success of support packages for individual countries, especially developing countries. The continuing uncertainties over the outcome of the Mexican effort, in addition to revealing substantial differences of view among G-7 countries, have added to such doubts. If the "star pupil" could not be rescued by a package of unprecedented magnitude, how great is the prospect for success elsewhere?

The Downgrading of the IMF

There is a final element of the G-7's new consensus that also reduces the prospects for effective international policy coordination: its unwillingness to lodge major new responsibilities in the International Monetary Fund. Since the IMF must be the primary locus for implementing any major systemic efforts, even if originated and steered by the G-7, its lessened status in the eyes of its key members is also a major problem.

Much of the "unwillingness to trust the IMF" is simply another manifestation of the nonaggression pact among the G-7. The G-7 countries have decided not only to abstain from criticizing each other in most circumstances but to block such criticisms elsewhere. As the dominant shareholders of the IMF, they can do so in that institution. The G-7 can also bar the IMF from participating in the most sensitive parts of its own meetings, including those that deal with exchange rates.[10]

This withholding of authority is extremely costly to the Fund. It has been inactive in the industrial countries for almost 20 years and has thus come to be widely viewed as a "foreign aid institution." Such limitations on IMF activity reduce its clout and hence the perceptions of its effectiveness. This image creates a vicious spiral that makes the G-7 even more reluctant to subject themselves to IMF surveillance.[11] Our proposals seek to reverse this, but it is a trend the G-7 undeniably fosters.

The G-7 concern about the Fund also rests on several more defensible propositions. One is that the IMF Executive Board is too low-level to carry

expanded further with the agreement of the other central banks in an emergency. The United States also has access to about $40 billion from the IMF, of which about $10 billion could be drawn virtually automatically and without any conditions. If the Treasury were ever to fully convert ESF dollars into foreign exchange, it could obtain more dollars by transferring its foreign exchange to the Federal Reserve in return (a transaction called warehousing). Limits on this procedure are established and changed by the Federal Open Market Committee.

10. Bryant (1995, 114) notes that "the G-7 governments have not wanted to establish a new secretariat to support the G-7 process and at the same time have been unwilling to allow existing international organizations such as the IMF or OECD to become actively enough involved to play that role."

11. Treatments of surveillance include Dobson (1991, 1994), Goldstein (1995), Bretton Woods Commission (1994), James (1996), and Pauly (1993 and forthcoming).

out serious surveillance and adjustment exercises. Another is that the board and the staff are too large to avoid leaks in sensitive policy areas, such as exchange rates. We will propose institutional changes to deal with these problems, which clearly add to G-7 doubts about the Fund.

Some of the G-7 hostility to the Fund stems from the view of many of its members that the United States dominates the institution. Some go so far as to characterize the grant of any additional authority to the IMF as "giving the Americans a blank check to pursue their national interests." Such a view would come as a great surprise to those American members of Congress who routinely seek to withhold US support on the grounds that the IMF impinges on American sovereignty. Nevertheless, at least part of the G-7's unwillingness to provide the IMF with more authority reverts to politics within the group—once again, notably between the United States and Germany.

The Abdication of Responsibility

The traditional *disagreements* within the G-7 over several key issues have thus become coupled with growing *agreements* over the difficulty, or even futility, of attempting to pursue some of the activities that have been central to the group's success in the past. The increasingly passive stance of the G-7 can largely be explained by these two sets of developments, especially the latter.

Some would argue that contemporary conditions preclude a repetition of the G-7's earlier successes. The group could coordinate macroeconomic policies in 1978—but the immobilization of fiscal policy and related implications for monetary policy now make that much harder. They could coordinate monetary policies in 1986—but that is now much more difficult because of the greater burdens on monetary policy and the central banks' jealous protection of their independence. They could coordinate exchange market policies in the mid-1980s—but the huge expansion of international capital flows renders that strategy far more problematic over extended periods, especially for any sizable adjustment effort like the Plaza Agreement and most of all for any systemic stabilization scheme like the Louvre Accord. Even some who are sympathetic to the goals of policy coordination, and agree that the G-7 has recorded notable accomplishments in the past, are skeptical of its prospects today.

But the new consensus of the mid-1990s sounds suspiciously like the "old consensus" of the early 1980s. During that period, the G-5 (and G-7) adopted an even more passive stance toward international coordination than is the case today. That passivity allegedly rested on the view that "convergence" of national policies and economic performance would eliminate all substantial international imbalances and related problems, at least over time, and that the world economy would function satisfactorily if each of the major national economies would simply put its own house in order.

The convergence thesis of that period, however, was largely an intellectual cover for the strong anticooperation bias of the first Reagan administration. American policy during that period produced the "twin deficits" that have had such negative effects on both the United States itself and the world economy. An important part of the reason was the administration's total rejection of any international cooperation—and any cognizance of the external impact of its own actions. In particular, it ignored the feedback on the American economy from the huge dollar overvaluation and current account deficits.[12] Other countries' initial resistance to the new American stance led the administration to justify its actions through the convergence thesis, which the others eventually swallowed when they realized that there was no prospect for altering Reagan policies and that public acrimony would further exacerbate their problems, including the strength of the dollar.

The G-5 inactivity of the early 1980s, under cover of the convergence approach, permitted the largest disequilibrium ever experienced by a key currency: the enormous overvaluation of the dollar. Overvaluation in turn produced both protectionist pressures, which threatened the entire world trading system, and the subsequent risk of a "hard landing," which could have devastated the world economy. Another result was the conversion of the United States into the world's largest debtor country, which, as noted in chapters 3 and 4, will have lasting consequences for the system as well as for the United States itself.

The G-5 explicitly repudiated this convergence thesis in its communiqué of the Plaza Agreement of September 1985. They admitted that "recent shifts in fundamental economic conditions, together with policy commitments for the future, have not been reflected fully in exchange markets" and that "these positive economic developments notwithstanding, there are large imbalances in external positions which pose potential problems." In other words, national "convergence" had produced international instability rather than the promised stability.

Most importantly, the G-5 agreed at the Plaza that "exchange rates should better reflect fundamental economic conditions than has been the case." They then intensified the process of direct intervention in the currency markets that was essential to resolve the problem. Convergence and noncooperation had been tried and had failed.

---

12. David Stockman, who was director of OMB at the outset of the Reagan administration and one of the chief architects of its economic policy, reveals that the administration's internal projections forecast quite accurately that the American current account imbalance would hit about $100 billion in 1984 as a result of their efforts. The problem was that they got the sign wrong: they predicted a surplus of $100 billion rather than the deficit of that magnitude that actually occurred. They obviously never gave the issue serious consideration (Stockman 1987).

Indeed, the most active and successful period of international coordination in the modern era ensued with the failure of the convergence principles. With this recent history in mind, two sets of questions arise for the present. First, are the G-7 governments correct to conclude that their traditional differences and especially their "new consensus" preclude effective coordination? Or are new approaches available that would overcome both and would resolve the widely shared doubts that have come to pervade the group? Second, what would be the impact of continued G-7 decline on the world economy and more specifically on its financial markets, on its trading system, and on the broader political relationships among the G-7 countries and between G-7 countries and nonmembers?

Having described the existing problems and analyzed their causes, we turn to a proposed response to those problems that could restore effective leadership to the world economy. This response may strike some readers as woefully inadequate to reverse the decline of the G-7 described in the preceding chapters and to address the needs that have been put forward. It is true that we make no sweeping proposals for a world central bank, or a G-7 equivalent of Economic and Monetary Union (EMU) in Europe, that would constitute a quantum jump in global coordination. This book does not endorse the "blueprint" for extensive coordination of fiscal and monetary policies that some of our colleagues have devised and that has been actively debated in academic circles (Williamson and Miller 1987).

The reason is simply that it would be unrealistic to expect the G-7 to embrace any of these ambitious coordination schemes in the short or even medium run. The analysis so far portrays an institution that has virtually given up on activist policies of any sort and that frequently makes substantive and tactical errors when it does decide to act. The most that a realistic agenda can attempt is gradual and evolutionary reform that will, over time, rebuild a systemic foundation for the kinds of cooperation that are needed.

The policy proposals in the last two chapters of this book are therefore deliberately designed to be incremental. They are also largely familiar, to officials as well as academic students of the topic, so should not require any extensive new studies before they can be understood and addressed. None would require major changes in existing policies and institutional arrangements. They are quite modest and evolutionary in both substantive and procedural terms.

It is nevertheless likely that even these proposals will be skeptically received by the monetary authorities at which they are primarily aimed. Our concluding chapters will in fact address the question of why the monetary authorities are so quick to oppose any changes in the status quo—indeed, why they have never agreed to major monetary reform in the postwar period, especially dealing with adjustment—despite its obvious shortcomings. The conclusion is that intervention by the top *political* authorities, operating through the G-7 summits, will probably be necessary to effect the proposed changes, in the same way that intervention by the political authorities in Europe was essential to spawn the EMS and now EMU.

We thus plead guilty to suggesting remedies that only begin to meet the problems we have specified. We do so explicitly and openly in the hope that the modest proposals that follow will commend themselves as a serious start in the needed direction. If these steps are adopted and succeed, the G-7 may regain some of its self-confidence and will to act. It may then become possible to build on the process to pursue more far-reaching and more comprehensive approaches over the longer run.

6

Reviving the G-7

Reviving the G-7 will require it to adopt new approaches in all the areas for which it is responsible: active surveillance and periodic coordination of economic activity within the group itself, leadership on "out of area" issues, and improvement in the systemic architecture. To do so, it will have to address the several problems, spelled out in the two preceding chapters, that are at the root of the G-7's decline.

These problems are not insurmountable. Indeed, some of the problems cited have declined greatly in importance. Some represent an erroneous understanding of the circumstances they address. Some of the problems are real but can be overcome by new policy approaches, the characteristics of which are laid out in this chapter. Building on this analysis, chapter 7 will then propose specific policy initiatives that the G-7 should undertake to resume effective leadership of the world economy.

Resolving the Traditional Differences

Chapter 4 suggested that no fundamental resolution of the "inflation versus unemployment" debate is likely. It also concluded, however, that the differences on this issue have diminished considerably. There is now intellectual consensus that there is little trade-off between the two, especially over the longer run. Pragmatically, the advent of large budget deficits everywhere has largely immobilized fiscal policy as a device for cyclical management. The G-7 should therefore focus more on creating systemic arrangements to improve world economic performance over time than on altering short-term cyclical prospects.

Underlying differences clearly remain on the relative responsibilities of surplus and deficit countries and are unlikely to dissipate as long as large imbalances persist. But, as discussed in chapter 4, there may be a growing consensus on the need to emphasize the contribution of exchange rate changes to the prevention or correction of these imbalances. This is because the three big economic areas—the United States, the European countries with their increasing focus on the international adjustment of the region as a whole, and Japan—are now quite similar with respect to the relatively modest dependence of their economies on trade. Hence all three, unlike more trade-dependent national economies such as Germany or the United Kingdom, will be reluctant to adjust their external imbalances via alterations in domestic demand (unless such alterations are needed for internal reasons as well). The systemic arrangements that should be the center of future G-7 attention should thus seek to maximize the effectiveness of currency adjustment techniques.

For some time, all G-7 members have in fact been seeking to devise exchange rate arrangements that will minimize the risk of both policy errors (especially the defense of overvalued parities) and market errors (prolonged misalignments due to private capital flows). The Europeans, of course, have been the most aggressive with their pursuit of regional arrangements. But the G-7 as a group continues to intervene actively in the exchange markets, albeit on an ad hoc basis, most recently to weaken the yen and strengthen the dollar in 1995. The main issue is the technical question of what arrangements will best avoid, or at least minimize, prolonged misalignments. The lesson, again, is to focus on building effective systemic structures.

The third traditional difference, regarding globalism versus regionalism as a focus for G-7 attention, has probably become both more acute and more significant. One problem is the lack of a new paradigm to guide security strategy in the post–Cold War period. Is it still necessary, or even desirable, for the G-7 to exercise global responsibility in the absence of a common global enemy? Or is it now acceptable, as well as more feasible pragmatically, for each major power to accept financial responsibility for its own region: the United States for Latin America, Western Europe for Eastern Europe and for the former Soviet Union, Japan for East Asia?

There are several obvious problems with the regional alternative. First, some regions are left out: no one would bear clear responsibility for the Middle East, South Asia, and Africa. Second, Western Europe itself may not be able to effectively handle the former Soviet Union—given the size of Russia, its continued status as a nuclear power, and the obvious interest of the United States in remaining deeply engaged there. Third, the United States would clearly be unwilling to restrict its leadership to the Western Hemisphere, and few Asian countries would accept regional leadership from Japan. Fourth, such an approach, even if feasible, would risk dividing the world into "spheres of financial influence" that could over time increase rather than quell international conflict.

These problems point toward the adoption of a global strategy for the G-7, rejecting "financial spheres of influence" in favor of global burden sharing by the group as a whole in responding to international economic problems wherever they may arise. That conclusion rests primarily on changes in global economic conditions, however, rather than broad foreign policy considerations. As noted in chapter 5, the most important structural change in the world economy over the past decade or so is the sharp increase in the magnitude of private capital flows and the globalization of capital markets. At least a dozen "emerging market economies," located in all parts of the world, now have the potential to disrupt the global system.

The Mexico crisis of late 1994–95 demonstrated that financial disruption in any one region can have pervasive "contagion effects" around the world. Argentina and a few other Latin American countries felt the most immediate and extensive spillover. But Eastern Europe was affected as well, and even some industrialized (including G-7) countries, including Canada and Italy (and maybe also the United States), suffered at least a bit of the "contagion."

There was an effect in East Asian markets, too, which was dramatic, if short-lived. Thailand experienced an enormous jump in domestic interest rates. The Hong Kong stock market plummeted. The central bankers of the region caucused nervously. Even Taiwan, with almost $100 billion of currency reserves, held an emergency cabinet meeting to consider the implications for its own markets. The crisis prompted several East Asian countries to begin setting up their own mutual support networks, and they are considering Australian proposals to create "an Asian BIS."

This globalization of financial markets suggests that the G-7 could not neatly compartmentalize the world economy even if it wanted to. Spillovers are simply too widespread to permit any rational assignment of regional spheres of financial influence. The case for policy cooperation applies globally rather than regionally.[1]

The G-7 should therefore work out a burden-sharing formula that would apply to all regions of the world. As suggested in chapter 7, the

---

1. Recent US initiatives to create regional free trade arrangements in the Asia Pacific (via APEC) and in the Western Hemisphere (via a Free Trade Area of the Americas, building on NAFTA) might be viewed as inconsistent with this proposal. Both efforts, however, particularly in APEC with its strong emphasis on "open regionalism," are in fact intended to set the stage for further liberalization on a global basis (Bergsten 1996). In addition, APEC seeks to join East Asia and North America together and thus *avoid* the evolution of regional blocs *within* each area. It will be essential, nevertheless, for both the United States and the other major trading countries (especially the European Union, with its far more extensive regional arrangements) to steer both the world trading system and the regional initiatives in directions that do not undermine the proper global focus.

IMF should be the locus of all international financial support operations, which would automatically entail use of the well-established quota relationships among its members. Supplements, where necessary, could be provided by the General Arrangements to Borrow (GAB)—whose national shares are also well-established (but need to be updated and augmented by new members, as is now being discussed and as is also addressed in chapter 7).

Where additional G-7 contributions are called for, one simple approach would be for each of the three main G-7 components (Europe, Japan, North America) to provide one-third of the total amount. If one of them wanted to retain some limited degree of special regional responsibility, an alternative would be for either Europe, Japan, or North America to pick up half the cost of an operation in "its area." The other half could be divided equally between the other two components of the G-7.

Nonmembers of the G-7 should increasingly be involved in any such operations, as were the Gulf countries and some others in financing the Gulf War. Several have already been approached to provide additional support to the IMF through the GAB. Engaging nonmembers in these ways would, in addition to helping finance the particular project, begin to involve such countries with the G-7. This would enhance the legitimacy of the G-7 and help pave the way for the eventual association of these countries with, and perhaps membership in, the group itself—a theme developed in some detail in chapter 7.

Immobilization of Fiscal Policy and Coordination of Monetary Policy

The more fundamental questions that challenge the future efficacy of the G-7 relate to the "new consensus" among its members that most coordination is neither desirable nor feasible. Three key elements in that "new consensus" are that the immobilization of fiscal policy precludes its incorporation in any meaningful coordination strategy, that monetary policy thus is fully occupied pursuing domestic targets and therefore its ability to address international purposes is severely limited or even obviated, and that the resultant preeminence of central banks in several of the key countries (including the United States and Germany) renders intergovernmental coordination infeasible because they are independent and protect this status so jealously.

There is obviously a good deal of truth in this line of argument. International coordination *would* be far more feasible, and far more promising, if the full range of policy instruments—including fiscal policy—were both available for that purpose and reasonably flexible to implement. Monetary policy *is* therefore called on to achieve an optimal mix of domestic objectives. Central banks *do* jealously guard their independence and resist coordination, foreign or domestic.

But these problems are not decisive, and remedies are both available and foreseeable for all of them. Part of the answer, of course, is to restore fiscal stability and thus renewed flexibility for budget policy within each country. The considerations cited here add to the long list of reasons for doing so.

Under the best of circumstances, this will take time. But both political parties in the United States put forward plans in early 1996 to eliminate the American budget deficit, which has already fallen to 2 percent of GDP, by 2002. All European members of the G-7 are striving to meet the Maastricht criterion for limiting their deficits to 3 percent of GDP by 1997, and the "stability pact" advocated by Germany would, if adopted, ensure that European budget deficits fall even further after EMU was established. Japan was running a structural budget surplus as recently as 1993 and also has a clear policy goal of restoring fiscal stability as quickly as its economic recovery (and financial crisis) will permit. Hence there is reason to hope that fiscal positions over the next few years will be restored to levels that will again permit at least some flexibility in their use, including through internationally coordinated efforts, though all of the G-7 countries face sizable unfunded liabilities in their public pension and other transfer programs that will require additional major efforts over the next decade or so to preserve fiscal stability.

But the attack of the "new consensus" on international coordination is fundamentally flawed because it misreads the implications for monetary policy. The critique concludes that monetary policy is already being used to pursue an optimal compromise between the major domestic policy targets, inflation and unemployment, and that it would simply be infeasible to add an external target as well. This, of course, assumes that such an external target would require a shift in monetary policy from what was appropriate for domestic purposes.

Under the proposals made in this book, the external target would be the exchange rate itself. There have been several studies that assess whether the targeting of domestic monetary policy toward an equilibrium exchange rate would have produced outcomes superior *on domestic grounds* to what has actually occurred over the last 25 years.[2] Most of the analyses that attempt to model the benefits of the specific policy proposals presented in this book conclude that exchange rate targeting is inferior to several theoretical alternatives. However, none of those alternatives are even being considered in the real world. Moreover, the authors of

---

2. They are cited and nicely summarized in Bryant (1995).

these studies candidly admit that their efforts have not yet produced a definitive reading of the issue and that their empirical evidence is limited (Bryant 1995, 53-54). The studies in fact suggest that exchange rate targeting might be preferable when policymakers want to address certain types of adjustment problems (particularly on the supply side), when they are more concerned with price stability than with output or employment, or when significant weight is attached to reducing the variability of key financial variables (including interest rates as well as the exchange rate itself).

In any event, most of these analyses cannot be directly applied to a regime of target zones, as will be proposed in chapter 7. This particular regime would require that monetary policy be directed to the exchange rate only on those occasions when a rate moved to the edge of the rather wide band. Such occasions should be relatively rare both because the bands would be quite wide (± 10 percent) and because coordinated, announced intervention within the margins would usually keep rates from moving to the extremes (Garber and Svensson 1995). Target zones should in fact be viewed as a technique for managing a system of flexible exchange rates and an alternative to the current ad hoc intervention, which occurs outside any agreed framework, rather than as a variant of fixed exchange rates. Studies of fixed (or narrow-band) exchange rates are thus largely irrelevant (Garber and Svensson 1995).

Another implication of the width of the target zones is that any need for monetary policy to address the exchange rate would arise only when the rate had moved substantially away from its agreed midpoint, or equilibrium level. Hence the signal that something was wrong would be rather strong. One possibility, of course, would be that the zone itself was incorrect and needed to be changed—an example of policy error by the authorities. Another possibility would be market error in interpreting the economics of the situation, in which case concerted intervention should usually suffice to move the rates away from the edges of the band.

The third possibility, which is most relevant here, is that the zones were correct but that the markets were also correct in sensing that current policies were jeopardizing their future maintenance. Monetary policy might be too expansionary, for example, generating new inflationary pressures and thus raising the prospect of a need for nominal depreciation of the zone to maintain its real value. The key point is that, under a regime of broad target zones, monetary policy would be called upon to address the exchange rate only when the rate had moved to a considerable extent and was thus signaling a significant question from the markets concerning the appropriateness of current policy. The country in question, and the

G-7 as a group, would, of course, have to determine which interpretation of the currency movement was correct in each specific case.

Unfortunately, no comprehensive analysis has been undertaken to discover whether targeting monetary policy on the exchange rate, under the conditions of a target zone regime, would help or hurt in achieving domestic economic objectives. Several episodes in the recent past, however, suggest that orienting monetary policy to the exchange rate induced substantially better outcomes, or would have done so had it been undertaken, both for the countries concerned (the United States and Japan in these examples) and for the world economy as a whole.

One spectacular example of a failure to incorporate exchange rate signals into domestic monetary policy, with adverse domestic effects, occurred during the breakdown of the fixed exchange rate regime. A tightening of American monetary policy was called for in mid-1972, if not earlier, but was not undertaken by the Federal Reserve. The dollar subsequently began to weaken and was formally devalued for the second time in February 1973. Because the devaluation was not accompanied by monetary tightening, however, the new level did not hold, and the United States and its partners agreed to move to flexible rates in early March 1973. By pursuing a domestic policy without regard to the signals emanating from the international movements of the dollar, US monetary authorities committed a gross error of monetary overexpansion, which delivered high inflation.

Paul A. Volcker, who was then Under Secretary of the Treasury for Monetary Affairs, laments the failure to tighten monetary policy:

> It seemed to me at the time, and it seems to me now, that we were at one of those points in economic history when [Federal Reserve Chairman Arthur] Burns's sensitivity (and many others') about the legitimacy of international considerations in conducting what is thought of as merely domestic monetary policy was misplaced. In the particular circumstances early in 1973, price increases were already beginning to accelerate in the United States. Within only a few weeks, monetary policy *was* tightened and the discount rate was raised. But it was all too late; too late to save the dollar exchange rate, and far too late to head off an incipient inflation that, amplified by repeated rises in world oil prices, soon reached an intensity beyond any seen in the life of the American republic. It presented me with my main challenge when I eventually assumed the position that Arthur Burns then held. I've often wondered whether the economy might not be stronger today if monetary policy in those days had not always carried the label "Made in Washington" and if the United States had responded to the international pressures on the dollar in the early 1970s with the vigorous monetary restraint that in any case was needed by the domestic economy (Volcker and Gyohten 1992).

Perhaps the clearest American example of both the failure to respond to the exchange rate signal, and the benefits of ultimately doing so, came in 1977–79—a period when inflation escalated rapidly from 5 percent in

1976, to almost 7 percent in 1977, to 9 percent in 1978, and then exploded into double digits with the second oil shock in 1979. The dollar weakened steadily throughout the period, prompting international calls for a strong response. But monetary policy remained lax through 1977 and most of 1978, apparently focused on maintaining domestic expansion despite relatively strong economic growth (5 percent in both years). The situation clearly called for substantial monetary restraint. The exchange rate was giving the proper signal throughout the period but was almost wholly ignored.

Monetary tightening finally occurred only when the plunge of the dollar in late 1978 required the Carter administration to launch a $30 billion "rescue package" and the Federal Reserve to raise its discount rate by a full percentage point for the first time in the postwar period. This reversal of monetary policy began to quell inflation (though that process was to require much stronger medicine shortly). It was driven by external considerations that clearly pointed American policy in the right direction, for domestic as well as international purposes. But the monetary authorities moved far too late to avoid double-digit inflation and would have done much better had they embraced the external signal much sooner.

A second, even more dramatic, dose of monetary restraint was added in late 1979. The new chairman of the Federal Reserve, Paul A. Volcker, instituted monetary targeting for the first time in American history—and, with it, a substantial cut in the permitted growth of the monetary aggregates—due partly to the continuing weakness of the dollar (though primarily due to the acceleration of inflation itself, as just noted). In light of the oil shock and the prior buildup of inflationary pressure, it took about three years and a sharp recession to bring inflation under control. But exchange rate considerations again pushed American monetary policy in the needed direction.

Another instance when American monetary conditions were driven wholly or largely by external considerations came in early 1987, when a sharp, renewed depreciation of the dollar triggered fears that the predicted "hard landing" might be at hand. Long-term interest rates rose sharply, prompting Treasury Secretary James Baker to conclude the Louvre Accord to halt the dollar's fall. In April and May, further dollar weakness "significantly contributed" to the Fed's decision to raise short-term interest rates—though the American economy would have been better served if the discount rate had been raised as well (Volcker and Gyohten 1992, 284).

Yet another case arose in the middle of 1989, when the dollar rose substantially against the yen and soared against the deutsche mark. A bargain could have been struck to both promote the domestic economic goals of all three countries and stabilize currencies with a signal from the Federal Reserve that easing would continue, coupled with increases in interest rates in Germany and Japan. But, owing in large measure to the central banks' resentment of the implied infringement of their independence under the Louvre Accord, this opportunity was missed. The G-7 agreed in late September that a depreciation of the dollar would be helpful, but its declaration was not supported by monetary policy. The Federal Reserve reduced interest rates later in the year but refused to do so after the G-7 meeting and publicly dispelled any suggestion that monetary policy would be used to nudge the dollar lower (Federal Reserve Board 1989; Henning 1994). The American recession of the early 1990s was longer than it might have been had rates been reduced earlier.

A more difficult case relates to the United States in the early 1980s. Massive budget deficits and resulting high real interest rates pushed the dollar to sharply overvalued levels. Reliance on monetary policy to resist the run-up of the dollar, through an easing of interest rates, would have impeded the effort to restore price stability to the American economy. Hence it would have been a mistake to orient monetary policy to the exchange rate during that period. No credible commentator at the time, or subsequently, has argued otherwise.

But a sensible injection of external considerations into the debate in the United States would have quickly focused it on reversing, or at least limiting, increases in the *fiscal* deficit, which were the source of both the internal and external imbalances. Skeptics doubt that any such considerations could have reversed the course of policy under the Reagan administration, which felt strongly about its "supply side" initiatives, and they may be right. But the situation was again clear-cut: fiscal restraint was needed for internal as well as external reasons, especially if internal needs were calculated over the longer run, when the budget deficits would have their most deleterious effects. Once again, serious attention to the external implications of American policy would have pushed it in the proper direction.

Similar conclusions obtain from other countries. As described in chapter 3, Japan in the late 1980s employed very expansionary monetary policy to stimulate recovery of its economy from the *endaka* (high yen) shock of 1985–87 and subsequent sharp decline in its external surplus. That use of monetary policy, however, generated the "bubble economy," which burst with a vengeance in the early 1990s and brought on the longest recession in Japan's postwar history. It also triggered a sharp yen depreciation that brought on the record trade surpluses of the early 1990s, with all their attendant problems, including the subsequent sharp yen *appreciation* in 1993–95, which prolonged Japan's recession.

Had Japan factored currency (and thus external) considerations into its policy determination in the late 1980s, whether informally or because of some formal international arrangement such as target zones, it would have relied much more heavily on fiscal policy to stimulate domestic demand in order to avoid yen depreciation. The outcome would have been much healthier both for Japan, over the medium and longer term, and for the world economy. Again, there was no policy dilemma, but Japan, happily accepting the short-run benefits for its economy of a weaker yen, ignored the external considerations that would have pointed its policy mix in a much more constructive direction. The G-7 totally failed to push Japan to do so.[3]

A recognition that external considerations generally point toward more sustainable, and thus more desirable, monetary and macroeconomic policies in the G-7 countries would provide a solid new basis for policy coordination. All the European members of the G-7 adopted such a stance when they joined the EMS and would embrace it comprehensively in creating EMU.

Another G-7 country, Canada, explicitly endorses a similar view. Its Monetary Conditions Index includes only two variables, one of which is the exchange rate. The index is not a rigid determinant of monetary policy, but the rule of thumb is that every change of 3 percent in the real effective exchange rate has about the same effect on real aggregate demand as a change of 1 percentage point in real interest rates (Freedman 1994). Norway and Sweden use a similar construct and, like Canada, make the calculated index publicly available. The United Kingdom and New Zealand also use the concept but do not publish the index.[4]

The US Federal Reserve Board has also recognized the close links between monetary policy and the external environment. Research at the Fed has revealed that 37 percent of the impact of changes in US monetary policy in the 1980s was transmitted to the economy through the exchange rate (Mauskopf 1990). This represents a doubling of the role of the exchange rate in the transmission mechanism from the earlier postwar period. Tighter money now dampens the domestic economy in large part by inducing an appreciation of the dollar that weakens the trade account, whereas the great bulk of the impact on the real economy was formerly conveyed through credit-sensitive changes in home building, purchases of automobiles and other consumer products, and other primarily domestic responses.[5]

---

3. As noted in chapter 4, some Japanese claim that they were forced by international considerations—the G-7 efforts of 1987 through early 1988 to stabilize or even strengthen the dollar—to *reduce* their interest rates. Once the yen began to weaken substantially in 1989–90, however, any sensible international arrangement would have pointed the Japanese policy mix in the opposite direction.

4. Communication to C. Fred Bergsten by C. Freedman, deputy governor of the Bank of Canada.

5. Robert Hall (Obstfeld 1995, 210) has in fact proposed that the United States should use the exchange rate as *the* intermediate target for stabilization policy.

The G-7 seemed to implicitly endorse the notion of keying monetary policy to external considerations a decade ago. After the Plaza Agreement, there was substantial coordination of national monetary policies within the group. Japan raised interest rates shortly after the Plaza to keep the yen rising. During 1986, the Federal Reserve, Bundesbank, and Bank of Japan reduced interest rates jointly on one occasion, and the Fed and Bank of Japan did so jointly on another (Funabashi 1989). The key countries recognized that international coordination of monetary policy was feasible and, at least in some cases, desirable.

These cases suggest that a country frequently can strengthen its economic prospects, especially over the longer run, by promoting greater consistency between its national policies and the global economy. In some cases, such as the United States in the late 1970s, the exchange rate may signal an erroneous thrust of overall economic policy. In other cases, such as the United States in the early 1980s and Japan in the late 1980s, the exchange rate may signal an erroneous mix between fiscal and monetary policy. Under both sets of conditions, paying attention to external considerations can contribute positively to national economic performance. If monetary policy needed to be altered to defend an exchange rate configuration, it would probably promote the long-term interest of the country in question.[6]

To be sure, the short-run flexibility of a country's monetary policy could be constrained as a result. Politicians understandably have short time horizons and seek to maximize that flexibility. But sound monetary policy should adopt a long-term horizon, and factoring external considerations into its determination is likely to help rather than hurt.

Most central bankers already take such a longer run view of policy. They should welcome the more extensive inclusion of international considerations in their policy deliberations, which should help them prevail

---

6. Volcker has reached a similar judgment. In his 50th Anniversary Stamp Lecture (1995), he concludes:

At some point a commitment to stabilizing exchange rates will indeed require the active use of monetary policy to that end. That requirement need not—*and I believe typically will not* [emphasis added]—be at odds with the posture of monetary policy on more purely domestic grounds, given a reasonable degree of exchange rate flexibility. . . . In looking back over the past quarter century or so, what strikes me in terms of United States experience is that at really critical junctures the exchange rate was given too little emphasis, not too much. Surely, with hindsight, the United States would have been better off with more restrictive monetary policies in the early 1970s as the fixed exchange system broke up and the dollar began its long depreciation. . . . When the United States in 1978 did mount a well co-ordinated intervention effort in response to another sinking spell for the dollar—an effort clearly supported by monetary tightening—it was late in the day. . . . The Super Dollar of the mid-1980s . . . conveyed a clear message about the excessive budget deficit. . . . Later in 1987, the ambitious effort at the Louvre . . . was, to my regret, not adequately supported by policy actions either in Japan or in the United States.

in the inevitable internal battles with their more politically oriented governments and parliaments. In countries where the central banks are independent, including Germany and the United States but now France as well, the politicians cannot determine monetary policy anyway so would experience little loss of influence if the monetary authorities were to attune their decisions more extensively to external considerations.

A country could, of course, decide to target monetary policy on its exchange rate, at least to the limited extent implied by a target zone regime, on a purely unilateral basis. We have just noted that several countries are in fact doing so. But the proposal in this book is for the G-7 to adopt target zones on a coordinated multilateral basis. The proposal thus raises the additional question, beyond whether targeting monetary policy to the exchange rate has a positive impact on the domestic economy, of the gains from coordination.

There is widespread agreement that international policy coordination will yield positive results. Most academic studies conclude that these results will be modest, but these studies miss a number of the beneficial features of such efforts and hence substantially underestimate the potential payoff (appendix A).

Moreover, there are no historical examples of countries' agreeing to explicitly coordinate their overall macroeconomic policies for extended periods, whereas there are at least three cases (the gold standard, the adjustable peg regime of Bretton Woods prior to 1971, and the EMS) in which countries have agreed to an exchange rate system that in turn has produced considerable policy coordination. It is thus highly unlikely that the G-7 could agree to a coordination regime addressed to their overall growth and inflation conditions. Exchange rate targeting seems much more feasible, and even the critics of that approach would agree that it is likely to produce better results than no coordination at all.

We could be more confident of the payoff from attuning a country's macroeconomic stance more closely to external factors if fiscal as well as monetary policy were likely to respond. The case of the United States in the early 1980s clearly illustrates the point, and every effort should be made to speed the day when fiscal flexibility will be restored so that it too can participate in the response. However, it is still superior for monetary policy to follow the external signals than to avoid systematic consideration of them. But as long as fiscal flexibility is so limited, it will be necessary to provide an "escape clause" to prevent a perverse reaction by monetary policy; our proposals below will include such a feature.

Even the most ambitious international agreement on exchange rates will not be implemented with total fidelity. Even if broken in some instances, however, an exchange rate arrangement would provide a benchmark for needed policy adjustment in participating countries and bolster domestic critics of erroneous policies. This is all that any international regime, via the G-7 or otherwise, can hope to accomplish. GATT rules are often violated, sometimes spectacularly as when the United States adopted its import surcharge in 1971, but no one doubts their value in pushing countries to adopt constructive trade policies. An international monetary regime that would enhance the role of external factors, particularly the exchange rate, in the determination of national monetary and eventually fiscal policies could help tilt domestic outcomes in desirable directions and play such a role.

The Role of the Central Banks

A corollary to this view of the importance of external factors in the formulation and execution of monetary policy is that the central banks will have to play a much more extensive role in the international coordination process. Such engagement would be particularly essential for Germany and the United States, where the monetary authorities are highly independent. The central banks would have to participate willingly and actively. The finance ministers would have to accept the authority of central banks in their policy domain.

To adopt such a regime, both the "supply" side (central banks) and the "demand" side (governments) of the equation would have to accept two concepts: that national economic performance would be improved by injecting external considerations more centrally into the formulation of monetary policy in support of new systemic structures, as just suggested, and that international coordination of those policies would further improve the outcome for monetary policy itself. However, the key central banks, conscious of the need to preserve their independence, will still be leery of "being coordinated by the finance ministers." They are well aware that their finance ministry colleagues used the Plaza-Louvre process to pressure them (Greider 1987, 686–87; Funabashi 1989, 56–58). The G-7, in concluding that coordination of monetary policy in support of new systemic structures should be one of its ongoing objectives, should thus candidly acknowledge that doing so is the responsibility of its central banks.

The central banks, for their part, should accept that they require a political context within which to operate—an agreement with their governments that establishes the basic framework. Governments provide a degree of political accountability that central banks, by virtue of their independence, generally lack. Only governments can establish an exchange rate to be defended, choose instead to let their currency float or adopt some other regime, or realign the exchange rate in response to changes in the economic fundamentals.

The tension between central bank independence and the need for a political framework established by governments need not undermine exchange rate and monetary cooperation if the principles just described are accepted. We recommend, in the next chapter, that the G-7 adopt target zones for their currencies. When implementing this recommendation, central banks and governments should implement the proposed principles through the following four-point formula.[7]

First, the G-7 finance ministers should establish the framework for the exchange rate regime. This would include such basic elements of the system as the central rates, the width of the target zones, and the commitment to defend the zones at the limits. The governments would retain the responsibility to make major changes in the regime, such as realignments of the zones, the departure of a currency from the system, and the induction of new currencies.

The central bank governors should be involved in all these decisions in an advisory capacity. They should participate in all meetings at which the finance ministers set the initial regime, review its progress, and consider alterations in its basic structure. The decisions on these topics, however, would clearly rest with the governments rather than with the central banks.

Second, the central banks would be given full independent discretion to manage exchange rates within this framework. They would have complete control over intervention operations and establish the arrangements for official financing of intervention. When adjustments of monetary policy were needed to defend the bands, the central banks would decide which of them should tighten or loosen.

Central bank governors should discuss these matters separately, at least in the first instance, from their finance ministers. The best forum would be their current arrangements through the Bank for International Settlements (BIS) in Basel. The usual group that meets in Basel is the G-10, however, so the G-7 central banks might have to meet separately on the margins of the larger group.

These arrangements would broadly parallel the institutional architecture of the EMS, wherein the economic and finance ministers meeting in the EU Council of Ministers (Ecofin) set the framework and the central banks implement it. The latter met as the Committee of Central Bank Governors, on the margins of the monthly meetings in Basel, and now meet as the Council of the European Monetary Institute in Frankfurt.

The third element of the bargain between central banks and finance ministers would apply when one or more countries' economic policies render the maintenance of the existing target zones irreconcilable with domestic monetary stability. Overexpansionary fiscal policy in a major country, in particular, might give rise to such a conflict. Under such circumstances, the central bank governors should confront their ministers

---

7. The formula draws on Henning (1994).

with a choice between changing the policy in question and realigning the target zones. They should have the formal right to initiate consideration of such issues among the governments—a right that would represent an important strengthening of the central banks over their position in the EMS (Williamson and Henning 1994).

Finally, to ensure close consultation between the governors and ministers, central banks should be fully involved in all G-7 meetings. They should be consulted whenever governments make decisions about the structure of the currency regime or realignments. The governors of the central banks must advise the finance ministers on the full range of monetary, as well as many nonmonetary, issues.

As an alternative to their existing forums in Basel, the G-7 central bank governors could split off from the finance ministers after the opening of G-7 sessions for separate discussions, at which the basic conversations on monetary policy would take place. The finance ministers would meet separately and concurrently to address the wide range of other G-7 issues for which they bear primary responsibility. The two "subcommittees" could then reassemble to report on each other's work so that all parties would be fully informed.

To backstop this process, the central bank deputies should attend all meetings of the G-7 deputies, where much of the operational work of the G-7 is conducted (Dobson 1991). The central bank deputies have recently begun to attend the preparatory sessions for G-7 ministerials. But they are still not engaged in important parts of the G-7 work and thus do not play—and do not feel they are playing—a full role.

Our proposed division of labor between finance ministries and central banks, and the arrangements for consultation among them, are broadly consistent with the understanding between the German government and Bundesbank governing German participation in the EMS. They are also, moreover, consistent with an important component of the exchange rate policymaking machinery of the future European monetary union. As laid down in Article 109 of the Maastricht treaty, the Council of Ministers will establish "general orientations" for exchange rate policy that the European Central Bank will observe, subject to the proviso that doing so does not endanger domestic price stability (Henning 1994, 1996).

Nonetheless, giving the central banks operational authority for implementing G-7 policies in the exchange markets would require a shift in the domestic allocation of responsibilities between finance ministries and central banks in several countries. These include the United States, where the authority is now shared by the Treasury and the Federal Reserve, and Japan.[8] In addition, Article 109 fails to provide the full institutional basis

8. For the United States, the Treasury should retain the authority to make commitments to participate in currency agreements while the Federal Reserve should be granted much greater leeway to intervene in the foreign exchange market without having to seek the Treasury's approval. The Fed's authority to conduct foreign exchange intervention could

for the international monetary policy of the EMU. These provisions will have to be developed and elaborated before the monetary union can serve as a full partner in the G-7 (Henning 1996).

Coping with Private Capital Movements

The final and perhaps most important aspect of the G-7's "new consensus" that deters it from effective policy coordination is the fear of many officials that private capital markets will overwhelm any efforts it might undertake. This conclusion rests, however, on several analytical errors.

The first is the view that recent currency crises demonstrate that official intervention cannot defeat the private speculators. The cases most frequently cited are those of the United Kingdom and Italy in 1992 and of Mexico in late 1994.

In all three cases, however, the governments involved were simply attempting to defend currency parities that were inconsistent with the underlying economic fundamentals and thus were demonstrably unsustainable. The United Kingdom set a clearly overvalued rate for sterling when it initially joined the EMU in 1990, as many observed at the time (Wren-Lewis et al. 1990; Williamson 1991). Cumulative inflation in Italy during 1987–91 exceeded cumulative inflation in Germany during the same period by 30 percent, as displayed publicly in the IMF's *World Economic Outlook* in early 1992, indicating that a sizable nominal depreciation of the lira would be necessary. Mexico's current account deficit reached 8 percent of its GDP in 1994, and numerous outside observers had pointed to the growing overvaluation of the peso as early as late 1992 (Dornbusch and Werner 1994; Williamson 1993).

These are examples of "policy error," where governments seek to defend an exchange rate that is inconsistent with the fundamentals. There is nothing new about it, and it has been a source of currency crises throughout the postwar period, whatever the size or speed of international capital flows. It is simply fallacious to blame "the speculators" or, less pejoratively, "the international markets" for conveying a message that is inherent in the economic conditions.

In fact, the chief mystery in each of these three cases is why the parities prevailed as long as they did and why the supposedly far-sighted markets failed to attack them much sooner. In addition, speculative attacks on the

in fact be established explicitly in law. It should also be able to initiate administration consideration of a realignment, in consultation with the G-7 partners, when fiscal policy, for example, makes maintenance of the existing target zones incompatible with domestic monetary stability (Destler and Henning 1989; Henning 1994).

French franc in 1993 and the Argentine peso in 1995 failed (even though the authorities of both countries had to raise interest rates sharply and accept very high rates of unemployment to hold their parities). Some of the same "speculators" who made huge profits from the earlier devaluations experienced sizable losses, usually with a good bit less public fanfare, from their failure to knock off these currencies. The markets are hardly omnipotent. The only reason to fear them is that they may bring home the unsustainability of a policy course more quickly and more forcefully than in the past. This is admittedly uncomfortable for sitting officials but hardly a reason to eschew national and international policies that are otherwise desirable.

The second key error in the hypothesis that "markets dominate" is the view that the monetary authorities must combat the totality of the private markets when they intervene to defend an exchange rate or for other purposes. In fact, they do not have to do so. If they did, their reserves, even augmented by swap lines and other borrowing arrangements, would indeed look puny by comparison.

But most exchange rates change very little on most days. The vast majority of the trillion dollars' worth of daily flows is self-balancing. The markets in fact display a high degree of stability despite their size and growth. Rates change only when market participants take large *uncovered* positions, thus upsetting the balance of supply and demand for a given currency at the prevailing exchange rate. It is the net uncovered position in the market, and only this position, that the monetary authorities must counter if their intervention is to be effective. Such uncovered positions can indeed become quite large when a rate clearly diverges from its fundamentals, but we are then back to the point just discussed—where the rate *should* change and *cannot* be defended by the authorities. During most periods, however, these positions are relatively modest and do not pose overwhelming challenges to the authorities.

In fact, recent studies show that intervention has been quite successful over the past decade (Dominguez and Frankel 1993; Catte, Galli, and Rebecchini 1994). The main reason is that the authorities can use intervention to alter market expectations by signaling their intentions to make future policy changes (Tietmeyer 1988). Intervention is particularly effective when it is coordinated among the key central banks, deployed when the rates are already moving in the desired direction ("leaning with the wind"), and made known to the markets. Intervention can fail when it ignores these criteria, but the magnitude of the private capital flows is not the governing factor.

The third error is the view that it would be a mistake for the major countries to set even fairly wide (say, ±10 percent) target zones for their currencies because such ranges would become targets for the speculators that would inevitably be attacked and defeated. Many G-7 authorities hold this view, and it is probably the single most important reason they have been unwilling to adopt explicit currency goals for almost a decade. There is, of course, a major exception: the EMS, which has become a target zone regime since 1993 (albeit with very wide ranges at ±15 percent) and which the Europeans argue is different because of the political commitment of the EU countries to achieve economic integration.

It has already been noted that "the speculators" are successful in pushing currencies off defined parities only when those parities are clearly inconsistent with the economic fundamentals. But there is good reason to believe that the authorities could determine and maintain equilibrium rates within the tolerances of target zones of ±10 percent (Williamson 1994). The IMF has demonstrated that its methodology can produce credible estimates (Bayoumi et al. 1994), and it has recently strengthened its internal procedures for reaching a consensus on equilibrium rates. Hence the fear of deviating from market realities should not be a deterrent to such an effort by the G-7.

There is another subtle but critical error in the current official resistance to more systematic exchange rate management: the extrapolation of behavior (speculative capital flows) under one regime (freely floating exchange rates) to behavior under a completely different regime (of ranges set and defended by governments). It is well known that systemic parameters can change abruptly and substantially when the rules of the system themselves are altered. The behavior of actors changes significantly when the regime under which they operate changes. Such a shift would surely occur in the exchange markets, just as it has been observed in the conduct of monetary policy and other key policy areas.[9]

The absence of official guidance to the currency markets is an important source of those markets' tendencies to produce disequilibrium exchange rates under a flexible rate system—the problem of "market error." This was demonstrably the case in the appreciation of the dollar in the early 1980s, the depreciation of the yen in the late 1980s, and the appreciation of the yen in early 1995. One should not assume that markets would continue to drive rates away from their equilibrium levels, or even necessarily test the limits of ranges set around those levels, if the authorities clearly identified and maintained credible ranges and demonstrated their resolve to defend them if and when necessary.

Krugman (1991) has demonstrated conceptually that the installation of a target zone system, for example, can convert destabilizing private capital flows into stabilizing flows. In their comprehensive review of the target zone literature, Garber and Svensson (1995, 20) conclude that "exchange

---

9. This analysis was pioneered by Robert Lucas, the winner of the Nobel Prize in Economic Science in 1995. It is known as the "Lucas critique" (Lucas 1981).

rates within the band, both theoretically and empirically, display strong mean-reversion."[10]

If the zones are based on underlying economic fundamentals and the authorities establish their credibility in defending them, speculators would have little incentive to push rates to the edges of the zones. As a rate approached the edge, there would be much greater potential for profit in pushing it instead back toward the center of the zone ("mean reversion") or even beyond. The officials would not have to intervene very often to "battle the speculators" nor frequently alter their domestic economic policy to defend the ranges.[11] The private capital flows that now seem so daunting to the officials would take on a wholly different countenance under an agreed monetary regime in which governments set and maintained the key parameters within which those flows take place.[12]

Finally, there is an even more fundamental error that most current officials make in considering the target zone alternative. They tend to see it as a variant of fixed exchange rates, on the view that the margins would frequently be attacked and that the usual problem of defending a fixed rate would then obtain.

This is simply wrong. Target zones should be viewed as an intermediate approach between fixed and flexible rates. But if one had to choose, it would be more appropriate to view target zones as a variant of flexible rates.[13] The reason, as just argued, is that properly chosen and credibly defended zones would prevent movement of spot rates to the margins on most occasions. Hence rates would fluctuate freely most of the time. The need to defend the bands would be relatively infrequent, as has proved to be the case in the (admittedly wider) EMS target zones.

---

10. They note, however, that most studies have not analyzed the type of currency regime advocated in this book. Krugman and most other analysts have addressed nominal rather than real zones, narrow rather than broad bands, and bilateral rather than multilateral systems of targeting. Hence the academic work to date neither confirms nor rejects, in any decisive manner, the benefits of target zones that are suggested here.

11. The previous section concluded that such changes in policy, when they did occur, would in most cases tend anyway to be in the long-term interest of the country so acting.

12. Based on his extensive practical experience, Volcker (1995) agrees: "[W]hen that credibility [of official intentions to stabilize the market] is established, markets will work with governments, not against them, to maintain a sense of equilibrium."

13. Garber and Svensson (1995, 23) reach a similar conclusion from their comprehensive review of target zone analyses:

[T]arget zones are better described as similar to managed floats with intra-marginal mean-reverting interventions, with additional marginal interventions defending the target zone in the rare cases when the exchange rate reaches the edge of the band . . . An official exchange rate band should consequently not be seen as a commitment to mostly marginal interventions, but as a practical way of expressing a verifiable general commitment to limit exchange rate variability with intra-marginal interventions.

Target zones should thus be viewed as an alternative technique for managing a system of flexible rates rather than as a weaker variant of fixed rates. Even G-7 officials do not support totally flexible rates any more, in light of the disastrous experience with them in the early 1980s. Consequently, policymakers should compare target zones with other techniques for managing flexibility—notably the ad hoc approach employed by the G-7 in recent years. We will make this comparison systematically in chapter 7.

This comparison leads some in the G-7 to yet another concern: even if they agreed with the analysis to this point, they would still reject announced target zones on the grounds that such a regime would destroy the main advantage that these officials believe they retain with respect to currency intervention—surprise. The view that surprise is the officials' only remaining defense in the markets is a corollary of the broader fear, outlined above, that private capital markets will inevitably swamp official intervention. We have already rejected that basic conclusion. In addition, we have noted that both theoretical and empirical research suggest that target zones would have positive rather than negative effects on the markets, converting the huge flows of private capital from destabilizing to stabilizing elements that would *help* the officials achieve their goals rather than hurt them.

More importantly from an operational standpoint, the authorities would always maintain the ability to surprise the markets with intramarginal intervention. If they believed that a rate was moving too rapidly toward one of its margins and wanted to take preemptive action, they could do so and thereby add to the credibility of their commitment to the zone itself. The EMS members have intervened frequently within their margins, with generally successful reversion of spot rates toward their midpoints. This is yet another reason why the margins would be tested fairly infrequently and why monetary policy would seldom need to be altered to defend the zones.

The success of a target zone system rests on two crucial variables. One is the ability of the authorities to set the ranges at levels that are, and remain, credible to the markets. This requires a mechanism for regular review of the zones to make sure that they remain appropriate, to change the zones if required, and to administer that review mechanism effectively.[14] Necessary realignments should be kept smaller than the width of the band, thereby obviating any need for changes in spot rates that would reward speculators.

Second, authorities must defend the zones effectively whenever the markets challenge them. Any new system of zones surely will be tested

---

14. For example, differential inflation rates between two participating currencies need to be offset by changes of equal amounts in the nominal bilateral zones to maintain real zones, the basis of the system as set out in chapter 7.

at least a few times in its early years. It will be essential to establish the determination of the authorities to sustain them, based on deliberate judgments of their continuing appropriateness and thus the erroneous nature of the market attacks. We will propose a target zone system in chapter 7 that meets these two central requirements.

The Bureaucratic Politics of Monetary Reform

There is a major institutional reason why monetary officials, in both finance ministries and central banks, display such remarkable unity in resisting exchange rate targeting. Freely flexible exchange rates have the great virtue, from the political or bureaucratic standpoints of these officials, of "leaving it to the market." Any undesirable outcomes can be blamed on the markets (or "the speculators") rather than on mistakes by the officials. They no longer take responsibility for exchange rates that may prove to be incorrect. No weekend meetings are needed to resolve the resulting crises.

We have seen that equilibrium exchange rates are as unlikely, or even more unlikely, to prevail under flexible rates as under "fixed" rates. The officials, however, have learned to prefer market error to policy error. Moreover, some of the costs of market errors under flexible rates, notably the pressures for trade protection that flow from excessive currency appreciations (as most clearly shown in the case of the United States in the mid-1980s), must be handled by trade policy officials rather than by the monetary authorities. Flexible rates do not prevent crises, but they often shift the locus of those crises—as well as the responsibility for dealing with them—from the monetary arena to trade policy.[15]

More generally, the present regime offers maximum flexibility to incumbent officials in their conduct of international monetary policy. They are not held responsible for any defined set of currency relationships. They are free to intervene, or not intervene, at will. It is not difficult to understand the zeal with which the officials defend the status quo despite its demonstrably poor results.

---

15. During the period of dollar overvaluation in the first half of the 1980s, the top trade officials of the first Reagan administration (US Trade Representative William Brock and Secretary of Commerce Malcolm Baldrige) repeatedly pleaded with Treasury Secretary Donald Regan and Under Secretary Beryl Sprinkel to halt or reverse the appreciation in order to counter its disastrous impact on American trade policy. The Reagan officials, and President Reagan himself, sincerely believed in free trade but wound up "protecting more American industries than any other Administration in the past half century" (Baker 1987) as a result of their own macroeconomic policies and the currency policies of their Treasury Department.

One of the implications of this powerful bureaucratic consideration is that neither finance ministries nor central banks are likely to be enthusiastic advocates of restoring more ordered international monetary arrangements. Hence it may become imperative for heads of government, with their broader responsibilities, to make such decisions. It is instructive that the EMS was created in 1979 by the chancellor of Germany and the president of France over the objections of most of their monetary experts. Political leadership has also been critical to the adoption of the Maastricht treaty and the drive for Economic and Monetary Union in Europe. The United States was motivated largely by the desirability of enhancing such political guidance of the economic system when, at the Tokyo summit in 1986, it pushed to link the financial leadership group much more closely to the summits of political leaders, including by converting the former from a G-5 to a G-7 so that the membership of the two groups would become identical.

The difficulty of achieving monetary reform through initiatives by monetary officials may even go beyond their desire to retain flexible exchange rates, or any particular substantive issue. The empirical fact is that the world's monetary authorities have never agreed on major systemic change in the absence of political direction. Markets forced the breakdown of the Bretton Woods system of fixed exchange rates, and the authorities were unable to work out any replacement despite almost two years of intensive effort through the Committee of Twenty created by the IMF/G-10 for that purpose (R. Solomon 1982; Williamson 1977). The monetary authorities seem to react only when forced to do so by crises, and they have even learned to duck the responsibility for most crises under current conditions.

It was therefore extremely encouraging that the G-7 summiteers at Naples in 1994 called for a thorough review of the institutional, and hence implicitly the substantive, foundations of the international monetary system. It was even more encouraging that at Halifax a year later, they took important initiatives to create a better early warning system and emergency financing mechanism to cope with "future Mexicos."

The summiteers at Halifax failed to follow through on the central currency and other adjustment issues, however. This was in large part because the follow-up to Naples was placed in the hands of the finance ministries and central banks, which, true to form, blocked any consideration of serious proposals to improve that more crucial component of the monetary system. It will probably be necessary for the heads of state and government to again address these issues themselves if the issues are to receive the careful attention and action they require.

The political leaders are especially likely to do so if they conclude that there are strong political, and even security, reasons for pursuing such controversial and technically complex initiatives. The economics of such projects must, of course, be substantively beneficial and accepted by the respective publics on their merits. But the enormous task of generating and selling such initiatives requires such a large expenditure of leaders' political capital that they must perceive an overriding reason for mounting the effort.

Most of the great "economic" initiatives of the postwar period were in fact driven by such broader purposes. The Bretton Woods institutions were developed while World War II was still being fought, as part of the strategy to maintain the subsequent peace, on the view that the trade and currency conflicts of the 1930s had been an important source of the subsequent conflagration. The European Economic Community was created primarily to obviate any possibility of another conflict between France and Germany, or within Europe more broadly. American support for European integration, and later for bringing Japan into a central role in all the international economic institutions (including the G-7), was similarly motivated by broad strategic as well as economic considerations. The G-7 and all its predecessors, dating from the early 1960s, evolved in part to solidify the anticommunist alliances by reducing the risk that economic conflicts would strain those critical relationships.[16]

The world now faces enormous new geopolitical challenges. The onset of economic multipolarity has altered the distribution of power that underpins global political relationships as well as world economic institutions and regimes. Old powers, notably Russia but also the United Kingdom, have declined sharply. New powers, notably Japan but especially now China, have risen to prominence. Huge regional shifts are occurring, with Asia ascendant and Europe—and some would say North America—proceeding less dynamically.

History suggests that new institutional architecture is needed to respond to such sweeping shifts. It also suggests that economic architecture can play a very useful role in recognizing new realities and coping with them. Such architectural reform is already occurring on trade issues, with the creation of the World Trade Organization and the dramatic regional initiatives to achieve free trade in the Asia Pacific (via the Asia Pacific Economic Cooperation forum, or APEC) and the Western Hemisphere (via the Free Trade Area of the Americas). It is even more essential in the monetary arena, however, in light of the centrality of finance to all economies—including the global economy.

There is thus a twofold political case for revival of the G-7. One element is the need for a stronger foundation for the world economy because of

---

16. The recent proposal for a Trans-Atlantic Free Trade Area (TAFTA) is the latest example of an economic initiative suggested for broader political and security reasons. The idea emanated almost wholly from foreign ministries and national security experts, who sought new institutional ties between North America and Europe in light of the fading of NATO (especially before its reinvigorated role in Bosnia), rather than from economic experts.

the obvious impact of economic developments on political conditions both within and among countries. The second is the adverse effect of failure to cooperate in the economic arena on overall relations among the G-7 countries and even on security cooperation between them. Since the G-7 countries continue to play a dominant role in the world economy, the responsibility for global progress on these issues rests squarely on their shoulders.

Hence the issue of G-7 reform is clearly worthy of attention by heads of state and government. They will in fact ignore it at their peril, in political and security as well as economic terms. Their addressing the matter at the two latest summits, at Naples and Halifax, is an encouraging sign that they recognize this reality. They now need to take the next steps and assure that their initiatives are adequate to the magnitude of the task at hand.

A Summing Up

An initiative for renewed international economic leadership by the G-7 appears to be both substantively feasible and quite desirable, despite the long-standing differences within the group and the more recent advent of agreed doubts about its prospects. The nature of that leadership must change, however. Given the widespread skepticism about the desirability of short-run macroeconomic management, and the even broader consensus on the need to orient monetary policy toward long-run stability targets, the new efforts should not focus primarily on global growth programs or other cyclical efforts. But the "new consensus," properly understood, could undergird efforts to build systemic arrangements that would promote the goals of all G-7 countries: fewer large currency misalignments, more constructive results and fewer crises from international capital flows, and greater stability of economic policy and economic performance.

New institutional devices will be needed to translate these concepts into practice. The central banks will have to play a much larger role in the process. Heads of state and government must assert their authority to overcome the institutional resistance of monetary officials. The G-7 will have to reform itself institutionally and accord a much larger role to the IMF.

The arrangements stressed in this chapter, to whose details we turn in chapter 7, relate primarily to the "internal" component of G-7 cooperation—among members of the group itself. They would seek to convert the current "nonaggression pact" among the G-7 members, which results in inaction and ineffectiveness, into a cooperative venture based on new substantive and institutional arrangements.

Separate systemic reforms will be needed to improve the "external" dimension of the G-7's responsibilities, and chapter 7 will address them as well. However, improvement of the G-7's internal coordination will contribute substantially to its external goals in two ways: directly, by strengthening the group's own economic performance and thus that of the world economy, and politically, by restoring the effectiveness of the G-7 and thus countering some of the doubts about its legitimacy. Moreover, some of the specific steps needed to strengthen the G-7's internal effectiveness—such as a larger role for the IMF in monitoring the G-7 economies themselves and thereby promoting a more effective adjustment process—are essential to improving the functioning of the world economy as a whole.

7

An Action Program

Chapter 6 concluded that the G-7 should focus on creating systemic arrangements that will strengthen the prospects for international economic prosperity and stability. Constructing such arrangements could help resolve both sets of problems confronting the group: the continuing traditional differences among its members, described in chapter 4, and the basic doubts about the efficacy of coordination that have beset the entire membership and were analyzed in chapter 5. Such systemic improvements should focus both on the adjustment process and on the financial dimensions of G-7 cooperation.

A better exchange rate regime could improve G-7 policy coordination as well as reduce currency misalignments and current account imbalances. Historically, there are very few cases where policy coordination has been achieved directly. By contrast, there are at least three fairly extended periods in which substantial coordination has been accomplished indirectly through implementation of currency regimes: the gold standard, the adjustable peg of Bretton Woods, and the European Monetary System (EMS) more recently with its impressive achievement of considerable inflation convergence among its members. Exchange rate reform could thus enable the G-7 to restore its leadership on a number of key issues and pave the way for more fundamental changes if the initial steps proved successful.[1]

---

1. Volcker (1995) reaches a similar conclusion:

It seems to me wrong to continue to argue, as typically has been done ever since floating began, that international currency reform and greater stability in exchange rates must await greater domestic stability and convergence among domestic econo-

The history of the G-7 itself supports this approach. Its agreements on exchange rate management during 1985–87 prompted joint interest rate reductions in 1986, several macroeconomic steps by Japan, and a serious effort to institutionalize coordination (including through the "objective indicators" adopted at the Tokyo summit in 1986). By contrast, the group achieved direct coordination of national policies only at the Bonn summit in 1978, and that agreement, while desirable and promising, had a fleeting effect and probably set back the entire process of coordination because of the sharp controversies it subsequently generated.

A New Exchange Rate Regime

In proposing a new currency regime to help revive the G-7, we start from the premise that both extremes—fixed and freely floating exchange rates—have been tried and found wanting. Fixed rates, even if implemented in practice as adjustable pegs, have turned out to be much too rigid. They have produced substantial policy errors—misalignments that created the problems discussed throughout this volume. This was the experience of the Bretton Woods global regime, the EMS after 1987, and numerous other country cases.[2]

Freely floating rates have also produced frequent and even more sizable disequilibria. The absence of governmental guidance permits market errors that push rates far from their underlying equilibria—as with the dollar in the early 1980s, when floating was close to its textbook ideal because of the resistance of the first Reagan administration to all intervention, and with the yen in the late 1980s and again in 1995.

With both extremes discredited, governments have been groping for intermediate regimes ever since the breakdown of Bretton Woods in the early 1970s. The Europeans quickly adopted the "snake in the tunnel" for their own currencies, elaborated it into the EMS in the late 1970s and formally converted the EMS into a system of broad target zones (± 15 percent) in response to their crisis of 1993.

---

mies. We need to examine at this point, it seems to me, the mirror image of that proposition: specifically, whether attaching greater priority to currency stability might also contribute over time to more consistent economic performance, growth, and productivity.

It is noteworthy that, in reaching this judgment, Volcker has moved significantly beyond the consensus reached by the Bretton Woods Commission (1994) that he had convened two years earlier.

2. The EMS appeared to solve the rigidity problem during its first phase, from 1979 through early 1987, when it successfully engineered a number of small, frequent realignments. Its subsequent evolution into excessive rigidity, however, reinforced the view that the dynamics of such systems usually point in such a direction and hence the systems themselves are unlikely to last.

Figure 7.1 Deutsche marks per dollar,[a] 4 January 1988 through 22 April 1996

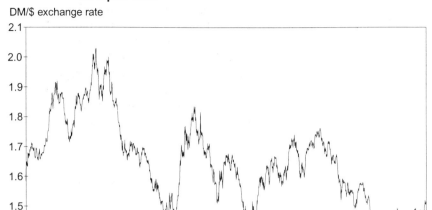

DM/$ exchange rate

1/4/88 9/22/88 6/16/89 3/12/90 11/30/90 8/22/91 5/15/92 2/8/93 10/28/93 7/2C/94 4/13/95 1/4/96

a. New York noon buying rate.

Source: Chicago Federal Reserve Bank.

The G-5 established a de facto regime of managed floating by undertaking substantial joint intervention activities in the middle 1970s, again in the late 1970s (to defend the dollar), and most ambitiously with the Plaza Agreement in the mid-1980s (to weaken the dollar). It adopted a more elaborate system of reference ranges in the Louvre Accord in 1987 to keep the dollar from falling too fast but was unable to maintain that effort very long, because the ranges were set before the dollar had completed its full decline from the overvalued level of 1985.

The G-7 has reverted to ad hoc intervention since that time, with results that could be characterized in some cases as de facto (or "quiet") target zones for some of the group's currency relationships. The trade-weighted dollar has fluctuated within ±5 percent of its end-1987 level against the currencies of its ±101 largest trading partners (figure 3.2) and within a 10 percent band against the other G-7 currencies in real terms since mid-1990 (figure 3.3). Since 1990, the dollar-deutsche mark rate has made two full swings within a band bordered by about 1.40:1 and 1.80:1 and was defended at each end by joint intervention on at least two occasions (figure 7.1).

The swings in the dollar-yen rate have been much larger, however, and have consistently created currency and current account problems as cited throughout this book (figure 3.1). Major problems emerged within the EMS that led to a series of currency crises there. A number of countries outside the G-7 also faced severe exchange rate problems—Mexico being only the most prominent example. So the de facto target zones maintained for the dollar-mark and perhaps a few other currency pairs, while revealing that G-7 officials, along with the Europeans, prefer a modicum of stability and are already moving toward a more structured regime, have failed to avoid severe problems of both policy error and market error.

Fortunately, more effective intermediate regimes are available that would both embody the virtues of the extreme systems and avoid their worst vices. The most desirable would be announced target zones with four key properties:[3]

■ agreement among the G-7 to set **ranges of ±10 percent around notional midpoints for real exchange rates** that would preserve equilibrium in each country's current account position;[4]

■ **public announcement of the zones** to inform the markets where the authorities intend to maintain them;

■ **constant reappraisal** of the appropriateness of the zones (including automatic adjustment of their nominal levels to offset inflation differentials and thus preserve their stability in real terms);

■ commitment to **policy action to defend the zones,** when and if necessary, through both concerted intervention in the markets themselves and changes in domestic economic (especially monetary) policy.[5]

These announced de jure target zones would be quite different from, and far superior to, the de facto target zones of recent years or the reference ranges established for a time at the Louvre. The ranges would be wider than those of the Louvre Accord—thereby permitting market forces to continue to play a major role in accommodating interest rate changes and other transitory phenomena—but considerably narrower than those of the current EMS and hence more helpful in preventing new misalignments. The public announcement of the ranges and the firm commitment to act when the rates reached their edges, assuming that the zones themselves are credible in terms of the underlying economics and effectively

---

3. Volcker (1995) has proposed a similar set of reforms.

4. Equilibrium need not and frequently will not mean a zero current account balance. For example, equilibrium for Japan during the current period probably means a surplus of about 1.5 percent of GDP, while equilibrium for the United States probably means a deficit of about 1 percent of GDP. The concept is explained in Williamson (1985) and these specific applications are developed in Bergsten and Noland (1993).

5. A detailed explanation of target zones is provided most recently in Bergsten and Williamson (1994). The most complete description is in Williamson (1985).

defended when initially tested, would convert destabilizing private capital flows into stabilizing elements in the system, as described in chapter 6. The zones would be explicitly denominated in real rather than nominal terms and thus adjusted both automatically to offset inflation differentials and occasionally when needed to counter large exogenous shocks (such as changes in world oil prices or German unification), thereby avoiding any buildup of misalignments and any transmission of inflationary pressures to surplus countries.

The goal of target zones is *not* to restore fixed exchange rates nor to fine-tune the currency markets. Target zones do not seek primarily to limit currency volatility, though they would probably help to do so.

The chief goal of a system of target zones is simple and modest: to avoid the periodic large misalignments of major currencies that will otherwise continue to produce sizable economic distortions, threaten the trading system by fostering protectionist trade policies, and jeopardize future financial stability by creating conditions that are bound to eventually produce a precipitate reversal in the misaligned currency. We know that such disequilibria have hit all of the world's major currencies in recent years and will continue to do so in the absence of systemic reforms. We know that these disequilibria become severe enough to threaten the entire system at least once every five to ten years: the dollar in the late 1970s and again in the middle 1980s, the yen in the late 1980s and perhaps the middle 1990s, the mark and other European currencies in the early 1990s. Target zones would seek to prevent such problems.

Had such a regime been in place and operating effectively over the last couple of decades, it would have tilted Japan toward expanding domestic demand via fiscal rather than monetary policy in the late 1980s and avoiding at least the worst of its "bubble economy." It would have added American and Japanese pressure for appreciation of the deutsche mark in the wake of German unification in the early 1990s, perhaps overcoming the opposition of Germany's European partners and thereby limiting the onset of high interest rates throughout Europe, which triggered prolonged stagnation for the entire continent. It could have totally avoided the excessive appreciation of the yen in 1995 that extended the Japanese recession and intensified the risk of global financial instability. It might even have pushed the United States to adopt less irresponsible fiscal policies in the 1980s, from which both it and the world economy continue to suffer.

To accept target zones, the G-7 members would need to recognize only three ideas:

- that target zones are a variant of flexible rather than fixed exchange rates, so that their adoption would not represent a change in the basic orientation of the current regime;
- that they are a better method for managing a regime of flexibility than the ad hoc intervention that now takes place;

- that occasionally addressing macroeconomic (usually monetary) policy to external objectives in order to defend the zones would promote rather than harm the long-term economic health of a country that does so.

An important goal of a target zone regime would be to focus the G-7 governments and central banks more systematically on the international position of their economies. This should improve national economic policy and performance over the long run, as described in chapter 6. In particular, monetary policy should perform better if it responds to signals emanating from an exchange rate's move toward one or the other edge of the target zone.

One important innovation of the proposed regime would be a new and explicit division of authority between finance ministries and central banks in managing it, as developed in chapter 6. The governments, operating largely via the finance ministries, would set up the system, decide on the initial zones, and alter them when needed. The central banks would advise on all these issues, very much as they do in the unstructured system that prevails now.

In addition, however, the central banks would be given clear and explicit authority to manage the system once the governments set its basic framework. The central banks would decide when and how to intervene to preserve the zones, including within the margins as well as at the extremes. They would be responsible for changing monetary policy if and when needed to preserve the zones, unilaterally or in concert. It would be their prerogative to weigh in with their governments on fiscal policy if they believed such changes were needed to preserve the zones, as would have been the case with the United States in the early 1980s; if the governments agreed with the central banks, it would be their responsibility either to alter fiscal policy or to realign the zones.

The central banks would carry out the international dimensions of all these activities through their own consultation devices, centered largely on the Bank for International Settlements (BIS). They would keep the governments informed of their decisions and activities and participate actively in all G-7 meetings, including at the level of deputies. But their autonomy in managing both exchange rates and monetary policy would be clear.

Officials in some key G-7 countries, notably Germany but also Japan, remain skeptical about the willingness and ability of other G-7 countries to manage their domestic economic policies in a fashion that would be consistent with more structured currency arrangements, even those as loose as wide target zones. Doubts are most frequently expressed about the United States' ability or willingness to play by the rules of a target-zone regime. Some other G-7 members, Germany in particular, seem to believe that the United States will never alter its economic policy in response to external constraints.

This view is simply wrong. The United States raised taxes to pay for part of the Vietnam War largely as a result of the sterling and gold crises of late 1967 and early 1968.[6] The Federal Reserve raised interest rates by a full percentage point, for the first time in the postwar period, as part of the dollar support package of late 1978. The Fed moved to monetary targeting a year later, and to its decisive attack on inflation, partly because of the continued weakness of the currency. The Fed let interest rates rise sharply in early 1987, thus bringing a halt to the Plaza strategy of dollar depreciation, in order to protect against the risk of a "hard landing."

Hence US policy clearly does respond to external pressures. Admittedly, it does so only in response to extreme conditions—when the damage has become severe or the risks intolerable. In recent practice, this has happened about once per decade. Moreover, US policy has often moved much later than would be desirable even in purely domestic terms. In participating in an international regime along the lines proposed, the United States would undeniably face charges at home that it was "giving up its sovereignty."

But the United States, like other countries, would benefit from an international regime that tilted its internal policy debates toward more timely reactions to international conditions. As to sovereignty, the basic case for policy coordination (appendix A) is premised on two key facts: that all countries have already lost much of their real independence, due to the advent of economic interdependence, and that they improve their national outcomes through coordination. Other countries would benefit at least as much from a regime that pushed the United States, as well as their own policies, toward greater international compatibility.

But some Europeans might still fear that exchange rate stabilization against the dollar would require them to "import inflation," as occurred under the Bretton Woods regime. We acknowledge that some of the European, particularly German, objections to the operation of the Bretton Woods regime in the second half of the 1960s are valid.

Target zones, however, differ fundamentally from that system. The two regimes differ, first of all, in the degree of exchange rate flexibility permitted. Target zones are a variation on a flexible rate regime rather than on fixed rates, as discussed in chapter 6 and below. Second, target zones are defined in real terms, which relieves low-inflation countries of any obligation to pursue an expansionary monetary policy to curb the

---

6. Then-Secretary of the Treasury Henry H. Fowler has indicated to the authors that these international events played a major role in enabling him to convince House Ways and Means Committee Chairman Wilbur Mills and other key members of Congress to finally approve President Lyndon Johnson's proposed income tax surcharge and additional budget cuts.

nominal appreciation of their currencies against high-inflation countries. Third, within a broad framework agreed by governments, our proposal would give central banks responsibility for managing the regime and thus the power to safeguard their stability concerns. Indeed, the proposal would give unprecendented authority to the central banks to formally initiate discussion among governments of a need for a currency realignment inter alia to avoid importing inflation. Surely these key features of the system will allay any reasonable fears that target zones would foist inflation on stability-oriented countries.

But the other G-7 countries would still like assurance that their partners will maintain responsible policies. Such assurance could be provided by drawing on the European experience. The European states agreed in the Maastricht treaty to use convergence criteria to assess their readiness for membership in Economic and Monetary Union (EMU). There are four key criteria: disciplined fiscal policies and moderate government debt, low inflation, long-term interest rates close to those of the low-inflation countries, and exchange rate stability (Commission and Council of the European Communities 1992; Kenen 1995). Inclusion of the criteria in the treaty addressed the concerns primarily of Germany, which feared entering into monetary union with countries that lacked an orientation toward price stability and fiscal discipline.

In addition, the Europeans have more recently begun to focus on the even more important question of how the EMU members would behave *after* the currency union was formed. The Germans have proposed a "stability pact" that would, for example, require even tighter fiscal management after entry. Whether this proposal is adopted by the European Union as a whole remains to be seen.

A modified set of such criteria among the G-7 could serve the same purpose, with the group agreeing that its members would have to meet certain "G-7 cooperation criteria" both before they could participate in any new exchange rate arrangement and to maintain their participation. The process of meeting the criteria would be healthy for the countries themselves, for the confidence of their G-7 partners in everyone's fealty to the system, and for the confidence of the financial markets in the whole arrangement. By promoting the reduction of fiscal deficits, it would also restore the flexibility of fiscal policy and hence return that instrument to the arsenal for possible active use (including through international coordination). Since the European members of the G-7 are already striving to meet the Maastricht criteria to qualify for EMU, the basic objective of the exercise would be to assure responsible performance by Canada, Japan, and the United States.[7]

---

7. Each of the three regions within the G-7 have moved toward fixed fiscal rules over the past decade. In addition to the Maastricht criteria now driving the European countries, the United States adopted Gramm-Rudman targets and continues to consider a balanced budget amendment. The Japanese Ministry of Finance has repeatedly invoked the principle of

The experience with the convergence criteria under EMU suggests, however, that the G-7 should not adopt the Maastricht formula uncritically. It is, for example, clearly inappropriate for countries with moderate fiscal deficits and debt to reduce them further in the face of recession and unemployment. The relevance of government debt to the ability of a country to stabilize its currency, except in extreme cases, is questionable in any event.

The cooperation criteria among the G-7 should instead refer to structural rather than unadjusted budget deficits to take account of the effect of the business cycle on the measured balance.[8] On the reasoning that countries that are far from internal balance might have a problem with the credibility of their using monetary policy to defend the target zone, it might be useful to include the rate of unemployment among the G-7 criteria. The level of internal savings also bears on fiscal convergence: the United States presently has the lowest budget deficit in the G-7, as a share of its GDP, but needs further improvement because its private saving is so low. The G-7 should choose criteria that underpin a country's ability to avoid severe tensions within the target zones and to use policy instruments, monetary policy in particular, to defend them. These cooperation criteria would thus be important not simply as conditions for entry into the target zone arrangement but for a country's continued membership as well.

Although we are not recommending that the G-7 adopt them unchanged, it is interesting to note that on the basis of the Maastricht criteria the economic policies and conditions of the United States, Germany, and Japan are reasonably convergent. American and German inflation rates are similar and will shortly be within about two percentage points of Japan's, which have been consistently low and even deflationary over the past couple of years (table 7.1). American and German long-term interest rates are also very close, with the Japanese rate correspondingly lower.

Table 7.1 also shows how the G-7 countries perform on the fiscal criteria set down in the Maastricht treaty. The deficit ratios, the more important of the two, are quite close. The United States has the lowest deficit ratio in the G-7, and its numbers are likely to move even lower over the next year or so. The debt ratios are also quite close for Germany and the United States, though somewhat higher for Japan.

The similarity of the key G-7 countries on these fundamentals bodes well for the sustainability of any new currency arrangements among them.

---

avoiding deficit bonds. This movement toward fiscal rules in the three regions has two important defects, however: the rules are highly arbitrary, and they are established independently of the policy stance in other regions of the world. Bringing fiscal rules under the rubric of the G-7 would help redress both deficiencies (Williamson and Henning 1994).

8. On this basis, all EU countries except Greece and Italy would probably meet the Maastricht fiscal deficit criterion in 1997 (*The Economist*, 20 April 1996, 43).

Table 7.1 G-7 performance on proposed cooperation criteria, 1995–97

G-7 member	Government debt[a]			Government balance[b]		
	1995	1996	1997	1995	1996	1997
United States	66.7	67.6	67.5	−2.0	−1.7	−1.6
Japan	87.0	92.2	94.7	−3.1	−4.1	−2.4
Germany	57.7	60.1	61.1	−3.5	−3.9	−3.4
France	52.3	55.0	56.4	−5.0	−4.2	−3.6
Italy	122.9	121.4	119.5	−7.2	−7.3	−5.9
United Kingdom	48.8	49.7	49.5	−5.1	−3.8	−2.5
Canada	96.3	99.7	97.3	−4.2	−2.4	−1.3

	Long-term interest rate[c]			Inflation rate using consumer price Index		
	1995	1996	1997	1995	1996	1997
United States	6.6	6.2	6.2	2.8	2.6	3.0
Japan	2.5	3.2	3.5	−0.1	0.4	1.3
Germany	6.5	6.3	6.3	1.8	1.5	1.5
France	7.6	6.9	6.8	1.8	1.8	1.8
Italy	12.2	10.8	10.4	5.4	4.4	4.0
United Kingdom	8.3	7.9	7.9	2.8	2.8	2.6
Canada	8.3	7.3	7.0	1.9	1.3	1.9

Source: IMF, World Economic Outlook, advance copy April 1996, except where noted.

a. General government gross debt as a percentage of GDP, Maastricht criteria use slightly different definition.
b. General government fiscal balance (actual) as a percentage of GDP.
c. 1995 figures from IMF, International Financial Statistics April 1996; 1996–97 from OECD Economic Outlook, December 1995.

Indeed, there is greater convergence among the United States, Germany, and Japan than there was within Europe at the start of the EMS or EMU efforts. Exchange rate stabilization might therefore proceed more smoothly globally than it has within the EMS.

Such a *systemic* initiative appears to be the best way to revive the G-7 as the informal steering committee of the world economy, as well as to provide a significant substantive improvement in international monetary arrangements. The ongoing differences among G-7 members, and the new consensus among them on the inefficacy of direct policy coordination, suggest that such an initiative may in fact be the *only* way to restore that role.

The present time may be uniquely appropriate for the G-7 to adopt a target zone system. Most analysts, and apparently the G-7 authorities themselves, believe that exchange rates are at roughly equilibrium levels. Hence current market rates could provide the basis for the agreed ranges.[9] This is important because, as illustrated by the G-7's own experience in setting reference ranges in 1986–87, it is far easier to reach agreement "around current levels" than to face the transitional problems that would occur if market rates had to be altered *before* the zones were set (Funabashi 1989).

For example, the United States and Japan should be able to agree on a target zone centered on 100:1 that would permit fluctuations between 90:1 and 110:1. This range would comprehend virtually all existing estimates of the equilibrium central rate, some of which range as high as 90:1 (Cline 1995b) and others as low as 110:1 (mainly in Japan). It would protect both countries against their deepest concerns: a renewed yen appreciation back to 80:1 or even beyond for the Japanese, and an excessive dollar appreciation back toward 120:1 or beyond for the Americans.

The United States and Japan would have been much better off over the past two years had they instituted such a range when the yen first rose to 100:1 in the summer of 1994.[10] Such an arrangement would almost certainly have prevented the subsequent excessive appreciation of the yen to above 80:1 in early 1995. That rise was fueled largely by market views that the United States *wanted* such an appreciation in order to pressure Japan to capitulate in the auto trade talks. American participation in a currency arrangement designed to avoid such extreme appreciation would clearly have obviated such a view. There would then have been no new currency shock to the Japanese economy and financial system, and no need for a new round of G-7 intervention to reverse the yen appreciation.

In fact, if the Europeans remain preoccupied with their regional initiatives, the United States and Japan might want to launch the new system with a "G-2" arrangement. Just such a sequence occurred when Treasury Secretary James Baker and Japanese Finance Minister (later Prime Minister) Kiichi Miyazawa agreed on a yen-dollar reference range in October 1986 before the Europeans joined in via the Louvre Accord in February 1987. As emphasized throughout this book, the yen-dollar rate has been the primary source of currency and trade imbalances in recent years and a major source of friction between the countries for over 25 years (Bergsten

---

9. The main exception is the view in some quarters in Europe that the dollar is undervalued. As indicated in chapter 4, this ignores the continued large US current account deficit and thus is incorrect. It may imply the existence of undervalued currencies elsewhere, however, perhaps in East Asia.

10. As proposed at that time by Bergsten (1994).

1982). Both countries have suffered substantially as a result. Responding to these problems and building on the precedent of the mid-1980s, they might therefore take the lead in forging new currency arrangements. They could thereby both repair their own frayed economic relationship and help revive the G-7.

Avoiding "Future Mexicos"

The G-7 should also erect new systemic mechanisms to avoid situations like the Mexican peso crisis that could reverberate worldwide, via either the private financial markets or the reversal of economic reform in emerging market economies. The central element in any such mechanism would be a better "early warning system" (Goldstein 1995), as was called for at the G-7 summit at Halifax in June 1995. The IMF should be the locus of such activities and should explicitly assign staff to regularly and systematically monitor the evolution of policy in all countries sizable enough to have potential systemic impact. This would obviously include all G-7 countries, as part of the process of implementing the target zones proposed in the previous section.

An effective early warning system will require countries to promptly transmit to the Fund full information on their economies. Mexico failed to provide key components of this data set in the runup to its recent crisis. The IMF has already worked out which data should be provided to it confidentially and which should be published. The questions now are whether all relevant countries will make the necessary revelations and how the markets will respond to those that do not.

Submission of data and recognition of pending problems are the easy parts; private economists, with or without all desirable information, pointed to the unsustainability of the Mexican external deficit and the associated overvaluation of the peso as early as 1992. Economists in key national governments (including Mexico itself) and the IMF obviously did so as well. The difficult question is how to translate such analyses into policy actions that will prevent a crisis.

The analyses must first be conveyed to policymakers in the country in question and to those with responsibility for surveillance of the entire system (in both the IMF and G-7). The preferred outcome, of course, would be for the country to then act promptly and effectively on the advice it was receiving. Failing that, however, the monitors from the IMF and/or G-7 would have to confront the country—with extensive discretion and privacy in the first instance—with the need for early action. If necessary, they should offer to provide external financial help—which could be much smaller and more effective at this early stage—to support the needed adjustment.

In addition, they should let the country know that they would respond to its continuing failure to act by a judicious and escalating public release of data and analysis. This would begin to inform the market that trouble was brewing. It would therefore trigger the most powerful sanction of all—initially an increase in the risk premium on the country's obligations and eventually a withdrawal of private capital (Goldstein 1995). Countries would thus have a powerful incentive to act.

The scheme could admittedly trigger the crisis that it seeks to prevent, but it is almost always better to have a market reaction sooner rather than later if one is inevitable. No mechanism of this type will be foolproof or costless in a world of sovereign countries that remain free to make mistakes. But it would provide a substantial improvement over the status quo. In the Mexican case, it might have led to early remedial action and avoided the huge costs to Mexico itself as well as the systemic threats that ensued.

But some problems of this type will still produce crises, even with the adoption of an effective preventive system. Hence a second and closely related reform is needed: creation of a rapid response mechanism, lodged in the IMF, to react promptly and effectively in such cases. The G-7 summit at Halifax endorsed such a reform and called it an emergency financing mechanism, which should be adopted, albeit with modifications, which we lay out below.

There is an established precedent among the industrial countries for providing additional resources to the IMF for such purposes, on which the G-7 has wisely sought to build: the General Arrangements to Borrow (GAB), which were created by the G-10 in the early 1960s to shore up the Bretton Woods system of fixed exchange rates. Its goal was to augment the financing available to the Fund to help the largest industrial countries defend their currencies. It was used on a number of occasions in the 1960s and 1970s (box 2.2).

The GAB operates on four key principles: that a sizable fund should exist to help handle major monetary crises, that it can be used only to counter genuine systemic threats, that all decisions to use it have to be made on the merits of the individual case, and that all lending is channeled via the IMF to assure that the borrowing country maintains an effective adjustment program. There is no automatic disbursement; each country in question must have adequate policies in place, as approved and moni-tored by the Fund. This avoids the risk of "moral hazard," whereby a country could be encouraged to misbehave (or the markets could continue to pour in money) if funds were automatically available for a bailout.

The decision at Halifax was to broaden the GAB to help avert "future Mexicos." The summiteers also decided to try to double the size of the facility, from its current level of about $27 billion to about $54 billion. The lending countries would provide the needed financing through the same techniques that they have used to convey resources to the GAB in the past, or to the IMF itself, avoiding any cost to national budgets.[11]

An important rationale for this proposal is international burden sharing. We have argued that it is a mistake to establish financial spheres of influence under which, for example, the United States takes responsibility for Mexico and Germany takes responsibility for Poland. The problems under discussion are global, systemic problems, and the entire international financial community has a responsibility to respond. Hence the IMF is the proper vehicle. Individual creditor countries could "top up" an international package if they believed that it was inadequate and that their national interests were particularly involved in a given case, but any such contributions should supplement the IMF package to maintain discipline and the global process.

Another important rationale is political. Shifting an important part of the responsibility for dealing with international financial problems from the G-7 into the IMF would enhance the legitimacy of both institutions, and of the system as a whole. The G-7 would retain its role as the informal leadership caucus of the Fund itself, and of the system more broadly, but in a way that should be both more acceptable to others and much more effective—thereby muting some of the concerns about its continued central position.

There is of course a close link between the improved early warning system and the added resources for the IMF. Effective prevention would limit the actual need for funds. But the existence of the additional funds could buttress the effectiveness of the early warning system by providing money to help countries that abided by its recommendations.

The structure of the Halifax proposal is sound. The level is grossly inadequate, however, because the Fund may need to deal with several countries at a time. Mexico alone required a package of almost $50 billion. Mexico and Russia together now have IMF programs that total almost $30 billion. An expansion of the GAB to at least $100 billion, almost double the magnitude called for at Halifax, would be desirable.

The second problem with the current G-7 program as devised at Halifax is that implementation has stalled badly as a result of the unwillingness of the G-7—operating in this case via the G-10, the custodian of the GAB—to offer new participants a decision-making role commensurate with their funding. The G-7/G-10 in fact adopted the ludicrous posture of asking nonmembers—industrial countries such as Austria and Spain, and developing countries such as Korea and Singapore—to provide funding with-

---

11. In the case of the United States, such funding would have to be both authorized and appropriated by Congress. But the contribution or even its subsequent activation would not count as a budget outlay that raises the overall deficit because the United States acquires equivalent claims on the Fund when it transfers dollars to it. The transaction is scored as an exchange of assets.

out any meaningful participation at all, let alone full membership in the group. We cited this episode in chapter 3 as one of the G-7's most notable recent failures—one where it snatched defeat from the jaws of victory, at least initially, by faulty implementation of a good idea.

The G-10 should offer full membership to countries that contribute additional funding to the new program. Indeed, the new program offers the G-7 a golden opportunity to enhance its legitimacy by creating a new group that would represent an intermediate step between its own informal steering committee and the universal membership of the IMF—a "middle tier" in the set of three concentric circles of international decision making described in chapter 2. This intermediate group would provide a convenient mechanism for G-7 consultations with the next most important participants in the international monetary system, and for offering a way station toward full membership in the G-7 for some of those countries as they become sufficiently important and experienced to join the innermost circle.[12]

Expansion of the G-10 to perhaps 15 or 20 countries should be based on several criteria. A minimum requirement would be a country's capacity and willingness to contribute financially to the new program. But a systemic criterion should be added: the importance of the country to the world economy, and especially to the international financial system, and thus its potential future role in the leadership of the world economy—and even the G-7 itself.

One key qualifier under these criteria, in addition to the countries that have already been approached to contribute, would be China. The G-7/G-10 has not invited China on the grounds that as a recipient of concessional lending from the World Bank's International Development Association (IDA) affiliate, it would not be an appropriate contributor to the new facility (as it could "profiteer" by borrowing soft money from one international financial institution and lending it on hard terms to another).

But Chinese reserves now exceed $70 billion, and given Chinese concerns about the risk of future financial instability in Hong Kong and other Asian markets, there is good reason to believe that the country might be willing to contribute. With the world's third largest economy and a growth rate that already enables it to play a major locomotive role for growth in Asia—the most dynamic region of the world economy—China is a necessary participant in future world economic leadership. Hence an intermediate group such as an expanded G-10 would provide a highly desirable opportunity to meet both China's desire for increased participa-

---

12. For these reasons, expansion of the G-10 would be far superior to creation of a "parallel group" as proposed by the G-10 itself in its continuing effort to mollify potential contributors without giving them much real role in the process. Any "parallel group" would inevitably be seen as second-class citizenship and would retard rather than enhance the legitimacy of the entire decision-making structure.

tion in global economic affairs (without the legal and political complications attending its bid to enter the World Trade Organization) and the interests of the current international economic leadership in engaging China in serious discussion of such issues.[13]

Enhancing the Legitimacy of the G-7

In addition to providing needed funding for Mexico-type problems, expanding the G-10 would help deal with one of the G-7's key problems, as described in chapter 3: its international legitimacy. Few legitimacy questions arise on matters that are primarily internal to the G-7, such as agreements to coordinate macroeconomic policies among its members. Few would arise with respect to any target zone (or other monetary) agreement governing relationships among the members' own currencies. Such a regime would have global ramifications and should of course be subject to IMF surveillance, but the rest of the world would greatly benefit from more effective exchange rate arrangements among the G-7 countries, and operational decisions such as within-group currency realignments would properly be made by the G-7 itself.

It is also legitimate for the G-7 to caucus on matters that confront the world economic system as a whole. The membership is relatively homogeneous in its levels of national economic development, its trade and financial policies, and its interest in maintaining an open world economy. It is wholly appropriate, therefore, that the G-7 establish common positions on systemic issues. The support of most of the G-7 is in fact necessary, although not sufficient, for important international economic initiatives and reforms of international organizations. International economic leadership requires that the G-7 agree on such initiatives, offer joint proposals, and set much of the agenda for broader negotiations.

In designing leadership groups, there is an inherent trade-off between efficient decision making and breadth of participation. Introducing developing countries, or countries in transition from command to market economies, into the G-7 would inject a great deal more heterogeneity into the group. That would make it even more difficult for the G-7 to establish common positions and then modify those positions when bargaining with countries outside the group. The economic organizations directly affiliated with the United Nations, not including the IMF and World Bank, have

---

13. Chinese entry into the IMF and especially the World Bank in the late 1970s, immediately after it began its economic reforms, played a major role in the success of those reforms and the steady increase in China's market orientation (Jacobson and Oksenberg 1990). As to the IDA problem, the superior approach would be to welcome Chinese financing for the GAB and then note the inconsistency of continued concessional lending to such a surplus/donor country.

broad participation but are notoriously inefficient in making decisions and managing their bureaucracies. Some of those shortcomings could be replicated by broadening the G-7. In any event, no countries outside the group meet the essential criteria of economic importance and global policy orientation at this time. The better course is to make the existing group work better before tampering with its membership.

By enhancing its effectiveness, the G-7 can restore at least some of the grudging acceptance of its role by nonmembers. Such a path is the only route to achieve a modicum of effective international economic leadership over the short to medium run. Our proposals seek to preserve the potential efficiency of the group by avoiding expansion at present while seeking the input of emerging new powers in other ways—including an expanded G-10 and an enhanced role for the IMF.

As the world economy evolves, however, the G-7 must be alert to the need to alter its membership. Some new countries will qualify by virtue of both their economic capability and their policy orientation. Some current members may become less important. Such an evolution will be essential to maintain both the effectiveness of the group and its legitimacy.

The revival of the G-7 should therefore include three institutional steps as well as the substantive program already outlined. First, the G-7 should make a major effort to bolster the IMF's capability and credibility so that it can move increasingly into the center of the action. This would permit a much wider range of countries to engage in international economic decision making in a meaningful way. The IMF's managing director should participate directly in all phases of the G-7's meetings—both to present the analytical work needed to run the proposed system and to enhance the group's legitimacy by representing the rest of the membership. All of our substantive proposals incorporate this objective.[14]

It is imperative for the G-7 to overcome its mistrust of the Fund (as described in chapter 5). No substantive progress is possible, whether in providing the analytical foundation for target zones or implementing a better early warning system, without the Fund's playing a central role. The G-7 must repudiate its current unwillingness to allow the IMF to carry out the responsibilities for which it was created.[15]

Second, the G-7 should streamline its own membership by becoming a G-3 as soon as the progression of monetary union in Europe permits

---

14. Bryant (1995) stresses the need to improve the analytical foundations for policy coordination and correctly concludes that this adds to the case for enhancing the role of the IMF. He proposes (115) "establishing a staff group . . . charged with the collective task of improving analytical knowledge about international macroeconomic interactions and diffusing that knowledge more widely." In essence, the IMF should staff the G-7 much more explicitly and much more extensively than it now does.

15. There are two real problems with the structure of the IMF, however. First, the Executive Board is fairly large, and leaks could occur. Hence it may be necessary to create a small subcommittee of the board to perform some of the more sensitive currency and country monitoring functions. Second, the IMF's exercise of the greatly increased responsibilities

that region to be represented by a single spokesperson on macroeconomic policy. This would replicate the evolution of decision making on trade policy, where the European Commission has represented the Community for over three decades—including in the trading system's international equivalent of the G-7, the Quad.[16] Restructuring the steering committee in this way would also create room for other countries to join the group over time without increasing its membership to an unmanageable size. Through a full presence at the group's meetings, the IMF managing director would represent the nonparticipants.

Third, the G-7 should consult much more actively with nonmembers in formulating its policies. The costs of failing to do so were demonstrated vividly in the IMF's rejection of the group's proposal on SDR allocation at Madrid in September 1994, and with the initial failures of its Halifax proposal to substantially augment the resources of the GAB. As noted above, an expanded G-10 would help achieve this objective.

Conclusion

As noted at the outset of this book, the gains from international policy coordination are substantial. Effective leadership of the world economy is essential to achieve such coordination, and for broader international economic purposes. With the advent of economic multipolarity, and in the absence of a global security threat that would require the United States to resume a dominant role, this leadership must be collective. The G-7 is the de facto informal steering committee and is likely to remain so for some time. But the performance of the G-7 has declined sharply over the past five to ten years.

World economic growth has been subpar throughout the 1990s. Currency crises are endemic and have hit every G-7 country. The Mexico crisis was permitted to erupt and caused widespread contagion. None of these financial disruptions has been handled effectively, let alone pre-

---

called for here would benefit from an upgrading of its board's level of representation. The best approach would be creation of the ministerial-level "Council" already provided for in the Second Amendment to the Articles of Agreement (Williamson and Henning 1994) to function as an intermediate governing body between the Executive Board and the Board of Governors. The Interim Committee was created to serve as a bridge to the creation of the Council, but because the Council has never been activated the Interim Committee remains. Replacing it with the Council would have the advantage of integrating its biannual ministerial meetings into the IMF's formal surveillance and decision-making machinery.

16. This change should be made even if the summits were to retain their G-7 character. Canada is arguably a legitimate member of the quadrilateral steering group for trade because of its weight in international trade flows and its traditional leadership role on those issues, but there will be no similar justification for its membership in the steering committee on macroeconomic and monetary policy once Europe is represented by a single spokesperson as there would then be a vast gap between the economic size of Canada and the other three members. Italy and the United Kingdom would find it increasingly difficult to justify their membership in the G-7 as well if they remained outside the EMU.

vented. Large current account imbalances recur. The trading system is threatened as a result. Numerous systemic disturbances can be easily envisaged. Hence the decline of the G-7 is extremely serious.

The G-7 should enhance its legitimacy both by increasing the IMF's role and by expanding the G-10 to engage countries that are newly important to the world economy though not yet ready for membership in the G-7 itself. But no alternative group is likely to function as the informal steering committee for the world economy. Hence the revival of the G-7, and indeed its conversion into a G-3 as soon as EMU proceeds far enough to make that possible, is essential both for the G-7 members and for the world economy as a whole.

There have always been deep-seated differences within the G-7 on several crucial issues. Some of those disagreements have eased in recent years; some have intensified. Effective G-7 cooperation thus will remain difficult.

Much more important, however, is the recent G-7 agreement—which we have dubbed the "new consensus"—that there is little that can be done, or even should be done, to address several key issues. The combination of long-standing disagreements and this new consensus have in fact produced a de facto nonaggression treaty among the G-7's members with respect to its internal activities, a pact that underlies the group's decline in recent years. That decline has been manifest along all three dimensions of the G-7's responsibilities: internally among its own members, externally toward other countries, and systemically with respect to the institutional architecture.

The action program proposed here can be pursued despite these hurdles. "Global growth programs" and other countercyclical initiatives would receive less emphasis than systemic reforms. Such systemic improvements, on the adjustment side, would aim simply to avoid large and sustained currency misalignments rather than to fix exchange rates or manage them continuously. A new set of G-7 cooperation criteria would assure that all participants in the arrangements were both capable of meeting, and committed to, their new international obligations.

In addition, adoption of a target zone regime for exchange rates could convert the massive international flows of private capital from destabilizing into stabilizing forces that support, rather than frustrate, the efforts of the monetary authorities. Occasional direction of monetary policy to external policy targets would generally strengthen rather than weaken national economies. The central bankers would play a much more extensive role in the new exchange rate regime.

On the financial side, creation of an early warning system and a sizable addition to available resources at the IMF would help head off, and deal with, problems triggered by huge capital flows like those that Mexico experienced. The IMF should monitor closely the policies of all countries with potential systemic effects and "blow the whistle" on such countries when they refuse to follow proposals for policy changes that would prevent Mexico-type crises. Such IMF activities should include all G-7 countries as well as emerging market economies.

The decision to implement such reforms can probably be made only by heads of state and government. Beyond the innate caution and conservatism of monetary officials, which have precluded their ever agreeing on basic monetary reform, they have a vested interest in maintaining a regime of freely flexible exchange rates that enables them to blame all mishaps on "the market" and transfers many of the resulting responsibilities (e.g., for countering trade protectionism) to other parts of their governments. Moreover, any adoption of a new regime implies the failure of the previous regime and thus of the officials themselves. It is no accident that the EMS was created by the heads of the key countries over the objections of most of their financial authorities and that, when negotiating the Maastricht blueprint for EMU, finance ministers operated under the political direction of their heads of government.

It is thus fortunate that the G-7 summit in Naples in July 1994 called for such institutional reform. A year later, the Halifax summit initiated several promising steps on the financial aspects of the problem. The summiteers at Halifax let their monetary officials deter them from considering more far-reaching proposals on the adjustment aspects of the problem, however, and the initial efforts of those same officials threatened to abort even the financial initiatives that were launched.

The Lyon summit in June 1996 should enhance the Halifax program on the financial issues by incorporating the proposals we make here: a more aggressive role for the IMF in implementing the early warning system, a clear mandate to the Fund to apply the surveillance system to the G-7 countries themselves, a much more ambitious expansion of the GAB to provide resources to the IMF to respond to financial crises, and an increase in the membership of the GAB/G-10 to engage the new contributors directly in international decision making.

In addition, the Lyon summiteers should begin the process of improving the international adjustment process and hence address the most central issues analyzed in this book. They could call for active consideration of a target zone regime, and perhaps other possible improvements in the exchange rate system or even the adjustment process more broadly, with decisions to made at the subsequent summit in the United States in 1997. They might want to appoint a wise persons' group to give them independent counsel on the issues, to provide an alternative view to the predictably cautious response that would emanate from their own monetary officials.

Such a program can provide the basis for reviving the G-7 as well as greatly improving the prospects for global prosperity and stability. It is both critical and urgent for the member countries to move in that direction as soon as possible. We hope that these analyses and proposals will help them do so.

Appendix A
International Economic Coordination

International economic coordination occurs when governments collaborate in setting their policies. More formally, it is "the process by which national policies are adjusted to reduce the adverse consequences (or reinforce the positive consequences) that the policies of one or more states have on the welfare of other states" (Putnam and Henning 1989, 15). With coordination, national policies differ from those that one would expect from purely national or autarkic policymaking. Because each country can benefit from the policy adjustments of its partners, coordination does not require giving precedence to other countries' concerns over one's own; it is a common enterprise of purely self-interested governments. Nor does coordination require giving precedence to international factors, such as exchange rates and the balance of payments, over domestic concerns such as growth and employment (Dobson 1991).

Why Coordinate?

Economic interdependence confers international effects on national policies. Through flows of trade and investment, monetary and fiscal policy changes in one country affect growth, employment, and inflation in others and feed back into the economy of the first country. Reaching a global or even national optimum for employment and inflation, therefore, requires that policy externalities be incorporated into the decision-making calculus (Frenkel, Goldstein, and Masson 1990, 10).

Coordination may ease an international constraint that would bind individual governments acting alone. A government facing high unemployment might fear that a fiscal expansion would hurt the country's current account position if it acted in isolation. If its partners agreed to stimulate their economies similarly, that current account constraint would be eased. This is what happened in the agreement at the Bonn summit of 1978. A similar dynamic applies to countries wishing to limit inflation. Coordination, in other words, is a mechanism for "internalizing" policy externalities.

In the absence of coordination, countries may be tempted to "export unemployment" by, for example, the serial devaluations and trade protectionism that occurred during the 1930s. Alternatively, countries, large ones in particular, might try to "export inflation," through competitive appreciations of their currencies and the imposition of export controls, as occurred after the first oil shock in 1973 (Bergsten 1974).

Obstacles and How to Overcome Them

Although the conceptual case for international coordination is widely accepted, several practical barriers exist (Cooper 1985; Feldstein 1988b;

Putnam and Henning 1989; Frenkel, Goldstein, and Masson 1990; Dobson 1991):

- **Enforcement of international bargains.** Because there is no global enforcement agency, governments lack the assurance that their counterparts will fulfill reciprocal commitments. Even the best-conceived packages may falter in practice, inducing countries to "cheat" or simply to forgo coordination out of fear that would-be partners will renege.

- **Time horizon of the exercise.** Coordination that seeks short-run payoffs can have adverse results over the longer run. Joint expansion programs, for example, can increase inflationary pressures over time—a charge that many Germans have leveled at the Bonn summit package.

- **Deflection of attention from more fundamental domestic policy requirements.** Policymakers could be tempted to seek international coordination to deal with symptoms of problems (e.g., the exchange rate) rather than their basic causes (e.g., budget deficits) and use coordination as an excuse to avoid the tougher actions that are needed.

- **Uncertainty over both the economic outlook and the impact of the proposed policies.** Such uncertainty pervades all economic policymaking, of course, but can be compounded when those efforts are extended to the international level.

- **Differences in party control of government give rise to conflicting policy preferences among countries with respect to economic performance.** Elections are not synchronized, and changes in party control occur with different frequencies and amplitudes across countries.

- **Differences in national institutions create international mismatches among ministers over the breadth of their domestic policy authority.** Finance ministers with restricted authority over fiscal policy within their countries, for example, could not credibly negotiate on this issue with counterparts that have broad authority. The independence of central banks, and hence the authority with which their governors can speak internationally, differs sharply across countries.

- **Conflicts over the distribution of joint gains can overwhelm the pursuit of optimal agreements.** Even in the presence of substantial absolute gains for all parties, distributive bargaining might scuttle coordination.

These obstacles are not arguments against coordination. Rather, each of these challenges to coordination identifies a purpose for institutions and procedures that seek to support coordination efforts.

The enforcement of agreements can be promoted by setting rules and building institutions. The GATT provides a striking example of success in this regard. Although regimes cannot establish at the international level the strong legal norms that prevail domestically, they can establish expectations and conventions that are costly to break. As Robert Keohane (1984) writes, "For reasons of reputation, as well as fear of retaliation and concern about the effects of precedents, egoistic governments may follow the rules and principles of international regimes even when myopic self-interest counsels them not to."

Adopting long-term rather than short-term targets for coordination will enhance the chances that it will produce optimal long-term outcomes. The European Monetary System (EMS), through setting and defending exchange rate targets, achieved an impressive reduction in inflation over the past 15 years. The European commitment to monetary union is helping to stiffen the resolve of governments to reduce budget deficits.

Attention diversion can be corrected by designing the coordination process so that it will encourage national policymakers to address their domestic problems directly rather than evade them via international gimmicks. The European experience again suggests, albeit imperfectly and with setbacks, that a serious commitment to exchange rate targets can induce countries to address their economic fundamentals more forcefully.

Despite uncertainty, countries *can* find policy packages that will improve their positions even if each country has a different view of the economic outlook and the impact of the measures chosen (Frankel and Rockett 1988, 275). Learning which model more nearly approximates the "true" model, moreover, can be stimulated by policy coordination (Ghosh and Masson 1994).

Ongoing, institutionalized information exchange, multilateral surveillance, and policy coordination would help surmount the three remaining obstacles. Effective surveillance would help to nudge "outlier" countries whose policies have been sidetracked by a change in party control back toward the group norm. The most dramatic case was France in 1982–83, where the new Socialist government jettisoned its "dash for growth" strategy when it became clear that pursuing this course further would endanger French participation in the EMS (and perhaps the European Community more broadly). Mismatches in ministerial competence can be addressed by selective broadening of meetings to include ministers with other portfolios or by elevating the exercise to the summit level. Meeting in an ongoing forum over the long term will raise governments' stake in maintaining a reputation for fulfilling agreements, increase trust among participants, and help them advance common interests despite intense distributive bargaining.

Empirical Significance

The main challenge to coordination is empirical. Some econometric studies have suggested that the benefits of coordination, though positive, are marginal (Oudiz and Sachs 1984; Oudiz 1985). The methods employed in such studies, however, cannot capture several critical dividends (Tietmeyer 1988).

First, the econometric models completely overlook the linkages between macroeconomic, trade, energy, and other economic policies. The United States successfully used the Bonn summit agreement of 1978 to reverse its domestic energy policy and begin phasing out energy price controls—with highly favorable effects on its own economy and the world economy, particularly over the longer run. That same summit produced a decisive political impetus for the completion of the Tokyo Round in the GATT; then-Special Trade Representative Robert Strauss has stated frequently that the round would never have succeeded in the absence of that impetus. These effects are not included in any of the econometric analyses of the summit's results (see, e.g., Holtham 1989). Coordination, and the summit process in particular, forces government officials to focus on the linkages among policies and thereby increases official awareness of these connections.

Second, the econometric models overlook the gains from avoiding crises or other costly outcomes through policy coordination. Because counterfactual outcomes are impossible to identify with certainty, such gains can never be definitively proved. But it is quite probable that the dollar correction set in train by the Plaza Agreement, for example, avoided an outbreak of American protectionism—including congressional legislation—that would have deeply damaged the entire international trading system. It may also have avoided a subsequent "hard landing" for the dollar that, like the precipitate yen appreciation of 1995 that resulted from that currency's previous undervaluation and consequent large external surpluses, could have levied sizable costs on the American and world economies.

Third, markets generally perform better when operating within the framework of consistent and effective political leadership. Monetary, fiscal, and exchange rate policies provide the macroeconomic framework within which corporations and individuals make economic decisions. When exchange rates become substantially misaligned and vary wildly, as the dollar did in the first half of the 1980s and the yen did at the end of the decade, they lose their value as guides for the allocation of resources. An effective system of international economic coordination would restore credibility to such price signals, the value of which escapes narrow conceptions of the benefits of coordination.

References

Ainley, Michael. 1984. *The General Arrangements to Borrow*. Pamphlet Series, no. 41. Washington: International Monetary Fund.

Alesina, Alberto, and Lawrence H. Summers. 1990. *Central Bank Independence and Macroeconomic Performance: Some Comparative Evidence*. Harvard International Economic Research Discussion Paper 1496, May. Cambridge, MA: Harvard University.

Armendariz de Aghion, Beatriz, and John Williamson. 1993. *The G-7's Joint-and-Several Blunder*. Essays in International Finance, no. 189 (April). Princeton, NJ: International Finance Section, Department of Economics, Princeton University.

Åslund, Anders. 1995. *How Russia Became a Market Economy*. Washington: Brookings Institution.

Baker, James A., III. 1987. Remarks at the Institute for International Economics, Washington, 14 September.

Bayoumi, Tamim, Peter Clark, Steve Symansky, and Mark Taylor. 1994. "The Robustness of Equilibrium Exchange Rate Calculations to Alternative Assumptions and Methodologies." In John Williamson, *Estimating Equilibrium Exchange Rates*. Washington: Institute for International Economics.

Bergsten, C. Fred. 1974. *Completing the GATT: Toward New International Rules to Govern Export Controls*. Washington and London: British-North American Committee.

Bergsten, C. Fred. 1975. *The Dilemmas of the Dollar: The Economics and Politics of United States International Monetary Policy*. New York: New York University Press. Forthcoming 2d ed. (Armonk, NY: M. E. Sharpe).

Bergsten, C. Fred. 1981a. "US International Economic Policy in the 1980s." Hearing before the Subcommittee on International Economic Policy and Trade of the Committee on Foreign Affairs. House of Representatives, 97th Cong., 1st sess. 24 February.

Bergsten, C. Fred. 1981b. "The Costs of Reagonomics." *Foreign Policy* 44 (Fall): 24–36.

Bergsten, C. Fred. 1982. "What to Do about the U.S.-Japan Economic Conflict." *Foreign Affairs* 60 (Summer): 1059–75.

Bergsten, C. Fred. 1986. "America's Unilateralism." In C. Fred Bergsten, Etienne Davignon, and Isamu Miyazaki, *Conditions for Partnership in International Economic Management*. Report to the Trilateral Commission 32. New York: Trilateral Commission.

Bergsten, C. Fred. 1990. "The World Economy after the Cold War." *Foreign Affairs* 69, no. 3 (Summer): 96–112.

Bergsten, C. Fred. 1993. "Good and Bad of Managed Trade." *Financial Times*, 18 August.

Bergsten, C. Fred. 1994. "Target Zones: Answer to Currency Volatility." *Nikkei Weekly*, 17 October.

Bergsten, C. Fred. 1996. "Globalizing Free Trade." *Foreign Affairs* 75, no. 3 (May–June): 105–21.

Bergsten, C. Fred, George Berthoin, and Kinhide Mushakoji. 1976. *The Reform of International Institutions*. A Report of the Trilateral Task Force on International Institutions to the Trilateral Commission. The Triangle Papers, no. 11. New York: Trilateral Commission.

Bergsten, C. Fred, William R. Cline, and John Williamson. 1985. *Bank Lending to Developing Countries: The Policy Alternatives*. POLICY ANALYSES IN INTERNATIONAL ECONOMICS 10. Washington: Institute for International Economics.

Bergsten, C. Fred, and Marcus Noland. 1993. *Reconcilable Differences? United States-Japan Economic Conflict*. Washington: Institute for International Economics.

Bergsten, C. Fred, and John Williamson. 1994. "Is the Time Ripe for Target Zones or the Blueprint?" In Bretton Woods Commission, *Bretton Woods: Looking to the Future*. Washington: Bretton Woods Commission.

Binaian, King, Leroy O. Laney, and Thomas D. Willett. 1986. "Central Bank Independence: An International Comparison." In E. F. Toma and M. Toma, *Central Bankers, Bureaucratic Incentives, and Monetary Policy*. Dordrecht and Boston: Kluwer.

Black, Stanley W. 1989. "Transactions Costs and Vehicle Currencies." *Journal of International Money and Finance* 10, no. 4 (December): 512–26.

Branson, William H., Jacob A. Frenkel, and Morris Goldstein. 1990. *International Policy Coordination and Exchange Rate Fluctuations*. Chicago: Chicago University Press for NBER.

Bretton Woods Commission. 1994. *Bretton Woods: Looking to the Future*. Washington: Bretton Woods Commission.

Bryant, Ralph C. 1987. "Intergovernmental Coordination of Economic Policies: An Interim Stocktaking." In *International Monetary Cooperation: Essays in Honor of Henry C. Wallich*. Princeton, NJ: International Finance Department, Department of Economics, Princeton University.

Bryant, Ralph C. 1995. *International Coordination of National Stabilization Policies*. Washington: Brookings Institution.

Bryant, Ralph C., Peter Hooper, and Catherine L. Mann, eds. 1993. *Evaluating Policy Regimes: New Research in Empirical Macroeconomics*. Washington: Brookings Institution.

Brzezinski, Zbigniew. 1996. "Summit of Impotence." *Washington Times*, 25 February.

Camdessus, Michel. 1994. "The IMF at Fifty—An Evolving Role but a Constant Mission." An address to the Institute for International Economics, Washington, 7 June.

Catte, P., G. Galli, and S. Rebecchini. 1994. "Concerted Interventions and the Dollar: An Analysis of Daily Data." In P. Kenen, F. Papadia, and F. Saccomani, *The International Monetary System in Crisis and Reform: Essays in Memory of Rinaldo Ossola*. Cambridge, UK: Cambridge University Press.

Caves, Richard E., Jeffrey A. Frankel, and Ronald W. Jones. 1996. *World Trade and Payments: An Introduction*, 7th ed. New York: HarperCollins.

Cline, William R. 1983. *International Debt and the Stability of the World Economy*. POLICY ANALYSES IN INTERNATIONAL ECONOMICS 4. Washington: Institute for International Economics.

Cline, William R. 1989. *American Trade Adjustment: The Global Impact*. POLICY ANALYSES IN INTERNATIONAL ECONOMICS 26. Washington: Institute for International Economics.

Cline, William R. 1995a. *International Debt Reexamined*. Washington: Institute for International Economics.

Cline, William R. 1995b. *Predicting External Imbalances for the United States and Japan*. POLICY ANALYSES IN INTERNATIONAL ECONOMICS 41. Washington: Institute for International Economics.

Cohen, Benjamin J. 1989. *Developing-Country Debt: A Middle Way.* Essays in International Finance, no. 173, May. Princeton, NJ: International Finance Section, Department of Economics, Princeton University.

Cohen, Benjamin J. 1992. "US Debt Policy in Latin America: The Melody Lingers On." In Robert Botteme et al., *In the Shadow of the Debt: Emerging Issues in Latin America.* New York: Twentieth Century Fund Press.

Cohen, Stephen D. 1988. *The Making of United States International Economic Policy: Principles, Problems, and Proposals for Reform,* 3d ed. New York: Praeger.

Collins, Susan, and Dani Rodrik. 1992. *Eastern Europe and the Soviet Union in the World Economy.* POLICY ANALYSES IN INTERNATIONAL ECONOMICS 32. Washington: Institute for International Economics.

Commission and Council of the European Communities. 1992. *Treaty on European Union.* Luxembourg: Office of the Official Publications of the European Communities.

Committee for the Study of Economic and Monetary Union. 1989. *Report on Economic and Monetary Union.* Luxembourg: Office of the Official Publications of the European Communities.

Cooper, Richard N. 1985. "Economic Interdependence and Coordination of Economic Policies." In R. W. Jones and P. B. Kenen, *Handbook of International Economics,* vol. 2. New York: North-Holland.

Cukierman, Alex, Steven B. Webb, and Filin Neyapti. 1992. "Measuring the Independence of Central Banks and Its Effect on Policy Outcomes." *World Bank Economic Review* (6 September): 353–98.

Destler, I. M. 1992. *American Trade Politics,* 2d ed. Washington: Institute for International Economics.

Destler, I. M., and C. Randall Henning. 1989. *Dollar Politics: Exchange Rate Policymaking in the United States.* Washington: Institute for International Economics.

Deutsche Bundesbank. 1994. *Annual Report.* Frankfurt.

de Vries, Margaret G. 1985. *The International Monetary Fund, 1972–1978: Cooperation on Trial.* Washington: International Monetary Fund.

Dobson, Wendy. 1991. *Economic Policy Coordination: Requiem or Prologue?* POLICY ANALYSES IN INTERNATIONAL ECONOMICS 30. Washington: Institute for International Economics.

Dobson, Wendy. 1994. "Surveillance and the International Monetary System: Ideals and Realities." Presented at IMF-World Bank conference on Fifty Years after Bretton Woods at Madrid, September.

Dominguez, Kathryn M., and Jeffrey A. Frankel. 1993. *Does Foreign Exchange Intervention Work?* Washington: Institute for International Economics.

Dornbusch, Rudiger. 1982. "Equilibrium and Disequilibrium Exchange Rates." *Zeitschrift fur Wirtschafts-und Sozialwissenshaften* 102: 573–99. Reprinted in R. Dornbusch, *Dollars, Debts, and Deficits* (Cambridge, MA: MIT Press, 1986).

Dornbusch, Rudiger. 1986. "Flexible Exchange Rates and Excess Capital Mobility." *Brookings Papers on Economic Activity* 1: 209–26.

Dornbusch, Rudiger, and Sebastian Edwards, eds. 1991. *The Macroeconomics of Populism in Latin America.* Chicago: University of Chicago Press.

Dornbusch, Rudiger, and Alejandro Werner. 1994. "Mexico: Stabilization, Reform, and No Growth." *Brookings Papers on Economic Activity* 1: 253–316.

Edwards, Richard W., Jr. 1985. *International Monetary Collaboration.* Dobbs Ferry, NY: Transnational Publishers.

Edwards, Sebastian, and Felipe Larraín. 1989. *Debt, Adjustment, and Recovery: Latin America's Prospects for Growth and Development.* Oxford: Basil Blackwell.

Eichengreen, Barry. 1989. "Hegemonic Stability Theories of the International Monetary System." In Richard N. Cooper, Barry Eichengreen, Gerald Holtham, Robert D. Putnam, and C. Randall Henning, *Can Nations Agree? Issues in International Economic Cooperation.* Washington: Brookings Institution.

Eichengreen, Barry. 1995. *International Monetary Arrangements for the 21st Century.* Washington: Brookings Institution.

Eichengreen, Barry, and Richard Portes. 1989. "Dealing with Debt: The 1930s and the 1980s. In Ishrat Husain and Ishac Diwan, *Dealing with the Debt Crisis.* World Bank Symposium. Washington: World Bank.

Eijffinger, Sylvester, and Jacob de Haan. 1995. *The Political Economy of Central Bank Independence.* Center for Economic Research, Tilburg University Discussion Paper, no. 9587. Tilburg, the Netherlands: Tilburg University.

Eijffinger, Sylvester, and Eric Schaling. 1993. "Central Bank Independence: Searching for the Philosophers' Stone." In Donald E. Fair and Robert J. Raymond, *The New Europe: Evolving Economic and Financial Systems in East and West.* Dordrecht and Boston: Kluwer.

Eijffinger, Sylvester, and Eric Schaling. 1995. "The Ultimate Determinants of Central Bank Independence." Center for Economic Research, Tilburg University Discussion Paper, no. 9505, January. Tilburg, the Netherlands: Tilburg University.

Emminger, Otmar. 1977. *The D-Mark and the Conflict between Internal and External Equilibrium.* Essays in International Finance, no. 122, June. Princeton, NJ: International Finance Section, Department of Economics, Princeton University.

Emminger, Otmar. 1986. *Dollar, D-Mark und Währungskrisen.* Stuttgart: Deutsche-Verlags Anstalt.

Engel, Charles, and James D. Hamilton. 1990. "Long Swings in the Dollar." *American Economic Review* 80: 689–713.

Federal Reserve Board of Governors. 1989. *Record of Policy Actions of the Federal Open Market Committee.* Washington.

Federal Reserve Board of Governors. 1994. *Record of Policy Actions of the Federal Open Market Committee.* Washington.

Feldstein, Martin. 1983. "The World Economy." *The Economist,* 11 June.

Feldstein, Martin. 1988a. "Thinking about International Economic Coordination: Distinguished Lecture on Economics in Government." *Journal of Economic Perspectives* 2, no. 2 (Spring): 3–13.

Feldstein, Martin, ed. 1988b. *International Economic Cooperation.* Chicago: Chicago University Press for the National Bureau for Economic Research.

Feldstein, Martin. 1994. "American Economic Policy in the 1980s: A Personal View." In Martin Feldstein, *American Economic Policy in the 1980s.* Chicago: University of Chicago Press.

Fischer, Stanley. 1987. "Sharing the Burden of the International Debt Crisis." *American Economic Review* 77 (May): 165–70.

Frankel, Jeffrey A. 1986. "The Dollar as an Irrational Speculative Bubble: A Tale of Fundamentalists and Chartists." *The Marcus Wallenberg Papers on International Finance* 1, no. 1. Washington: International Law Institute.

Frankel, Jeffrey A. 1988. *Obstacles to International Macroeconomic Policy Coordination.* Studies in International Finance, no. 64, December. Princeton, NJ: Princeton University Press.

Frankel, Jeffrey A. 1992. "International Nominal Targeting (INT): A Proposal for Overcoming Obstacles to Policy Coordination." In M. Baldassarri, J. McCallum, and R. Mundell, *Global Disequilibrium in the World Economy.* London: Macmillan Press; New York: St. Martin's Press.

Frankel, Jeffrey A. 1993. *On Exchange Rates.* Cambridge, MA: MIT Press.

Frankel, Jeffrey A. 1996. "Recent Exchange Rate Experience and Proposals for Reform." Paper presented at the American Economics Association meeting, San Francisco, 6 January. Forthcoming in *American Economic Review Papers and Proceedings.*

Frankel, Jeffrey A., and Richard A. Meese. 1987. "Are Exchange Rates Excessively Variable?" *NBER Macroeconomics Annual* 2: 117–53.

Frankel, Jeffrey A., and Katharine Rockett. 1988. "International Macroeconomic Policy Coordination When Policymakers Do Not Agree on the True Model." *American Economic Review* 78, no. 3 (June): 318–40.

Frankel, Jeffrey A., and Andrew Rose. 1995. *A Survey of Empirical Research on Nominal Exchange Rates*. NBER Working Paper, no. 4865. Cambridge, MA: National Bureau of Economic Research.

Frankel, Jeffrey A., S. Erwin, and K. Rockett. 1992. "A Note on Internationally Coordinated Policy Packages Intended to Be Robust Under Model Uncertainty." *American Economic Review* 82 (September): 1052–56.

Freedman, C. 1994. "The Use of Indicators and of the Monetary Conditions Index in Canada." In Tomás J. T. Baliño and Carlo Cottarelli, *Frameworks for Monetary Stability: Policy Issues and Country Experiences*. Washington: IMF Institute and Monetary and Exchange Affairs Department.

Frenkel, Jacob A., Morris Goldstein, and Paul R. Masson. 1990. "The Rationale for, and Effects of, International Economic Policy Coordination." In William H. Branson, Jacob A. Frenkel, and Morris Goldstein, *International Policy Coordination and Exchange Rate Fluctuations*. Chicago: Chicago University Press for the National Bureau for Economic Research.

Frieden, Jeffry A. 1991. *Debt, Development, and Democracy: Modern Political Economy and Latin America, 1965–1985*. Princeton, NJ: Princeton University Press.

Funabashi, Yoichi. 1989. *Managing the Dollar: From the Plaza to the Louvre*, 2d ed. Washington: Institute for International Economics.

Furstenberg, George M. von, and Joseph P. Daniels. 1992. *Economic Summit Declarations, 1975–1989: Examining the Written Record of International Cooperation*. Princeton Studies in International Finance, no. 72, February. Princeton, NJ: International Finance Section, Department of Economics, Princeton University.

Garber, Peter, and Morris Goldstein. N.d. *Overseeing Global Capital Markets*. Washington: Institute for International Economics. Forthcoming.

Garber, Peter, and Lars Svensson. 1995. "The Operation and Collapse of Fixed Exchange Rate Regimes." In Gene M. Grossman and Ken Rogoff, *Handbook of International Economics*, vol. 3. Amsterdam: North Holland.

Ghosh, Atish R., and Paul R. Masson. 1994. *Economic Cooperation in an Uncertain World*. Cambridge, MA: Blackwell.

Gilpin, Robert. 1981. *War and Change in World Politics*. Cambridge and New York: Cambridge University Press.

Gilpin, Robert. 1987. *The Political Economy of International Relations*. Princeton, NJ: Princeton University Press.

Goldstein, Morris. 1995. *The Exchange Rate and the IMF: A Modest Agenda*. POLICY ANALYSES IN INTERNATIONAL ECONOMICS 39. Washington: Institute for International Economics.

Goodhart, Charles. 1988. "The Foreign Exchange Market: A Random Walk with a Dragging Anchor." *Economica* 55: 437–60.

Goodman, John B. 1991. *Central Bank-Government Relations in Major OECD Countries*. Prepared for the US Congress, Joint Economic Committee, 102nd Cong., 1st sess. Washington: GPO.

Goodman, John B. 1992. *Monetary Sovereignty: The Politics of Central Banking in Western Europe*. Ithaca, NY: Cornell University Press.

Greider, William. 1987. *Secrets of the Temple: How the Federal Reserve Runs the Country*. New York: Simon and Schuster.

Grilli, Enzo. 1988. "Macroeconomic Determinants of Trade Protectionism." *World Economy* 11 (September): 313–26.

Grilli, Vittorio, Donato Masciandaro, and Guido Tabellini. 1991. "Political and Monetary Institutions and Public Financial Policies in the Industrial Countries." *Economic Policy* 13 (October): 342–92.

Group of Five. 1985. Communiqué. Washington: US Treasury Department (22 September).

Haggard, Stephan, and Robert R. Kaufman, eds. 1992. *The Politics of Economic Adjustment: International Constraints, Distributive Conflicts, and the State*. Princeton, NJ: Princeton University Press.

Handelsblatt. 1995. "Germans Are the World's Top Nay-Sayers" and "The Germans Should Not Always Say No and Step on the Brakes." (25 April): 1 and 39.

Henning, C. Randall. 1994. *Currencies and Politics in the United States, Germany, and Japan.* Washington: Institute for International Economics.

Henning, C. Randall. 1996. "Europe's Monetary Union and the United States." *Foreign Policy* 102 (Spring): 83–100.

Henning, C. Randall, Gary Clyde Hufbauer, and Eduard Hochreiter. 1994. *Reviving the European Union: Prospects for Recovery.* Washington: Institute for International Economics.

Holtham, Gerald. 1989. "German Economic Policy and the 1978 Bonn Summit." In Richard N. Cooper, Barry Eichengreen, Gerald Holtham, Robert D. Putnam, and C. Randall Henning, *Can Nations Agree? Issues in International Economic Cooperation.* Washington: Brookings Institution.

Husain, Ishrat, and Ishac Diwan, eds. 1989. *Dealing with the Debt Crisis.* World Bank Symposium. Washington: World Bank.

Ikenberry, G. John. 1993. "Salvaging the G-7." *Foreign Affairs* 72, no. 2 (Spring): 132–39.

Ikenberry, G. John. 1996. "The Myth of Post-Cold War Chaos." *Foreign Affairs* 75, no. 3 (May–June): 79–91.

International Spectator. 1994. Vol. 29, no. 2 (April–June).

James, Harold. 1996. *International Monetary Cooperation since Bretton Woods.* Washington: International Monetary Fund; New York: Oxford University Press.

Jacobson, Harold, and Michel Oksenberg. 1990. *China's Participation in the IMF, the World Bank, and the GATT.* Ann Arbor: University of Michigan Press.

Kahler, Miles, ed. 1986. *The Politics of International Debt.* Ithaca, NY: Cornell University Press.

Kapstein, Ethan B. 1994. *Governing the Global Economy: International Finance and the State.* Cambridge, MA and London, UK: Harvard University Press.

Kenen, Peter B. 1990. "Organizing Debt Relief: The Need for a New Institution." *Journal of Economic Perspectives* 4, no. 1 (Winter): 7–18.

Kenen, Peter B., ed. 1994. *Managing the World Economy: Fifty Years after Bretton Woods.* Washington: Institute for International Economics.

Kenen, Peter B. 1995. *Economic and Monetary Union in Europe: Moving beyond Maastricht.* Cambridge, MA: Cambridge University Press.

Keohane, Robert O. 1984. *After Hegemony: Cooperation and Discord in the World Political Economy.* Princeton, NJ: Princeton University Press.

Keohane, Robert O., and Joseph S. Nye, eds. 1971. *Transnational Relations and World Politics.* Cambridge, MA: Harvard University Press.

Kindleberger, Charles P. 1973. *The World in Depression, 1929–39.* Berkeley: University of California Press.

Kristof, Nicholas D. 1993. "The Rise of China." *Foreign Affairs* 72, no. 5 (November–December): 59–74.

Krugman, Paul R. 1991. "Has the Adjustment Process Worked?" In C. Fred Bergsten, *International Adjustment and Financing: The Lessons of 1985–1991.* Washington: Institute for International Economics.

Krugman, Paul R., and Marcus Miller, eds. 1992. *Why Have a Target Zone?* CEPR Discussion Paper, no. 718, October. London: Centre for Economic Policy Research.

Lohmann, Susanne. 1992. "Optimal Commitment in Monetary Policy: Credibility Versus Flexibility." *American Economic Review* 82 (March): 273–86.

Lucas, Robert E. 1981. "Econometric Policy Evaluation: A Critique." In Robert E. Lucas, *Studies in Business-Cycle Theory.* Cambridge, MA: MIT Press.

Marris, Stephen. 1983. "Crisis Ahead for the Dollar." *Fortune,* vol. 108 (26 December): 25–26.

Marris, Stephen. 1985. *Deficits and the Dollar: The World Economy at Risk.* POLICY ANALYSES IN INTERNATIONAL ECONOMICS 14. Washington: Institute for International Economics.

Mauskopf, Eileen. 1990. "The Transmission Channels of Monetary Policy: How Have They Changed?" *Federal Reserve Bulletin* 76 (December): 985–1008.

Meese, Richard A. 1986. "Testing for Bubbles in Exchange Markets." *Journal of Political Economy* 94: 345–73.

Mussa, Michael. 1994. "Exchange Rate Policy." In Martin Feldstein, *American Economic Policy in the 1980s*. Chicago and London: University of Chicago Press.

Nau, Henry R. 1990. *The Myth of America's Decline: Leading the World Economy into the 1990s*. New York: Oxford University Press.

Nölling, Wilhelm. 1993. *Monetary Policy in Europe after Maastricht*. New York: St. Martin's Press.

Nye, Joseph N. 1990. *Bound to Lead: The Changing Nature of American Power*. New York: Basic Books.

Obstfeld, Maurice. 1995. "International Currency Experience: New Lessons Relearned." *Brookings Papers on Economic Activity*, 1: 119–20.

Odell, John S. 1982. *US International Monetary Policy: Markets, Power, and Ideas as Sources of Change*. Princeton, NJ: Princeton University Press.

Odell, John S. 1988. "From Bretton Woods: Sources of Change in Bargaining Strategies and Outcomes." *Journal of Public Policy* 8 (July–December): 287–315.

Oudiz, Gilles. 1985. *European Policy Coordination: An Evaluation*. Centre for Economic Policy Research Paper, no. 81. London: CEPR.

Oudiz, Gilles, and Jeffrey Sachs. 1984. "Macroeconomic Policy Coordination Among Industrial Economies." *Brookings Papers on Economic Activity* 1: 1–76.

Oye, Kenneth A. 1993. *Economic Discrimination and Political Exchange: World Political Economy in the 1930s and 1980s*. Princeton, NJ: Princeton University Press.

Pauly, Louis W. 1993. "The Political Foundations of Multilateral Economic Surveillance." In Janice Gross Stein and Louis W. Pauly, *Choosing to Co-operate: How States Avoid Loss*. Baltimore: Johns Hopkins University Press.

Pauly, Louis W. N.d. *Who Elected the Bankers?* Ithaca, NY: Cornell University Press. Forthcoming.

Pöhl, Karl Otto. 1987. "Are We Moving towards a More Stable International Monetary Order?" Speech to the American Institute for Contemporary German Studies, Washington, 7 April.

Posen, Adam S. 1993. "Why Central Bank Independence Does Not Cause Lower Inflation: There is No Institutional Fix for Politics." In Richard O'Brien, *Finance and the International Economy: 7*. Oxford: Oxford University Press.

Putnam, Robert D., and Nicholas Bayne. 1987. *Hanging Together: Cooperation and Conflict in the Seven-Power Summits*, 2d ed. Cambridge, MA: Harvard University Press.

Putnam, Robert D., and C. Randall Henning. 1989. "The Bonn Summit of 1978: A Case Study in Coordination." In Richard N. Cooper, Barry Eichengreen, Gerald Holtham, Robert D. Putnam, and C. Randall Henning, *Can Nations Agree? Issues in International Economic Cooperation*. Washington: Brookings Institution.

Richardson, J. David, and Karin Rindal. 1996. *Why Exports Matter: More!* Washington: Institute for International Economics and The Manufacturing Institute.

Rose, Andrew K. 1994. "Exchange-Rate Volatility, Monetary Policy and Capital Mobility: Empirical Evidence and the Holy Trinity." Berkeley: University of California. Photocopy.

Sachs, Jeffrey, ed. 1989. *Developing Country Debt and Economic Performance: The International Financial System*, vol. 1. Chicago: University of Chicago Press for the National Bureau for Economic Research.

Sachs, Jeffrey, ed. 1990. *Country Studies: Argentina, Bolivia, Brazil, Mexico*, vol. 2. Chicago: University of Chicago Press for the National Bureau for Economic Research.

Sachs, Jeffrey. 1994. "Life in the Economic Emergency Room." In John Williamson, *The Political Economy of Policy Reform*. Washington: Institute for International Economics.

Sazanami, Yoko, Shujiro Urata, and Hiroki Kawai. 1995. *Measuring the Costs of Protection in Japan*. Washington: Institute for International Economics.

Smyser, W. R. 1993. "Goodbye, G-7." *The Washington Quarterly* (Winter): 15–28.

Solomon, Anthony. 1983. "A Personal Evaluation." In George de Menil and Anthony Solomon, *Economic Summitry*. New York: Council on Foreign Relations.

Solomon, Robert. 1982. *The International Monetary System, 1945–1981*. New York: Harper & Row.

Stark, Jürgen. 1995. "The G-7 at Work." *International Economy* 9, no. 5 (September–October): 52–57.

Stockman, David A. 1987. *The Triumph of Politics: The Inside Story of the Reagan Revolution*. New York: Avon Books.

Stoltenberg, Gerhard. 1987. "The United States and Europe: Main Objectives for Economic Policies and International Cooperation." Speech at Georgetown University, Washington, 10 April.

Summers, Lawrence H. 1994. "Shared Prosperity and the New International Economic Order." In Peter B. Kenen, *Managing the World Economy: Fifty Years after Bretton Woods*. Washington: Institute for International Economics.

Tietmeyer, Hans. 1988. "Some Comments on the New Commitment to International Cooperation since the Plaza Accord of 1985." Manuscript.

Tietmeyer, Hans. 1993. *National Monetary Policy and European Monetary Union*. Konrad Adenauer Stiftung Occasional Papers, no. 23-93. Bonn and Washington: Konrad Adenauer Stiftung.

The Twenty G-7 Summits: The History, the Issues, the Protagonists, and all the Official Declarations of the G-7 Summits from Rambouillet to Naples. 1994. Naples: Adnkrono Libri.

Volcker, Paul A. 1995. "The Quest for Exchange Rate Stability: Realistic or Quixotic?" Stamp 50th Anniversary Lecture, Senate House, University of London, 29 November.

Volcker, Paul A., and Toyoo Gyohten. 1992. *Changing Fortunes: The World's Money and the Threat to American Leadership*. New York: Time Books.

Whyman, William E. 1995. "We Can't Go on Meeting Like This: Revitalizing the G-7 Process." *Washington Quarterly* 18 (Summer): 139–65.

Williamson, John. 1977. *The Failure of World Monetary Reform, 1971–1974*. New York: New York University Press.

Williamson, John. 1985. *The Exchange Rate System*, 2d ed. POLICY ANALYSES IN INTERNATIONAL ECONOMICS 5. Washington: Institute for International Economics.

Williamson, John. 1988. *Voluntary Approaches to Debt Relief*. POLICY ANALYSES IN INTERNATIONAL ECONOMICS 25. Washington: Institute for International Economics.

Williamson, John. 1991. *Britain's Role in EMU*. Open Forum Series No. 10. Dorchester, UK: Liberal Democrat Publications.

Williamson, John. 1993. "Exchange-Rate Policy in Mexico." Testimony to the US House of Representatives, Committee on Small Business, 20 May.

Williamson, John. 1994. "Introduction." In John Williamson, *Estimating Equilibrium Exchange Rates*. Washington: Institute for International Economics.

Williamson, John. 1995. *What Role for Currency Boards?* POLICY ANALYSES IN INTERNATIONAL ECONOMICS 40. Washington: Institute for International Economics.

Williamson, John, and C. Randall Henning. 1994. "Managing the Monetary System." In Peter B. Kenen, *Managing the World Economy: Fifty Years after Bretton Woods*. Washington: Institute for International Economics.

Williamson, John, and Marcus H. Miller. 1987. *Targets and Indicators: A Blueprint for the International Coordination of Economic Policy*. POLICY ANALYSES IN INTERNATIONAL ECONOMICS 22. Washington: Institute for International Economics.

Woolley, James T. 1985. "Central Banks and Inflation." In Leon N. Lindberg and Charles S. Maier, *The Politics of Inflation and Economic Stagflation*. Washington: Brookings Institution.

World Economic Forum and IMD International. 1995. *The World Competitiveness Report 1995*. Geneva and Lausanne.

Wren-Lewis, Simon, Peter Westaway, Soterios Soteri, and Ray Barrell. 1990. *Choosing the Rate: An Analysis of the Optimum Level of Entry for Sterling into the ERM*. London: National Institute of Economics and Social Research.

Wyplosz, Charles. 1995. "Links between Monetary Policy and the Exchange Rate." Paper presented at the Bank for International Settlements, 9 December, Basel, Switzerland.

Index

Accounting standards, lack of international, 19
Adjustable pegs, 9, 20, 52, 69, 123
Adjustment
  apportioning costs of, 63
  Bonn program for, 57, 144
  via changes in domestic demand, 63, 98
  via exchange rates, 63, 64, 66n, 98
  future problems for, 7
  objective indicators to guide, 22
  Plaza program for, 21, 30, 34, 56, 107, 125, 147
  process, 20, 22, 39, 83
  program for Mexican, 35–37
  question of who initiates, 65, 98
African Development Bank (AfDB), 3
Ainley, Michael, 23
Alesina, Alberto, 87n
Argentina, 99
Armendariz de Aghion, Beatriz, 37
Asia Pacific Economic Cooperation (APEC) forum, 44, 48, 50, 68, 99n, 119
Asian Development Bank (ADB), 3
Åslund, Anders, 37
Automobile and automobile parts negotiations, 30, 63, 78, 133

Baker, James, 76, 79, 85, 104, 117n, 133
Baker Plan, 24, 76

Bank for International Settlements (BIS), 14, 36n, 88, 110, 128
Bank of England, 87
Bank of Japan, 67, 77n, 87
Banking crises
  frequency of, 18
  reducing risk of, 18–19
Banque de France, 87
"Bear squeeze" of 1988, 23
Bayne, Nicholas, 14n
Bayoumi, Tamim, 114
Bentsen, Lloyd, 77n
Bergsten, C. Fred, 15n, 24n, 33n, 50n, 66n, 74, 79, 99n, 126n, 133, 133n, 144
Berthoin, George, 15n
Big Emerging Markets, 68
Binaian, King, 87n
BIS *See* Bank for International Settlements
Black Monday, stock market crash on, 6, 78
Bonn summit agreement of 1978
  finance ministers' role in, 21
  Germany and Japan's negative view of, 57–58, 78
  heads of state's role in, 21
  as impetus to conclusion of Tokyo Round, 17, 21, 147
  as key G-7 success, 20–21, 57, 124, 144
  oil shock's effect on, 24, 57, 147

Brady, Nicholas, 24
Brady Plan, 24, 78
Brazil, 44, 53
Bretton Woods Commission, 39, 91*n*, 124*n*
Bretton Woods system *See also* Adjustable pegs
    collapse of, 20, 40, 117
Bryant, Ralph, 91*n*, 139*n*
Brzezinski, Zbigniew, 48*n*
Bubble economy in Japan, 6, 28, 29, 51, 52, 58, 78, 79, 105
Budget deficits *See also* Fiscal policy
    European criticism of US, 33, 73, 83
    European resolve to eliminate, 57–58, 86, 100, 146
    financing for US, 67
    as limiting scope for coordination, 56, 84, 86–87
    as percentage of GDP, 131, 132*t*
Bundesbank
    as advocate of stability, 56, 71, 75
    autonomy of, 75–76, 87
    cooperation with Federal Reserve, 75, 75*n*
    raised interest rates after unification, 28, 29
Burden sharing, 24, 35, 68, 72, 78, 99, 136
Bush administration, 56, 78, 79, 83
Bush, George, 29, 51

Canada, 17, 44, 106, 140*n*
Capital flows *See* Private capital markets
Carter administration, 56, 104
Carter, Jimmy, 21
Catte, P., 24, 30, 113
Central banks
    coordination with finance ministries, 87–88, 109, 111, 128
    defense of independence, 5, 100, 109
    deputies of, 111
    effect of primacy of monetary policy on, 87, 100
    increased importance of, 5, 14, 84, 87–89,
    interest rate reductions after the Plaza, 21–22, 87, 107
    need for increased role in G-7, 10, 14, 88, 109–12, 141
    need to take international considerations into account, 107–08
    preference for central bank coordination, 88

resistance to coordination with finance ministries, 87–88, 105
    as target zone managers, 10, 110, 128
Central and Eastern Europe, 69, 69*n*, 99
Chernomyrdin, Victor, 37
China
    barriers to G-7/G-10 membership, 48, 137–38, 138*n*
    conflict with US, 51
    economic weight of 44, 48, 119
Chirac, Jacques, 11, 76
Cline, William R., 24, 24*n*, 32*n*, 66*f*, 133
Clinton administration, 10, 29, 56, 77*n*, 78, 80, 83, 85*n*
Cohen, Benjamin J., 24*n*
Cold War, 4, 37, 71*n*, 73, 74, 84
Collins, Susan, 69*n*
"Competitive depreciation," 40*n*
Consensus for inaction, 5, 31, 83–95, 100
Contagion effects, 7, 35, 53, 71*n*, 99
Convergence thesis, 5, 92–93
Cooper, Richard N., 144
Cooperation criteria, 10, 130–32
Coordination, international economic
    barriers to, 55–82, 83–95, 144–45
    case for, 129, 144
    versus cooperation, 13*n*, 19*n*, 20
    costs of failure to engage in, 6, 53, 120
    desirability of, 6,
    difficulties of collective management of, 84
    examples of currency regimes leading to, 9, 20, 52, 108, 123
    long-term targets for, 146
    political weakness as excuse for precluding, 85
    primacy of domestic goals as excuse for precluding, 85
    as promoting better domestic outcomes, 85, 101–09
    US failure to engage in, 4, 33, 36, 78, 93
Cukierman, Alex, 87*n*
Currency crises *See also specific currency*
    contagion effects of, 7, 35, 53, 99
    endemic nature of, 4, 39, 50–51, 126, 127, 140
    support for countries experiencing, 89–91
Currency management
    ad hoc, 9, 42, 102, 116, 125
    failures of, 30–33, 51
    goals of, 30

impact of currencies outside G-7 on, 67
successes of, 20–24
Currency overvaluation, as policy error,
40, 98
Current account imbalances *See also*
specific countries, 60f–62f
conflicts over, 16, 59–68, 98
distribution of world surpluses, 66f
financing for, 67
G-7 disinterest in, 67
G-7 failure to avoid, 33–34, 63

Daniels, Joseph P., 14n
Debt crisis, developing country
G-7 role in resolving, 3, 24, 76, 79
in Poland, 71
Deficit versus surplus countries, 59–68,
81, 98
de Gaulle, Charles, 75
Derivatives markets, 19
Destler, I. M., 112n
Deutsche mark
dollar exchange rate, 104, 125, 125f,
126
effect of dollar's weakness on, 31n
failure to appreciate in wake of
unification, 28, 29, 31, 40n
Developing countries
debt crisis, 24, 76, 79
lack of representation in G-7, 44
rejection of new SDR allocation in
1994, 38
de Vries, Margaret, 23
Diwan, Ishac, 24n
Dobson, Wendy, 91n, 111, 144, 145
Dollar, US
decline in mid-1994, 33, 34, 88
deutsche mark exchange rate, 31n, 125,
125f, 126
devaluation in early 1970s, 20
European desire to strengthen, 32, 53,
67
"G-2" target zone with the yen, 11,
133
means for defending, 9n
overvaluation in 1980s, 3, 39, 41, 93,
104–05
risk of hard landing for, 6, 7, 53, 93,
104, 129, 147
stability of trade-weighted, 49, 49t, 50t,
125
yen exchange rate, 23, 31f, 104, 125,
133

Dominguez, Kathryn, 24, 30, 113
Dornbusch, Rudiger, 24n, 112

Early warning system
application to developing countries, 8,
42, 52, 134, 141–42
application to G-7, 8, 42, 52, 134, 142
creation of, 8, 42, 52, 118
requirements for improved, 42
Economic and Monetary Union (EMU)
fiscal criterion for membership in,
57–58, 86, 100, 130
political drive for, 76, 118
G-7 failure to consider impact, 10, 31,
32
as single entity for adjustment
purposes, 64, 140
Edwards, Richard W. Jr., 23
Edwards, Sebastian, 24n
Eichengreen, Barry, 24n, 80, 80n, 90
Eijffinger, Sylvester, 87n
Emergency funding mechanism, 4, 8, 39,
42, 43, 118, 135, 136
Euro, 7, 32, 70
European Bank for Reconstruction and
Development (EBRD), 3
European Commission, 16, 140
European Monetary System (EMS)
coordination within, 9, 52, 123
creation by heads of state, 7, 117, 142
crises of 1992–93, 31–32, 39, 89–90, 126
effect of dollar's weakness on, 31n
success in reducing inflation, 123, 146
as target zone regime, 89–90, 114, 115,
124
European Union
ensuring German engagement in, 74,
75
Germany as leader of, 4, 74
impact of higher German interest rates
in 1991 on, 28, 29, 51
monetary regime at odds with rest of
G-7, 69
recession of early 1990s, 28
regional focus of, 68–70, 72, 98
responsibility for Eastern Europe and
former Soviet republics, 72, 98
single currency in, 7, 64, 69, 71, 74–75
trade in goods and services, 64, 64f
unemployment in, 6, 7, 28, 50, 57
Exchange markets, settlement risk in, 19
Exchange Rate Mechanism, 89

Exchange rates *See also specific currencies*
effectiveness of intervention in
managing, 5, 21–24, 30, 113
failures in managing, 30–33, 51, 78
as guide for resource allocation, 147
as preferred vehicle for adjustment, 63,
64, 98
as signals for needed changes in
domestic policy, 85, 101–09
successes in managing, 21–24, 124
targeting of, 101–03, 108
as transmission mechanism for
monetary policy, 106
Exchange Stabilization Fund, 36, 90
Exports, impact on wages, 28
External relations
G-7 failures in, 35–39
with Mexico during peso crisis, 35–37,
74, 89, 90
with Russia, 4, 37–39

Federal Reserve Board
autonomy of, 87
cooperation with Bundesbank, 75, 75n
failure to tighten monetary policy in
1970s, 103–04, 129
failure to ease monetary policy in
1989, 104–05
research on exchange rates, 106
Feldstein, Martin, 21n, 144
Finance ministries *See also specific
ministry*
alignment of G-5 membership with G-
7, 22, 118
coordination with central banks, 87–88,
109, 111, 128
deputies of, 14, 111
Gulf War burden-sharing agreement
among, 24, 68
reduced power of, 88
reluctance to reform system, 10, 39
summit role of, 14, 39
"Financial spheres of influence," 70–72,
98–100, 136
Fiscal policy *See also* Budget deficits
effects of contraction in, 86n
fixed rules for, 130n
immobilization of, 57, 86–87, 97, 100,
108
Maastricht criterion on, 57–58, 86, 130,
131, 131n
Fischer, Stanley, 24n
Fixed-rate currency regime
breakdown of, 103, 117

as nominal anchor, 40
policy error induced by, 41, 124
Fowler, Henry H., 129n
Framework Talks of 1993–95, US-Japan,
67, 77
Franc, French, 32, 58
France
abandonment of independence in G-7,
75–76
current account, 58, 59
"dash for growth" strategy, 58, 146
franc fort policy, 58
GAB activation for, 23
merchandise trade balance, 62f
monetary policy, 75–76, 87n
shift to emphasis on stability, 58,
75–76
trade balance, 62f
Frankel, Jeffrey A., 24, 30, 41, 113, 146
Free Trade Area of the Americas
(FTAA), 44, 50, 68, 99n, 119
Freedman, C., 106, 106n
Freely flexible currency regime
with ad hoc coordination, 9, 42, 98,
102, 125
in early 1980s, 30, 69, 124
market error induced by, 41, 42, 98,
117
Frenkel, Jacob A., 144, 145
Frieden, Jeffry A., 24n
Funabashi, Yoichi, 21, 76n, 87, 107, 109
Furstenberg, George M. von, 14n

"G-2" yen-dollar target zone, 11, 133
G-3, evolution of G-7 into, 5, 10, 139
G-5, 16, 30, 124
role in debt crisis, 24
share of foreign exchange reserves, 46t
G-6, accord at Louvre, 75
G-7 *See also specific countries*
benign neglect in 1980s, 6, 79, 92–93
blocking of criticism, 91, 91n
consensus for inaction, 5, 31, 52, 83–95,
132, 140
consultation among, 35, 36n, 37, 78–79
convergence of key members'
economies, 131–32
cooperation criteria for, 10, 130–32,
132t, 141
creation of, 16
currency crises throughout, 4, 39,
50–51, 126, 127, 140
current account imbalances, 17, 33–34,
59–68, 98, 141

delayed recognition of need for debt reduction, 24
distrust of IMF, 10, 42, 91
exchange rate management, 16, 21–24, 30–33, 51, 124
extent to which fault lies with, 49–53
external relations, 4, 16, 35–39
global growth strategy of, 21, 29
inactivity of 1980s compared to early 1990s, 5, 92–93
leadership of, 1–2, 10, 15, 15n, 80–81, 84, 95, 117–18, 138–39, 140
legitimacy, 9, 10, 15, 43–49, 138–40, 141
membership criteria, 44–48
microeconomic issues outside the competence of, 18
need for systemic arrangements, 11, 17, 52, 97, 120–21, 123, 132, 141
political case for reviving, 117–20
rejection of coordination, 5, 86–95
reluctance to criticize other members, 83, 91
renewed risk of recession in, 6, 53
responsibilities of, 15–20, 52, 92–95
share of currencies dominating private transactions, 45, 46t
share of IMF quotas, 15, 45, 47t
share of reserve holdings, 45, 47t
share of world output, 1, 15, 17f, 44
share in world trade, 44, 45t
support programs of, 89–91
traditional differences among, 4, 55–81, 132
unwillingness to share decision making with nonmembers, 9, 43, 136–37, 140
willingness to act in international interest, 45
world growth and, 16, 27–29, 50, 59, 83
G-10, 14, 16, 30
Basel Committee of bank supervisors, 18
central bankers' meeting, 88
creation of GAB by, 16, 20, 22
Eurocentricity of, 44
expanded membership of, 9, 137, 142
launch of Special Drawing Rights, 20
membership criteria for, 137
as way station to G-7 membership, 9, 137
GAB See General Arrangements to Borrow

Galli, G., 24, 30, 113
Garber, Peter, 19, 90, 102, 114, 115n
GATT See General Agreement on Tariffs and Trade
General Agreement on Tariffs and Trade (GATT), 1, 52, 145
General Arrangements to Borrow (GAB)
G-10 creation of, 22–23
Halifax decision to double funding, 8, 43, 135, 140
invitation to non-G-7 to contribute to, 43, 136
as supplement to IMF support programs, 100
Germany
abstention on vote for Mexican support, 36, 74
anti-inflationary stance, 55, 70
ascendance in G-7 of, 4, 74
budget deficits, 28, 57
conflicts with US, 4, 33, 55, 73–75, 83
as a creditor country, 59
current account, 35, 59, 60f
disillusion with past coordination, 78
employment in, 56
fear of hyperinflation, 56
fiscal policy, 29, 56, 86
fiscal tightening as part of global growth strategy, 29
impact on Europe of higher interest rates in 1991, 28, 29, 51
Länder's role in, 57, 86
merchandise trade balance, 60f
role in Eastern Europe and former Soviet republics, 72
"stability pact" proposed by, 101, 130
unification of, 28, 51, 56n, 57, 59, 65, 86
Ghosh, Atish R., 146
Gilpin, Robert, 80n
Globalism versus regionalism, 4, 68–73, 81, 98
Gold regime, 52, 74, 123
Goldstein, Morris, 19, 42, 91n, 134, 135, 144, 145
Goodman, John B., 87n
Great Depression, 1, 56
Greider, William, 109
Grilli, Enzo, 34
Grilli, Vittorio, 87n
Group of Seven See G-7
Growth
failure to generate, 27–29, 50
versus price stability, 4, 55–59

prospects for strategy for, 59
strategy, 4, 29, 83
Gulf War, 3, 28, 71, 76, 78, 100
Gyohten, Toyoo, 103, 104

Haan, Jacob de, 87n
Haggard, Stephan, 24n
Halifax summit
  decision to double GAB, 8, 43, 135
  initiative to prevent financial crises, 10,
    11, 39, 42, 118, 134, 142
Hall, Robert, 106n
Hard landing, of the dollar
  1987 risk of, 6, 93, 104, 129, 147
  renewed risk of, 7, 53
Henning, C. Randall, 21, 57, 63–64, 79n,
    87, 131n, 105, 110n, 111 140, 144, 145
Holtham, Gerald, 57
Husain, Ishrat, 24n

Ikenberry, G. John, 1, 14n
IMF See International Monetary Fund
Income stagnation, 27–28, 50
Incumbents, rejection of, 51
India, 44
Indonesia, 44
Inflation
  differentials, 31, 70, 112
  exporting, 144
  fighting versus emphasis on growth,
    55–59
  rates in 1995–97, 132t
  success in reducing, 123, 129, 146
  trade-off between unemployment and,
    57, 58
Inter-American Development Bank (IDB),
  3
Interest rates, 7, 132t
International Development Association
  (IDA), 3, 137
International economic coordination See
  Coordination, international economic
International Finance Corporation, 3
International Monetary Fund (IMF), 1, 2,
  13
  advice to countries in trouble, 8, 42,
    134
  charges of US dominance of, 23, 92
  countries' submission of data to, 134
  estimates of equilibrium exchange
    rates, 114
  Executive Board, 92, 139n

expanded resources to handle crises, 4,
    8, 10, 22–23, 39, 42, 43, 118, 135,
    136, 141
G-7 distrust of, 10, 42, 91
G-7 limits to participation of, 91
as locus for early warning system, 8,
    42, 100, 120, 134, 135, 136, 139,
    141–42
Mexican support package and, 35, 36,
    74, 134
public release of country information,
    8, 42, 135
quotas, 9, 15
reduced clout of, 91
surveillance of developing economies,
    42, 52, 134, 141–42
surveillance of G-7 economies, 8, 42,
    52, 134, 141–42
US Congress' distrust of, 92
vote on G-7's SDR proposal in 1994,
    39, 140
International Trade Organization, 1
Intervention
  criticism of US, 33, 73, 79
  effectiveness of, 5, 21–24, 30, 113
  G-7 role in, 89
  within the margins, 102, 116
  monetary authorities' reluctance to
    attempt, 85, 112, 124
  restoration in 1985 of, 69
  to stem dollar's decline in 1994, 33, 88
  sterilized, 85
  to strengthen dollar in 1995, 98
  surprise as advantage in, 116
  to weaken yen in 1995, 77, 77n, 98
Italy
  current account, 59
  economic size, 43
  GAB activation for, 23
  inflation, 32, 112
  merchandise trade balance, 62f
  refusal to participate at Louvre, 75n

Jacobson, Harold, 138n
James, Harold, 91n
Japan
  alliance with Germany on monetary
    issues, 5
  antipathy for budget deficits, 77–78
  bad-loan problem, 6, 18, 51
  bubble economy, 6, 28, 29, 51, 52, 58,
    78, 79, 105
  as creditor country, 76

current account surplus, 28, 29, 30, 34, 59, 86
disillusion with past coordination, 78
dominant role of Ministry of Finance in, 58, 86
East Asian orientation, 68, 71
East Asia's reluctance to accept leadership of, 98
failure to play strong international role, 76
financial system's fragility, 6, 32, 66
fiscal expansion as part of global growth strategy, 29
fiscal policy, 28, 29, 58, 86, 100
funding for Gulf War, 76
funding for Russia, 77
goods and services trade, 64, 64f
increased independence in G-7, 76
Kuril Islands dispute, 77
merchandise trade balance, 61f
recession of early 1990s, 6, 7, 28, 29, 31, 34, 50, 105
reliance on monetary rather than fiscal expansion, 29, 58, 77n, 105
resentment of US pressure, 76
share of world current account surpluses, 65, 66f
trade barriers, 66, 77n
trade conflict with the United States, 33, 51, 58, 63, 77
trade policy, 17, 28
trade surplus, 7, 63, 105
unemployment in, 50

Kahler, Miles, 24n
Kantor, Mickey, 77n
Kapstein, Ethan B., 24n
Kaufman, Robert R., 24n
Kawai, Hiroki, 77n
Kenen, Peter B., 24n, 130
Keohane, Robert O., 80, 80n, 88n, 146
Kindleberger, Charles P., 80n
Kohl, Helmut, 51
Krugman, Paul R., 21, 114, 115n
Kuril Islands, 77

Laney, Leroy O., 87n
Larraín, Felipe, 24n
Leadership
  absence of hegemon to provide, 15n, 80–81
  difficulties of collective, 84
  importance of initiative by heads of state, 10, 95, 117–18, 142

importance of small core group, 1–2, 15, 138–39, 140
US, 47, 68, 72, 80, 98
"Leaning with the wind," 113
Legitimacy
  IMF's role in enhancing, 138–40
  rise of new powers as challenge to, 9, 10, 15, 43–49, 119
Lira, 32, 40, 89, 112
Lohmann, Susanne, 87n
Louvre Accord, 78, 87, 104
  adoption of reference ranges, 22, 76, 125, 126, 133
Lucas, Robert E., 114n
Lyon summit, 11, 142

Maastricht treaty, 10, 69, 74, 111
  fiscal criterion of, 57–58, 86, 101, 130, 131
Market error, 39, 40–41, 102, 114, 117, 126
Marris, Stephen, 41
Masciandaro, Donato, 87n
Masson, Paul R., 144, 145, 146
Mauskopf, Eileen, 106
Mexico
  current account deficit, 112
  debt crisis, 71
  peso crisis, 8, 35, 51, 53, 71, 71n, 74, 85n, 89, 99, 112, 134, 136
  trade barriers in, 53
Miller, Marcus H., 65n, 94
Ministry of Finance, Japan, 58, 77–78, 86
Miyazawa, Kiichi, 76, 79, 85, 133
Monetary authorities See also specific authority
  blaming the market, 32, 112, 117, 142
  preference for status quo, 117, 142
  reluctance to intervene, 142
Monetary policy See also specific countries
  extra burden in face of fiscal immobility, 86, 100
  increased role of exchange rate in, 106
  need for long-term view in, 107
Mulford, David, 69
Mulroney, Brian, 51
Multilateral Investment Guarantee Agency (MIGA), 3
Mushakoji, Kinhide, 15n

Naples summit, 10, 39, 42, 118, 142
Nau, Henry, 80n
"New consensus" See Consensus for inaction

Neyapti, Filin, 87n
Noland, Marcus, 33n, 66f, 126n
Nonaggression pact, See Consensus for inaction
Nonbanks, 19
Nye, Joseph S., 80, 80n, 88n

"Objective indicators," 22, 124
Obstfeld, Maurice, 27n, 106n
Odell, John S., 80n, 81
Oil
    price controls, 21, 147
    shocks, 24, 56, 86, 104, 144
Oksenberg, Michel, 138n
Oudiz, Gilles, 27n, 147
Oye, Kenneth A., 80n, 81

Pauly, Louis W., 91n
Persian Gulf War See Gulf War
Peso crisis, in Mexico
    contagion effects, 7, 35, 71n, 89, 99
    early signs of, 112
    East Asian reaction to, 99
    Eastern Europe's reaction to, 99
    G-7 mishandling of, 35–37
    Latin American reaction to, 99
    support package in wake of, 35–36, 74, 85n, 91
    as systemic threat, 37, 99, 134
Plaza Agreement
    correction of dollar overvaluation, 21, 30, 34, 125, 147
    as key G-7 success, 21, 94, 107
    as repudiation of convergence thesis, 5, 69
Policy error, 39–41, 78, 102, 112, 126
Polish debt crises, 71
Portes, Richard, 24n
Posen, Adam S., 87n
Pound sterling See Sterling
Private capital markets
    attack of overvalued currencies, 112–13
    challenge to net uncovered positions of, 113
    globalization of, 7, 99
    growth of, 84, 89–91, 99
    IMF release of information to, 8, 42, 135
    inadequacy of national supervision and regulation of, 7, 18
    increased number of countries involved in, 90
    risk of sudden shifts in, 6–7, 37

    size of flows vis-à-vis official intervention, 112–13
    systemic effects of, 37, 90, 99
    threat to currencies during Bretton Woods period, 20
Protectionism, 6, 7, 34, 53, 93, 117, 117n
Putnam, Robert D., 14n, 21, 57, 144

Quad, the, 17, 140

Rapid response facility See Emergency funding mechanism
Rational speculative bubbles, 41
Reagan administration, 84, 79, 93, 105, 117n, 124
Reaganomics, 6, 51, 52, 86
Rebecchini, S., 24, 30, 113
Reference ranges, 22, 11, 75, 76, 125, 126, 133
Regionalism, versus globalism, 68–73, 81, 98
Richardson, J. David, 28
Rindal, Karin, 28
Rockett, Katharine, 146
Rodrik, Dani, 69n
Russia
    G-7 mishandles support for economic reform of, 4, 37–39
    IMF program for, 8, 136
    participation in summits, 14, 43, 48n
    US role in supporting, 71, 72, 77, 98

Sachs, Jeffrey, 24n, 27n, 147
Saudi Arabia, 23, 48
Sazanami, Yoko, 77n
Schaling, Eric, 87n
Schmidt, Helmut, 57n
Sherpas, 14
Smithsonian Agreement, 20
Smyser, W. R., 14n
Solomon, Robert, 22, 118
Sous-sherpas, 14
Soviet Union, former republics of, 69, 69n
Special Drawing Rights (SDRs)
    creation of, 20
    rejection of proposal for new allocation, 4, 38, 140
Speculators, officials' tendency to blame, 32, 112, 117, 142
Stark, Jürgen, 19n, 36n
Sterilized intervention, 5
Sterling, 32, 40, 51, 76, 89, 112
Stockman, David, 93n

Stoltenberg, Gerhard, 79, 85
Strauss, Robert, 16, 147
Strauss-Ushiba Agreement, 58
Summers, Lawrence H., 36n, 38n, 74n,
    87n
Summits *See also specific summit*
    Bonn, 17, 20–21, 24, 57–58, 78, 124,
        144, 147
    central bankers' role in, 14, 111
    finance ministers' role in, 14, 39
    Halifax, 8, 10, 11, 39, 42, 43, 118, 134,
        135, 142
    heads of state's role in, 13–14, 89n, 95
    Lyon, 11, 142
    Naples, 10, 39, 42, 118, 142
    Tokyo, 19–20, 22
Support packages
    for beleaguered countries, 89–91
    as target for speculators, 90
Surplus versus deficit countries, 4, 59–68,
    81, 98
Svensson, Lars, 90, 102, 114, 115n
Switzerland, 23
Systemic arrangements
    versus ad hoc reactions, 2, 9, 42
    G-7 responsibility to design, 11, 18, 52,
        97, 120–21, 123, 132, 141

Tabellini, Guido, 87n
Takeshita, Noboru, 79
Target zones
    of ±10 percent, 9, 113, 114, 126
    announcement of, 9, 126
    authority to manage, 110–12, 128
    commitment to defend, 116–17, 126
    conversion of destabilizing into
        stabilizing capital flows, 9, 114,
        126–27, 141
    credibility of, 116
    de facto, 124–26
    doubts of US willingness to stick to,
        128, 130
    EMS as example of, 89–90, 106, 114,
        115, 124
    equilibrium rates within, 114
    "G-2" target zone, 11, 133
    goals of, 127–28
    introduction while exchange rates are
        at equilibrium, 133
    mean reversion in regime of, 115
    officials' critique of, 112–17
    paving the way for more extensive
        cooperation, 9, 123

as promoting better domestic
    outcomes, 9, 101, 127–28
proposal for, 124–34
reappraisal of, 126
as variant of flexible exchange rates,
    102, 115, 115n, 116, 127, 129
Telephone accord of 1987, 23
Thatcher, Margaret, 58
Tietmeyer, Hans, 38n, 113, 147
Tokyo Round, Bonn summit's role in
    concluding, 17, 21, 147
Tokyo summit
    "objective indicators" adopted at, 22
    statement of objectives, 19–20
Trade
    dependence and adjustment policy
        preferences, 63, 98
    G-7 lack of direct responsibility for, 7,
        17
    goods and services, 64f
    merchandise, 60f–62f
    protection, 6, 7, 34, 53, 93, 117, 117n
Trading system, 3, 6, 29, 34, 50, 51, 145
Trans-Atlantic Free Trade Area (TAFTA),
    119n

Unemployment
    exporting, 29, 34, 144
    rates as cooperation criterion, 131
    rates in Europe, 27–28, 50, 56
    trade-off between inflation and, 57, 58
United Kingdom
    abstention on vote for Mexican
        support, 36
    current account, 59
    fading G-7 role in, 76
    GAB activation for, 23
    reduced emphasis on growth
        programs in, 58
    trade balance, 61f
United States
    adjustment via exchange rates, 63
    and bilateral imbalance with Japan, 63
    budget deficits, 67, 83, 100, 105
    budget deficit reduction as part of
        global growth strategy, 29
    competitiveness of firms in, 67
    conflicts with Germany, 4, 33, 55,
        73–75, 83
    current account deficits, 28, 29, 34, 59,
        60f, 67, 71
    as debtor country, 6, 51, 74, 93
    decline in international clout, 4, 69, 73,
        79

export sector's role in increasing
wages in, 28
failure to seek coordination, 4, 33, 36,
78, 93
fiscal policy, 4, 56, 58, 86, 105
full employment, 28, 58
German concessions to, 74
global leadership, 47, 68, 72, 80, 98
goods and services trade, 64, 64f
inconsistency of policies, 4, 33, 79
"locomotive strategy" of, 56
low saving rate in, 67, 131
merchandise trade balance, 60f
monetary policy in 1970s, 103–04
monetary policy in 1980s, 6, 51, 92–93,
104–05
preference for expansionary policy,
55–56, 71
productivity problem, 28
protectionism in, 6, 7
recession of 1990s, 28, 105
recession of late 1970s, 104
reduced interest in fiscal expansion in
1990s, 4, 58, 86
response to external constraints,
103–05, 128–29
standards of living, 27
trade conflict with China, 51
trade conflict with Japan, 30, 33, 51, 63,
77, 77n
trade deficit, 7
trade policy, 6
unemployment in 1950s and early
1960s, 56
wage stagnation, 6, 27–28, 50
Urata, Shujiro, 77n
Uruguay Round, 29, 50, 51
US Congress, 35, 51
US Council of Economic Advisers, 88

US National Economic Council, 88
US Office of Management and Budget,
88, 93
US Treasury, shared authority of, 88–89

Volcker, Paul A., 103, 104, 107n, 115n,
123n, 124n, 126n

Wage stagnation, 27–28, 50
Webb, Steven B., 87n
Werner, Alejandro, 112
Whyman, William, 14n,
Willett, Thomas D., 87n
Williamson, John, 24n, 32, 65n, 94, 111,
112, 114, 118, 126n, 131n, 140n
Woolley, James T., 87n
World Bank, 1, 2–3, 13, 137
World Trade Organization, 1, 3, 13, 50,
52
Wren-Lewis, Simon, 32, 112
Wyplosz, Charles, 90

Yen
appreciation leading to recession in
early 1990s, 29, 34, 66, 105
depreciation in the late 1980s, 28, 39,
41, 105
dollar exchange rate, 23, 31f, 104, 125,
133
endaka shock of 1985–87, 105
"G-2" target zone with the dollar, 11,
133
G-7 failure to manage exchange rate
of, 30, 33, 78
relationship to Japan's current account
balance, 31n, 66n-67n
at undervalued level in late 1980s, 67
US refusal to weaken, 77
Yen-dollar agreement, 23, 76

Other Publications from the
Institute for International Economics

POLICY ANALYSES IN INTERNATIONAL ECONOMICS Series

1   The Lending Policies of the International Monetary Fund
    John Williamson/*August 1982*
                    ISBN paper 0-88132-000-5   72 pp.

2   "Reciprocity": A New Approach to World Trade Policy?
    William R. Cline/*September 1982*
                    ISBN paper 0-88132-001-3   41 pp.

3   Trade Policy in the 1980s
    C. Fred Bergsten and William R. Cline/*November 1982*
    (out of print)   ISBN paper 0-88132-002-1   84 pp.
    Partially reproduced in the book *Trade Policy in the 1980s.*

4   International Debt and the Stability of the World Economy
        William R. Cline/*September 1983*
                    ISBN paper 0-88132-010-2   134 pp.

5   The Exchange Rate System, Second Edition
    John Williamson/*September 1983, rev. June 1985*
    (out of print)   ISBN paper 0-88132-034-X   61 pp.

6   Economic Sanctions in Support of Foreign Policy Goals
    Gary Clyde Hufbauer and Jeffrey J. Schott/*October 1983*
                    ISBN paper 0-88132-014-5   109 pp.

7   A New SDR Allocation?
    John Williamson/*March 1984*
                    ISBN paper 0-88132-028-5   61 pp.

8   An International Standard for Monetary Stabilization
    Ronald I. McKinnon/*March 1984*
    (out of print)   ISBN paper 0-88132-018-8   108 pp.

9   The Yen/Dollar Agreement: Liberalizing Japanese Capital Markets
    Jeffrey A. Frankel/*December 1984*
                    ISBN paper 0-88132-035-8   86 pp.

10 Bank Lending to Developing Countries: The Policy Alternatives
    C. Fred Bergsten, William R. Cline, and John Williamson/*April 1985*
                    ISBN paper 0-88132-032-3   221 pp.

11 Trading for Growth: The Next Round of Trade Negotiations
    Gary Clyde Hufbauer and Jeffrey J. Schott/*September 1985*
    (out of print)   ISBN paper 0-88132-033-1   109 pp.

12 Financial Intermediation Beyond the Debt Crisis
    Donald R. Lessard and John Williamson/*September 1985*
    (out of print)   ISBN paper 0-88132-021-8   130 pp.

13 The United States-Japan Economic Problem
    C. Fred Bergsten and William R. Cline/*October 1985, 2d ed. January 1987*
    (out of print)   ISBN paper 0-88132-060-9   180 pp.

14 Deficits and the Dollar: The World Economy at Risk
    Stephen Marris/*December 1985, 2d ed. November 1987*
    (out of print)   ISBN paper 0-88132-067-6   415 pp.

15 Trade Policy for Troubled Industries
Gary Clyde Hufbauer and Howard F. Rosen/*March 1986*
ISBN paper 0-88132-020-X   111 pp.

16 The United States and Canada: The Quest for Free Trade
Paul Wonnacott, with an Appendix by John Williamson/*March 1987*
ISBN paper 0-88132-056-0   188 pp.

17 Adjusting to Success: Balance of Payments Policy
in the East Asian NICs
Bela Balassa and John Williamson/*June 1987, rev. April 1990*
ISBN paper 0-88132-101-X   160 pp.

18 Mobilizing Bank Lending to Debtor Countries
William R. Cline/*June 1987*
ISBN paper 0-88132-062-5   100 pp.

19 Auction Quotas and United States Trade Policy
C. Fred Bergsten, Kimberly Ann Elliott, Jeffrey J. Schott, and
Wendy E. Takacs/*September 1987*
ISBN paper 0-88132-050-1   254 pp.

20 Agriculture and the GATT: Rewriting the Rules
Dale E. Hathaway/*September 1987*
ISBN paper 0-88132-052-8   169 pp.

21 Anti-Protection: Changing Forces in United States Trade Politics
I. M. Destler and John S. Odell/*September 1987*
ISBN paper 0-88132-043-9   220 pp.

22 Targets and Indicators: A Blueprint for the International Coordination
of Economic Policy
John Williamson and Marcus H. Miller/*September 1987*
ISBN paper 0-88132-051-X   118 pp.

23 Capital Flight: The Problem and Policy Responses
Donald R. Lessard and John Williamson/*December 1987*
(out of print)   ISBN paper 0-88132-059-5   80 pp.

24 United States-Canada Free Trade: An Evaluation of the Agreement
Jeffrey J. Schott/*April 1988*
ISBN paper 0-88132-072-2   48 pp.

25 Voluntary Approaches to Debt Relief
John Williamson/*September 1988, rev. May 1989*
ISBN paper 0-88132-098-6   80 pp.

26 American Trade Adjustment: The Global Impact
William R. Cline/*March 1989*
ISBN paper 0-88132-095-1   98 pp.

27 More Free Trade Areas?
Jeffrey J. Schott/*May 1989*
ISBN paper 0-88132-085-4   88 pp.

28 The Progress of Policy Reform in Latin America
John Williamson/*January 1990*
ISBN paper 0-88132-100-1   106 pp.

29 The Global Trade Negotiations: What Can Be Achieved?
Jeffrey J. Schott/*September 1990*
ISBN paper 0-88132-137-0   72 pp.

30 Economic Policy Coordination: Requiem or Prologue?
    Wendy Dobson/*April 1991*
                        ISBN paper 0-88132-102-8   162 pp.

31 The Economic Opening of Eastern Europe
    John Williamson/*May 1991*
                        ISBN paper 0-88132-186-9   92 pp.

32 Eastern Europe and the Soviet Union in the World Economy
    Susan M. Collins and Dani Rodrik/*May 1991*
                        ISBN paper 0-88132-157-5   152 pp.

33 African Economic Reform: The External Dimension
    Carol Lancaster/*June 1991*
                        ISBN paper 0-88132-096-X   82 pp.

34 Has the Adjustment Process Worked?
    Paul R. Krugman/*October 1991*
                        ISBN paper 0-88132-116-8   80 pp.

35 From Soviet disUnion to Eastern Economic Community?
    Oleh Havrylyshyn and John Williamson/*October 1991*
                        ISBN paper 0-88132-192-3   84 pp.

36 Global Warming: The Economic Stakes
    William R. Cline/*May 1992*
                        ISBN paper 0-88132-172-9   128 pp.

37 Trade and Payments After Soviet Disintegration
    John Williamson/*June 1992*
                        ISBN paper 0-88132-173-7   96 pp.

38 Trade and Migration: NAFTA and Agriculture
    Philip L. Martin/*October 1993*
                        ISBN paper 0-88132-201-6   160 pp.

39 The Exchange Rate System and the IMF: A Modest Agenda
    Morris Goldstein/*June 1995*
                        ISBN paper 0-88132-219-9   104 pp.

40 What Role for Currency Boards?
    John Williamson/*September 1995*
                        ISBN paper 0-88132-222-9   64 pp.

41 Predicting External Imbalances for the United States and Japan
    William R. Cline/*September 1995*
                        ISBN paper 0-88132-220-2   104 pp.

42 Standards and APEC: An Action Agenda
    John S. Wilson/*October 1995*
                        ISBN paper 0-88132-223-7   176 pp.

43 Fundamental Tax Reform and Border Tax Adjustments
    Gary Clyde Hufbauer assisted by Carol Gabyzon/*January 1996*
                        ISBN paper 0-88132-225-3   108 pp

BOOKS

IMF Conditionality
John Williamson, editor/*1983*   ISBN cloth 0-88132-006-4   695 pp.

Trade Policy in the 1980s
William R. Cline, editor/*1983*
(out of print)   ISBN paper 0-88132-031-5   810 pp.

Subsidies in International Trade
Gary Clyde Hufbauer and Joanna Shelton Erb/*1984*
                ISBN cloth 0-88132-004-8   299 pp.

International Debt: Systemic Risk and Policy Response
William R. Cline/*1984*   ISBN cloth 0-88132-015-3   336 pp.

Trade Protection in the United States: 31 Case Studies
Gary Clyde Hufbauer, Diane E. Berliner, and Kimberly Ann Elliott/*1986*
(out of print)   ISBN paper 0-88132-040-4   371 pp.

Toward Renewed Economic Growth in Latin America
Bela Balassa, Gerardo M. Bueno, Pedro-Pablo Kuczynski,
and Mario Henrique Simonsen/*1986*
(out of stock)   ISBN paper 0-88132-045-5   205 pp.

Capital Flight and Third World Debt
Donald R. Lessard and John Williamson, editors/*1987*
(out of print)   ISBN paper 0-88132-053-6   270 pp.

The Canada-United States Free Trade Agreement:
  The Global Impact
Jeffrey J. Schott and Murray G. Smith, editors/*1988*
                ISBN paper 0-88132-073-0   211 pp.

World Agricultural Trade: Building a Consensus
William M. Miner and Dale E. Hathaway, editors/*1988*
                ISBN paper 0-88132-071-3   226 pp.

Japan in the World Economy
Bela Balassa and Marcus Noland/*1988*
                ISBN paper 0-88132-041-2   306 pp.

America in the World Economy: A Strategy for the 1990s
C. Fred Bergsten/*1988*   ISBN cloth 0-88132-089-7   235 pp.
                ISBN paper 0-88132-082-X   235 pp.

Managing the Dollar: From the Plaza to the Louvre
Yoichi Funabashi/*1988, 2d ed. 1989*
                ISBN paper 0-88132-097-8   307 pp.
235 pp.
United States External Adjustment and the World Economy
William R. Cline/*May 1989*   ISBN paper 0-88132-048-X   392 pp.

Free Trade Areas and U.S. Trade Policy
Jeffrey J. Schott, editor/*May 1989*   ISBN paper 0-88132-094-3   400 pp.

Dollar Politics: Exchange Rate Policymaking in the United States
I. M. Destler and C. Randall Henning/*September 1989*
(out of print)   ISBN paper 0-88132-079-X   192 pp.

Latin American Adjustment: How Much Has Happened?
John Williamson, editor/*April 1990*
                ISBN paper 0-88132-125-7   480 pp.
The Future of World Trade in Textiles and Apparel
William R. Cline/*1987, 2d ed. June 1990*
                ISBN paper 0-88132-110-9   344 pp.

Completing the Uruguay Round: A Results-Oriented Approach to the GATT Trade Negotiations
Jeffrey J. Schott, editor/*September 1990*
ISBN paper 0-88132-130-3 256 pp.

Economic Sanctions Reconsidered (in two volumes)
Economic Sanctions Reconsidered: Supplemental Case Histories
Gary Clyde Hufbauer, Jeffrey J. Schott, and Kimberly Ann Elliott/*1985, 2d ed.*
December 1990 ISBN cloth 0-88132-115-X 928 pp.
ISBN paper 0-88132-105-2 928 pp.

Economic Sanctions Reconsidered: History and Current Policy
Gary Clyde Hufbauer, Jeffrey J. Schott, and Kimberly Ann Elliott/*December 1990*
ISBN cloth 0-88132-136-2 288 pp.
ISBN paper 0-88132-140-0 288 pp.

Pacific Basin Developing Countries: Prospects for the Future
Marcus Noland/*January 1991* ISBN cloth 0-88132-141-9 250 pp.
(out of print) ISBN paper 0-88132-081-1 250 pp.

Currency Convertibility in Eastern Europe
John Williamson, editor/*October 1991*
ISBN paper 0-88132-128-1 396 pp.

International Adjustment and Financing: The Lessons of 1985-1991
C. Fred Bergsten, editor/*January 1992*
ISBN paper 0-88132-112-5 336 pp.

North American Free Trade: Issues and Recommendations
Gary Clyde Hufbauer and Jeffrey J. Schott/*April 1992*
ISBN paper 0-88132-120-6 392 pp.

Narrowing the U.S. Current Account Deficit
Allen J. Lenz/*June 1992*
(out of print) ISBN paper 0-88132-103-6 640 pp.

The Economics of Global Warming
William R. Cline/*June 1992* ISBN paper 0-88132-132-X 416 pp.

U.S. Taxation of International Income: Blueprint for Reform
Gary Clyde Hufbauer, assisted by Joanna M. van Rooij/*October 1992*
ISBN cloth 0-88132-178-8 304 pp.
ISBN paper 0-88132-134-6 304 pp.

Who's Bashing Whom? Trade Conflict in High-Technology Industries
Laura D'Andrea Tyson/*November 1992*
ISBN paper 0-88132-106-0 352 pp.

Korea in the World Economy
Il SaKong/*January 1993*
ISBN paper 0-88132-106-0 328 pp.

Pacific Dynamism and the International Economic System
C. Fred Bergsten and Marcus Noland, editors/*May 1993*
ISBN paper 0-88132-196-6 424 pp.

Economic Consequences of Soviet Disintegration
John Williamson, editor/*May 1993*
ISBN paper 0-88132-190-7 664 pp.

Reconcilable Differences? United States-Japan Economic Conflict
C. Fred Bergsten and Marcus Noland/*June 1993*
ISBN paper 0-88132-129-X   296 pp.

Does Foreign Exchange Intervention Work?
Kathryn M. Dominguez and Jeffrey A. Frankel/*September 1993*
ISBN paper 0-88132-104-4   192 pp.

Sizing Up U.S. Export Disincentives
J. David Richardson/*September 1993*
ISBN paper 0-88132-107-9   192 pp.

NAFTA: An Assessment
Gary Clyde Hufbauer and Jeffrey J. Schott/*rev. ed. October 1993*
ISBN paper 0-88132-199-0   216 pp.

Adjusting to Volatile Energy Prices
Philip K. Verleger, Jr./*November 1993*
ISBN paper 0-88132-069-2   288 pp.

The Political Economy of Policy Reform
John Williamson, editor/*January 1994*
ISBN paper 0-88132-195-8   624 pp.

Measuring the Costs of Protection in the United States
Gary Clyde Hufbauer and Kimberly Ann Elliott/*January 1994*
ISBN paper 0-88132-108-7   144 pp.

The Dynamics of Korean Economic Development
Cho Soon/*March 1994*   ISBN paper 0-88132-162-1   272 pp.

Reviving the European Union
C. Randall Henning, Eduard Hochreiter and Gary Clyde Hufbauer, editors/
April 1994
ISBN paper 0-88132-208-3   192 pp.

China in the World Economy
Nicholas R. Lardy/*April 1994*   ISBN paper 0-88132-200-8   176 pp.

Greening the GATT: Trade, Environment, and the Future
Daniel C. Esty/*July 1994*   ISBN paper 0-88132-205-9   344 pp.

Western Hemisphere Economic Integration
Gary Clyde Hufbauer and Jeffrey J. Schott/*July 1994*
ISBN paper 0-88132-159-1   304 pp.

Currencies and Politics in the United States, Germany, and Japan
C. Randall Henning/*September 1994*
ISBN paper 0-88132-127-3   432 pp.

Estimating Equilibrium Exchange Rates
John Williamson, editor/*September 1994*
ISBN paper 0-88132-076-5   320 pp.

Managing the World Economy: Fifty Years After Bretton Woods
Peter B. Kenen, editor/*September 1994*
ISBN paper 0-88132-212-1   448 pp.

Reciprocity and Retaliation in U.S. Trade Policy
Thomas O. Bayard and Kimberly Ann Elliott/*September 1994*
ISBN paper 0-88132-084-6   528 pp.

The Uruguay Round: An Assessment
Jeffrey J. Schott, assisted by Johanna W. Buurman/*November 1994*
ISBN paper 0-88132-206-7   240 pp.

Measuring the Costs of Protection in Japan
Yoko Sazanami, Shujiro Urata, and Hiroki Kawai/*January 1995*
ISBN paper 0-88132-211-3   *96 pp.*

Foreign Direct Investment in the United States, Third Edition
Edward M. Graham and Paul R. Krugman/*January 1995*
ISBN paper 0-88132-204-0   232 pp.

The Political Economy of Korea-United States Cooperation
C. Fred Bergsten and Il SaKong, editors/*February 1995*
ISBN paper 0-88132-213-X   128 pp.

International Debt Reexamined
William R. Cline/*February 1995*
ISBN paper 0-88132-083-8   560 pp.

American Trade Politics, Third Edition
I. M. Destler/*April 1995*
ISBN paper 0-88132-215-6   360 pp.

Managing Official Export Credits: The Quest for a Global Regime
John E. Ray/*July 1995*
ISBN paper 0-88132-207-5   344 pp.

Asia Pacific Fusion: Japan's Role in APEC
Yoichi Funabashi/*October 1995*
ISBN paper 0-88132-224-5   312 pp.

Korea-United States Cooperation in the New World Order
C. Fred Bergsten and Il SaKong, editors/*February 1996*
ISBN paper 0-88132-226-1   144 pp.

Why Exports Really Matter! ISBN paper 0-88132-221-0   34 pp.
Why Exports Matter More!   ISBN paper 0-88132-229-6
J. David Richardson and Karin Rindal/July 1995; February 1996   36 pp.

Global Corporations and National Governments
Edward M. Graham/*May 1996*   ISBN paper 0-88132-111-7   168 pp.

Global Economic Leadership and the Group of Seven
C. Fred Bergsten and C. Randall Henning/*June 1996*
ISBN paper 0-88132-218-0   192 pp.

SPECIAL REPORTS

1   **Promoting World Recovery: A Statement on Global Economic Strategy
     by Twenty-six Economists from Fourteen Countries**/*December 1982*
     (out of print)   ISBN paper 0-88132-013-7   45 pp.

2   **Prospects for Adjustment in Argentina, Brazil, and Mexico:
     Responding to the Debt Crisis** (out of print)
     John Williamson, editor/*June 1983*   ISBN paper 0-88132-016-1   71 pp.

3   **Inflation and Indexation: Argentina, Brazil, and Israel**
     John Williamson, editor/*March 1985*   ISBN paper 0-88132-037-4   191 pp.

4   **Global Economic Imbalances**
     C. Fred Bergsten, editor/*March 1986*   ISBN cloth 0-88132-038-2   126 pp.
                                    ISBN paper 0-88132-042-0   126 pp.

5   **African Debt and Financing**
     Carol Lancaster and John Williamson, editors/*May 1986*
     (out of print)   ISBN paper 0-88132-044-7   229 pp.

6   **Resolving the Global Economic Crisis: After Wall Street**
     Thirty-three Economists from Thirteen Countries/*December 1987*
                                    ISBN paper 0-88132-070-6   30 pp.

7   **World Economic Problems**
     Kimberly Ann Elliott and John Williamson, editors/*April 1988*
                                    ISBN paper 0-88132-055-2   298 pp.

     Reforming World Agricultural Trade
     Twenty-nine Professionals from Seventeen Countries/*1988*
                                    ISBN paper 0-88132-088-9   42 pp.

8   **Economic Relations Between the United States and Korea: Conflict or Cooperation?**
     Thomas O. Bayard and Soo-Gil Young, editors/*January 1989*
                                    ISBN paper 0-88132-068-4   192 pp.

WORKS IN PROGRESS

Private Capital Flows to Emerging Markets after the Mexican Crisis
Guillermo Calvo, Morris Goldstein, and Eduard Hochreiter

Trade, Jobs, and Income Distribution
William R. Cline

Trade and Labor Standards
Kimberly Ann Elliott and Richard Freeman

Regionalism and Globalism in the World Economic System
Jeffrey A. Frankel

Transatlantic Free Trade Agreement
Ellen Frost

Forecasting Financial Crises: Early Warning Signs for Emerging Markets
Morris Goldstein and Carmen Reinhart

Overseeing Global Capital Markets
Morris Goldstein and Peter Garber

Global Competition Policy
Edward M. Graham and J. David Richardson

Flying High: Civil Aviation in the Asia Pacific
Gary Clyde Hufbauer and Christopher Findlay

Toward an Asia Pacific Economic Community?
Gary Clyde Hufbauer and Jeffrey J. Schott

The Economics of Korean Unification
Marcus Noland

The Case for Trade: A Modern Reconsideration
J. David Richardson

The Future of the World Trading System
John Whalley and Colleen Hamilton

Crawling Bands: Lessons from Chile, Colombia, and Israel
John Williamson

For orders outside the US and Canada please contact:

Longman Group UK Ltd.
PO Box 88, Fourth Avenue
Harlow, Essex CM 19 5SR UK

Telephone Orders: 0279 623923
Fax: 0279 453450 Telex: 81259

Canadian customers can order from the Institute or from either:

RENOUF BOOKSTORE
1294 Algoma Road
Ottawa, Ontario K1B 3W8
Telephone: (613) 741-4333
Fax: (613) 741-5439

LA LIBERTÉ
3020 chemin Sainte-Foy
Quebec G1X 3V6
Telephone: (418) 658-3763
Fax: (800) 567-5449

Visit our website at: http://www.iie.com   **E-mail address: orders@iie.com**

Global Economic Leadership and the Group of Seven

C. Fred Bergsten
C. Randall Henning

Sluggish global growth, frequent currency crises, huge trade imbalances and the Mexican financial collapse all reveal the failure of the Group of Seven industrial nations to provide effective leadership of the world economy. The G-7 has played this role effectively in the past and must do so again to assure global prosperity.

Part of the G-7's decline is due to continuing policy differences among the United States, Germany, and Japan. The bigger problem, however, is a new "consensus for inaction" based on fears of trying to counter the huge flows of international private capital, the existence of large budget deficits everywhere, and the resistance of central banks to coordination by anyone.

The study offers a comprehensive analysis of all these changes in the world economy and reaches a much more optimistic reading of the prospects for effective G-7 leadership. It proposes an action program that includes reforming the exchange rate regime, instituting an early warning system to prevent new monetary crises, augmenting the resources of the IMF to deal with private capital flows, and institutional reform of the G-7 itself.

"Fred Bergsten has a special knack for focusing on the right issues at the right time. This new book challenges the policymakers to respond to the need for fresh thinking to deal with financial volatility." —**Paul A. Volcker**, former Chairman of
The Board of Governors, The Federal Reserve System

"This is an important book. [Its] analysis of the decline of the G-7 . . . is disturbingly accurate. Restoring G-7 cooperation is essential to strengthening world growth without inflation or currency instability." —**David C. Mulford**, Chairman, CS First Boston,
and former Under Secretary of the Treasury for International Affairs

"The G-7 is fast becoming a ceremonial artifact. So it is timely that [this book] explains why, and offers ideas of what could be done to revive international economic cooperation among the major players." —**Robert B. Zoellick**, Executive Vice President and General Counsel, Federal National
Mortgage Association, and former Under Secretary of State and Economic Summit "Sherpa"

". . . makes a strong case for a 'revised G-7' as the best available option to provide effective economic leadership to the world when it will be most urgently needed. He outlines an agenda for improvements that is both ambitious and realistic."
—**Wolfgang Rieke**, former Head
of the International Division, Deutsche Bundesbank

"After sharply criticizing the present G-7, this book presents dynamic proposals to revitalize it as the effective steering committee for global economic management."
—**Shijuro Ogata**, former Executive Director, Bank of Japan

C. Fred Bergsten is Director of the Institute for International Economics. He has also been Chairman of the Competitiveness Policy Council since 1991, and Chairman of the APEC Eminent Persons Group dur-ing 1993-95. He was Assistant Secretary for International Affairs of the US Treasury (1977-81); Assistant for International Economic Affairs to the National Security Council (1969-71); and a Senior Fellow at the Brookings Institution (1972-76), the Carnegie Endowment for International Peace (1981), and the Coun-cil on Foreign Relations (1967-68). This is his 25th book on a wide range of international economic issues.

C. Randall Henning, Visiting Fellow at the Institute for International Economics, is Associate Professor at the School of International Service, American University. He is the author of *Currencies and Politics in the United States, Germany, and Japan* (1994), coeditor of *Reviving the European Union* (1994), and coauthor of *Dollar Politics: Exchange Rate Policymaking in the United States* (1989).

INSTITUTE FOR INTERNATIONAL ECONOMICS

11 Dupont Circle, NW
Washington, DC 20036-1207
(202) 328-9000
fax: (202) 328-5432
http://www.iie.com

ISBN 0-88132-218-0

90000>

9 780881 322187